KINGDOM FINANCE

KINGDOM FINANCE

HOW TO RADICALLY SHIFT FROM LACK AND DEBT INTO DIVINE FINANCIAL FREEDOM

MELISSA VAN SCHAIK

LIFEWISE BOOKS

KINGDOM FINANCE

HOW TO RADICALLY SHIFT FROM LACK AND DEBT
INTO DIVINE FINANCIAL FREEDOM

MELISSA VAN SCHAIK

Published by:

LIFEWISE BOOKS
PO BOX 1072
Pinehurst, TX 77362
LifeWiseBooks.com
To contact the author visit MelissaVanSchaik.com

Print - 978-1-958820-62-9
Ebook - 978-1-958820-63-6

DEDICATION

This book is dedicated to my sister, Lahoma, whose lifelong dream was to become a published author and who taught me that life can be way shorter than expected, so write it now.

SPECIAL THANKS

I would like to thank my husband, Chris, who has always believed in and supported every dream and goal I've had and without whom this book would not have been possible. I would also like to thank Pastor Gary Keesee who helped me find the language to communicate many of the concepts presented and who gave me the inspiration and courage to share my story.

CONTENTS

INTRODUCTION

MY TESTIMONY

Revelation 19:10 (NKJV) says, "...*For the testimony of Jesus is the spirit of prophecy.*" That means when we open our mouths and testify about what Jesus has already done, it also speaks prophetically that He will do it again. For this reason, it's vitally important to share the testimony of what Jesus has done in my life, in this case, from a financial standpoint.

If one were to look at my early years, there would be nothing to indicate I would experience the level of prosperity and financial freedom I now walk in. I was the second child of a young single mother who had left my alcohol and drug-addicted father and had to work incredibly hard to support me and my sister. My mom's mother was a literal orphan who grew up in an orphanage and worked hard her whole life just to spend retirement in poverty as well and die with no inheritance to leave to her children. You've probably heard the saying that some people are just born with a silver spoon in their mouth; well, I like to joke that I was born with a plastic spoon in mine. My early childhood was filled with poverty, hardship, and lack as my parents struggled to even keep food on the table, sometimes selling their own plasma for milk and bread money.

My husband and I married at eighteen and had three babies within the first four years of our marriage. To say we struggled financially was an understatement. However, my husband has always had extreme favor on his life, which caused him to be promoted continuously, even at a very young age. Nevertheless, it seemed that no matter how much money we made, we could never get "ahead" in our finances. We were in our mid to late twenties, bringing in over six figures per year and still couldn't seem to stop the paycheck-to-paycheck cycle and using debt to provide for our needs, being late on our bills, getting constant phone calls from bill collectors, and continuously having to evade the repo man when we would fall behind on our car payments.

It was in the middle of this frustration that my prayers began to change from "Lord, bless me" to "Lord, teach me" because, at this point, it was apparent that having more money was not the solution to our problems. No matter how much money we had or how much our income went up, our situation never changed. Looking back, I can clearly see the issue wasn't lack of money alone but from having no financial literacy or education on how to properly handle and steward it.

The Lord then began to show us principles in His Word that, when obeyed faithfully and consistently over time, bring incredible breakthroughs. He also showed us that having a poverty mindset has nothing to do with how much money we might have, and this mindset, once in place, doesn't go away with having more money. He began to challenge us to change many of the beliefs we had about money, even though many of those beliefs had been forged through the teachings at church, ironically. Nevertheless, we woke up to the fact that our way wasn't working, and we were ready to do things God's way.

If nothing changes, then nothing changes, and we knew we had to be willing to change. However, we also had to learn that trying to change our behavior without first changing our beliefs is an uphill battle we would probably lose. On the flip side, if a person changes their beliefs, behavior automatically changes as a result, so it became our mission to figure out what we believed and let God show us what needed to change about those beliefs.

Once we were ready to listen and obey, the Lord brought us through a journey of replacing those false beliefs with His truths and replacing our bad habits with new disciplines, except these new disciplines weren't as much behavior-focused as they were spiritually guided and purposed. He showed us how to walk in financial integrity according to His Word, not of other financial gurus. He took us on a wilderness journey of pruning away possessions (including but not limited to our home), pruning away positions (my husband was laid off from his six-figure job), pruning away spending habits that were consuming our wealth, and teaching us how to truly trust in Him for our provision because now there was literally no other source for us to trust in.

In the wilderness, there is no other choice but to trust God, and the wilderness trains our hearts to have a God-first attitude in all things, especially around money and provision. The wilderness trains foolish habits out of us and expels false beliefs. The wilderness is where we learned to live obediently to God's Word in the areas of finances and principles like tithing are not optional or feelings-based like we used to believe. We learned that we don't get the benefits provided and promised in God's Word for things like tithing without being obedient. Even though the wilderness was harsh, fierce, and unrelenting, we knew it was God's loving way of rescuing us from slavery, and we had to trust the process.

I don't regret the wilderness; I became grateful for it before ever even leaving it. As much as it hurt at first to have everything stripped away, simultaneously, it was also like a huge weight had been lifted. There was no more burden of working to support and keep afloat a sinking ship. Once the ship sunk, we could finally see clearly enough to wonder why the heck we worked so hard to keep it anyway. In the wilderness, as we took steps of faith to honor God, even if it meant we couldn't pay our bills, we saw God show up in miraculous ways we would have never seen otherwise. Like someone showing up on our doorstep with $1000 cash because they felt led, which happened to be the exact amount we needed to make rent because we chose to tithe before paying any bills.

If I have any regret, it is simply that God had to resort to such drastic measures to turn us around. During this time, the Lord instructed us to start a business that seemed crazy. Start a construction company? God, don't you know that it's 2008, and the construction industry has literally tanked here in Florida? Okay. You're the boss here. That very business was the vehicle through which God opened the windows of heaven within just a few short years and poured out such blessings we still can't contain them.

Today, our lives look completely different and not just in that we are living debt-free, with the ability to pay cash for almost anything—including cars. As cool as that is, that isn't even the real miracle. The real miracle is that WE are completely different, not just our situation. We are not tied to any amount of money, any possessions, or any position. We no longer see these things as our provider. Although we have and enjoy nice things, we don't live extravagantly because we would rather fund God's kingdom assignments than our own personal lifestyle.

We now know what it means to seek His kingdom first and live by His principles, and we find it exciting when God tells us to give extravagantly because we are in a place where God can do that through us. It's funny how suffering extreme poverty and lack can birth such generosity in a person's heart. I think it's because when you know the struggle, you never forget what it feels like. We literally had three years in a row where we had to look our teenage children in the faces and say, "There are no Christmas presents this year. None. Not because we don't love you but because we do. We can buy Christmas presents, or we can have electricity, that is the choice here. We also are not going to take tithe money that belongs to God just to buy things you don't need that you will probably even forget about by next Christmas."

As a parent, it was crushing to have to have that conversation with our children. However, God honored that sacrifice, and the very next Christmas, we were able to pay cash and buy our son a car. We never expected to be able to help our children with such things. After years of not being able to buy birthday or Christmas gifts, we can buy each other almost anything. But the ironic thing is that we don't. We don't have the desire to fill our lives with more useless stuff. Our favorite thing at Christmas time is to secretly bless other struggling families because we so vividly remember that pain.

As a result of our journey, God revealed to us key principles and strategies in His Word that, when obeyed, unlock kingdom provision, open windows, and give us access to our financial inheritance in Christ. Where most well-meaning programs, Christian or otherwise, focus on behavior modification, God is a God of belief modification. When He can change our beliefs, our behavior changes as a result. Trying to change our behavior without first changing our beliefs will keep us on a hamster wheel of frustration. There will be a lot of activity and movement but no progress. It is God's desire for His children to be free from every burden—finances are no exception. It is our heart's desire that the keys we learned and are sharing with you will be used to unlock others to be set free financially as well.

HOW TO GO THROUGH THIS BOOK

This book is a roadmap to financial freedom. We must become free on the inside before we will ever experience freedom on the outside. This book is meant to help expose and tear down many of the most common strongholds keeping God's people in financial bondage, which has nothing to do with how much money we may have. It is meant to be a marathon, not a sprint.

Have your Bible, a pen, and a highlighter with you so you can get the most out of this study. It is best to go through it slowly, really digging into and studying the scriptures discussed and planting them deeply into your heart. There are self-reflection questions designed to uncover the beliefs that keep us in bondage that we can replace with the truth and be set free.

CLASS 1

WHAT IS A POVERTY SPIRIT AND HOW DOES IT WORK?

"For as he thinks in his heart, so is he..."

PROVERBS 23:7 NKJV

Why do some Christians seem to have the Midas touch when it comes to finances, money, and provision, while others seem to barely scrape by no matter how hard they work? Why can some people, even Christians, amass great wealth and yet still feel like it is never enough? Why are some Christians plagued with constant feelings of unworthiness, no matter how much God, in His Word and through other people, affirm their value? Perhaps the reason is a poverty spirit is working like an unseen undercurrent directing the course and flow of their lives?

It is important for Christians to know how our enemy, the devil, uses poverty as a strategy and tactic to derail God's plan for our lives. Before we dive into unmasking the goal and strategies our enemy uses to accomplish this, I would like to clarify that when I say the term "poverty spirit," I am not necessarily talking about a spiritual entity. I am speaking more of an internal condition or an ingrained mindset that runs like a background program influencing our thoughts, decisions, and therefore, our actions when it comes to dealing with finances and provision. However, many times, there can be a spiritual entity behind the thoughts that pop into our minds or behind losses we suffer, but that is not always the case. Many times, when it is an actual spiritual entity at work, it can continue its influence in our lives because we think the thoughts we are thinking are originating from our own minds and we end up believing they are our own thoughts, so we never even consider we could be dealing with a wicked spirit we have God-given authority over.

There was definitely a spiritual entity behind the financial and personal losses suffered by Job, as told in the biblical account of his life in the Bible. In Job 1, we read that Satan, who is also referred to as "the devourer," was able to cause catastrophic losses for Job as a means of testing Job's devotion to God. We see another account in Mark 8:33, where Jesus looked His disciple Peter in the face and rebuked Satan! Peter gave voice to a thought that came from Satan. Even though we can see by these examples that spirits can be behind the natural poverty we suffer or even behind things we think or say, other times, the thoughts and beliefs come from our experiences, upbringing, or other teachings that have formed into subconscious thought patterns. Because we have never taken the time to challenge these thoughts and beliefs with the Word of God, they act like the rudder of our ship, steering the course of our lives by influencing our decisions.

For the sake of much of this discussion, when I refer to a "poverty spirit," I am speaking of ingrained mindsets rooted in poverty thinking, and not necessarily a spiritual entity seeking to cause financial losses. Every demonic spirit is a poverty spirit because the goal of these spirits is always to steal, kill, devour, and destroy anything and everything that belongs to us. However, much of the time, it is our own "stinkin' thinking" that has created thought patterns we've held for so long that we don't even realize they are there. Many times, this poverty thinking influences our decisions, which results in losses, setbacks, and the lack we suffer.

If one were to look at the financial situations of most modern-day believers in the church, there would be little to indicate that the Bride of Christ is betrothed to the King of Glory. There is little distinguishing her royal position as heir to the promises of God. In fact, in most cases, financially speaking, there is little to no difference between the financial situations of believers and the rest of the world. The reason for this is the enemy has infected the church with a poverty spirit, even getting many to adopt a false doctrine that money is evil, and poverty is some sort of virtue that pleases God. The enemy has been able to get away with this because most believers are scripturally illiterate, and as a result, few know and walk in their royal identities, positions, authority, and the provisions that come with it.

Thinking that believers living in poverty pleases God could not be further from the truth. Psalm 35:27 tells us that the Lord "*...has pleasure in the prosperity of His servant.*" The Hebrew word used for prosperity here is *shalom*[1], which means "completeness, soundness, welfare/health, peace, safety, security." This word is not only describing financial prosperity, although that is included, it is an all-encompassing prosperity far beyond just financial. This verse is saying that it gives God pleasure when His servants experience this all-encompassing prosperity, which goes far beyond financial prosperity. If our prosperity pleases our Lord, why are we not seeking to bring Him such pleasure?

Notice that it does not say God takes pleasure in the poverty of His servants. How, then, has it been so easy for so many in the church to adopt a poverty spirit and live so far below the standard God desires for His children? As human parents, we desire to see our children be successful and have all the provision they could ever need. We just do not want them to be corrupted by those possessions or for money and possessions to have the wrong priority in their hearts. It is no different with our heavenly Father. Throughout Scripture, we see the blessing of the Lord and financial prosperity tied together. Any warnings about riches and possessions have to do with giving those things the wrong priority in our lives, not with wealth itself. Giving wealth and material possessions the wrong priority is a heart condition, and we can be guilty of this no matter how much or how little we possess.

Now, before we go further in teaching what the Bible actually says about the financial prosperity of God's servants, it is important to note that I am not advocating a "name-it-and-claim-it, bless-me prosperity gospel" that has been used to justify greed and treating God like some genie in the sky whose job it is to grant our wishes and give us every little thing we ask for. The prevalence of a false doctrine like this has caused the pendulum of acceptable doctrine to swing completely in the opposite direction, causing many of us to adopt the false belief that forsaking money, wealth, and possessions will make us more righteous. Neither of these two ways of thinking could be more opposed to what God desires for us.

Throughout this book, we will discover that poverty and wealth have little to do with the number of possessions or amount of money we have and much more to do with our internal condition. We are going to learn that owning possessions and wealth can be the blessing God intends them to be if those things don't own us, or they could be our downfall causing us to be unable to truly surrender all that we have to follow Jesus.

Read Matthew 19:16-22.

We do not want to be like the rich young ruler who encountered Jesus. When Jesus asked this young ruler to sell his possessions and give the money to the poor so that he would have treasure in heaven, it was a test meant to expose the priority this man placed on his possessions and the grip they had on his life. Jesus was asking this young ruler if he could give up the temporary (his earthly wealth) for the eternal (heavenly wealth). The disciples surrendered everything—walking away from their homes, businesses, and their entire lives to follow Jesus. Belief in Jesus is free but following Him comes with a cost. To follow Christ, we must be willing to surrender all to the cause and make Him first above all we possess.

The problem in this parable was not that this young man had great wealth and many possessions. It was that this rich young ruler was too attached to his possessions to give them up to follow Jesus. He wanted a formula he could follow instead of living a lifestyle of sacrifice and relationship. Jesus did not tell him to sell his possessions because there was something wrong with owning possessions; it was this man's attachment to his possessions that kept him from following Jesus. His possessions had the wrong priority in his life.

Scripturally speaking, the problem is not with owning things or amassing great wealth. If it is a sin or a problem to be wealthy, why does God equate and promise financial increase with His blessings for obedience? We see many examples of God bestowing great wealth on the lives of many people, including but not limited to Abraham, Isaac, Jacob, Joseph, David, Solomon, and more. We also see, in the book of Job, that God bestows double-portion wealth as a blessing on Job for his patient endurance during testing. In Scripture, prosperity is always spoken of as a positive reward for obedience to the Word of God, and poverty is always spoken of with a negative connotation. Poverty was usually the result of a curse for disobedience to the Word of God. Deuteronomy 28 strongly compares prosperity and poverty, connecting prosperity with obedience and poverty with disobedience, as do many verses in Proverbs as well. Not one scripture mentions poverty as a blessing.

Please note that just because someone is experiencing poverty, does not necessarily mean they are living in disobedience to the Word of God. In many instances, if a believer continuously lives in poverty, the reason could have more to do with their lack of knowledge about what their biblical inheritance contains, so they don't have the faith to reach for great wealth. We can't believe God for something when we don't know it is His will for us to have it.

Other times, continuous poverty in the life of a believer could be because the person has unknowingly adopted a poverty mindset, which causes them to expect and, therefore, settle for way less than what God desires for them. It is important for every believer to examine themselves for the possibility that they could be believing lies about prosperity. Once we have become a child of God by professing faith in Jesus Christ, our lives change jurisdiction. We come under the rulership of the kingdom of God instead of the god of this world. This means we now have access to everything contained within the kingdom of God; however, it is our responsibility to bring the provision of heaven to the earth.

Read Colossians 1:13-14.

This passage tells us that when we accepted Christ, we came out from being under the jurisdiction of the kingdom of darkness ruled by Satan and are now under the kingdom of God. To get a natural picture of this, I currently live in the state of Florida. That means I live under the jurisdiction of the laws that govern the state of Florida. If I transfer to a different state, like Ohio, that means my life would now be under the jurisdiction of the laws of Ohio, and the laws governing Florida no longer apply to me. The same thing happens when our lives change spiritual jurisdiction. Satan and the kingdom of darkness no longer have authority or rulership over us. This means Satan can only steal, kill, or cause direct destruction if we give him a legal foothold. Ephesians 4:27 explains how anger is just one type of foothold we can give the enemy.

Just like Florida law enforcement wouldn't be able to invade my home in Ohio unless I gave them a legal justification to do so, the same is true with our enemy, the devil. He cannot just waltz into our lives and do whatever he wants.

Now, being the thief he is, he may try some illegal tactics, hoping we won't know how to exercise our authority over him, but often, he is going to look for a legal way to gain a foothold to confiscate our blessings. He does this by bringing charges against us before the throne of God. If he can get us to sin by disobeying God, he can petition God to legally be able to confiscate our blessings. We can see from the account of Job that even when we haven't sinned, just by bringing charges of accusation against us, until those charges are cleared, he will have free reign to devour our earthly wealth, our health, or whatever else he can get his hands on. 1 Peter 5:8 warns us of this and tells us to stay sober and keep watch because Satan is actively looking for someone to devour. This warning was written to the Church! We wouldn't have been warned if it wasn't possible for Satan to find a way to devour our lives.

If Satan can't gain the legal foothold to devour our finances by getting us to disobey the Word of God, his next best strategy is to get us to embrace a different truth. Notice, I did not say embrace an outright lie. Satan is tricky and knows we usually will reject an outright lie, which is why he tries to mix his lies with some truth, making them appear scriptural, even though they are not. This is why we must have our own firm grasp of the scriptures and take responsibility for our own learning. It is great to attend church services and to learn from others, but that cannot and should not ever be a replacement meal for our daily bread.

We must feast on the Word of God daily, dining at the table with the Holy Spirit and allowing the Spirit of Truth to speak to us and teach us all things as Jesus promises us in John 14:26. Here, Jesus tells us Holy Spirit will teach us all things and will bring us to remember the things Jesus Himself said. Teachers and pastors are great and are a gift to the Church from Christ Himself. However, most of our learning should not be secondhand. Without a relationship with the Living Word and the written Word, we won't be able to discern if what's being taught is correct. We need to be in daily communication with the Holy Spirit, allowing Him to have the final say on things we learn, even when it comes to this book. Please do not just take my word for it. Look up the scriptures, write down questions, and ask the Holy Spirit to clarify what is correct.

For example, many Christians have adopted the belief that money is evil because of certain teachings from some pulpits. Is this what the Bible says? No. It says, "For *the love of money is the root of all evil...*" (1 Timothy 6:10 KJV). We can commit that sin without a dime to our name. This is exactly how a poverty spirit works in the background of our minds. Satan tries to get us to embrace a doctrine that poverty is a virtue that pleases God because money is evil, going as far as getting us to buy into the lie that even Jesus was poor, proving God wants us poor. (We will dispel that myth later.) By doing this, Satan gets us to repel wealth and prosperity, which accomplishes the exact same effect as if he came right up and stole our provision out of our hands. However, by operating in our minds, Satan doesn't have to steal a thing! He gets us to do his dirty work for him by simply getting us to agree with a lie!

Some of the greatest examples in Scripture of a right relationship with the Lord are shown in the lives of men such as Job, Abraham, Joseph, and King David, and yet, these men were vastly wealthy. One thing these men had in common besides their wealth was they lived life with a God-first mindset and kept Him the priority in every aspect of their lives, including but not limited to their wealth. We can clearly see that wealth in and of itself is not the problem. The problem lies with giving wealth the wrong place in our hearts, the wrong priority in our lives, and developing an unhealthy attachment to wealth and possessions.

If this truth is obvious in Scripture, why then has it been so easy for the enemy to get God's children to fear and repel wealth and develop the false belief that wealth is bad and poverty is good? Why has it been so easy to get God's children to adopt a poverty spirit? To understand, we must look at who or what the spirit of poverty really is and what its goal is. The spirit of poverty is a stronghold established for the purpose of keeping us from walking in victory—the full, complete victory of the cross. We will get into what a stronghold is and how it works in a little bit. For now, it's important to know Satan will use spiritual entities when he can, or he will develop and use ingrained beliefs and mindsets to establish a poverty stronghold because he wants to keep us from enforcing the victory of the cross on him.

He seeks to keep us from everything Christ's victory gained for us, including all the blessings of our inheritance in Christ. The cross of Jesus purchased us an inheritance that is just as much for this life as it is for eternal life. Luke 10:19 tells us part of that victory is that we now have authority over *"all the power of the enemy."* If we are stuck in poverty-thinking because of these poverty strongholds, the enemy keeps us from using our Christ-given authority over him.

For some reason, we mistakenly believe our salvation, restoration, and inheritance are solely for the afterlife in eternity. We will dive deeper into this subject in the lesson dedicated to the truth of our inheritance. However, until then, know the belief that our inheritance in Christ is only about eternity is a lie perpetrated on believers by the enemy and designed to keep us from having the provision God desires us to have in this life to fulfill every kingdom assignment He gives us. Satan, through a poverty spirit, seeks to keep us living as orphans and peasants and from knowing our true identities, instead of rising to our rightful place as the heirs of the King. His goal is not just to keep provision out of our hands. The real goal is that by keeping provision out of our hands, he can keep us from doing the will of God.

HOW TO RECOGNIZE THE PRESENCE OF A POVERTY STRONGHOLD

A poverty spirit has several strategies it can use to keep us from the will of God. These strategies include, but are not limited to:

- keeping us focused on what we lack
- keeping us focused on our own "unworthiness"
- establishing false beliefs about money, wealth, prosperity, and property

- having us terrified of loss
- giving us great wealth, ironically, and keeping us focused on amassing and hoarding great fortunes

Let's dive into each of these strategies a little bit deeper so we can see and determine whether a poverty spirit is operating in our lives. This can't be determined by the amount of wealth or possessions we do or don't have. The presence of this stronghold manifests in our thoughts and behaviors as follows:

The first strategy is to keep us focused on what we lack, what we wish we had, and always feeling like we will never have enough. We will feel trapped by the lack of provision and will make decisions based on the provision we already do or don't have. We have a constant underlying fear of lack or never having enough or running out of provision. It will cause us to stockpile and hoard out of fear of being without. (Sidenote: Like in the story of Joseph, God can lead us to store up provision for a coming season instead of using it freely. This is not fear-based hoarding when it is in obedience to a direct command of the Lord. However, keep in mind that the provision the Lord had Joseph stockpile was for other people, not just for himself. It was to preserve the nation through a time of famine. More on this later.)

When motivated by a poverty spirit, most of our time will be consumed with chasing and stockpiling provision, over-working, and yet, stepping into "more than enough" provision will always elude us. In addition, Satan will employ legal or illegal strategies to steal our provision through troublesome circumstances or outright steal our provision to keep us in a constant state of lack. He keeps us so busy working just to pay the bills we are always behind on that we don't even have the energy to pursue our inheritance, which is doing our part to advance the kingdom through the assignments God wants to give us.

The second strategy is to struggle with persistent feelings of unworthiness: unworthy to receive from the Father, undeserving of His goodness, or dressed in this garment of false humility that says, "we're not worthy." Feelings of unworthiness keep us from being able to receive God's grace or His provision, causing us to try to work for both instead.

Read Luke 15:11-24.

Even though he was genuinely repentant, his feelings of unworthiness kept him from returning to his identity as a son who could simply receive provision from his father and made him want to work for both his provision and his place in the house. In other words, he felt like he had to work for both his salvation and provision. This is what Satan does with many of us. He traps us into working for God for our salvation instead of simply receiving God's grace by faith. What we don't realize is that this "humility" is actually pride because our focus is on our own works and what we can do to make up for the bad things we've done instead of focusing on what Christ did on our behalf and now we don't feel indebted to God because we worked for what He gives us.

The third strategy the enemy uses to establish a poverty stronghold is the enemy will seek to establish false beliefs around money and possessions. We've already discussed one of those beliefs—money and prosperity are evil. Other false beliefs are things like: "Money management is too hard," or "I want just enough to pay my bills; I don't need great wealth." Again, it sounds good and humble, and yet, it's still pride. Saying we don't need great wealth is assuming our wealth is about us anyway. Wanting just enough for our own house is one of the most selfish attitudes we can have.

Who, then, should feed the hungry? Who, then, should build orphanages, send missionaries, or ship Bibles all over the globe? By not having our own wealth to participate in providing for these global needs, when it comes to us, the kingdom doesn't advance beyond our own house. Do we think that's better or honors God more than having the guts to ask for the ability to build the wealth it takes to do these things? I can't think of anything more selfish. I don't say this in condemnation but rather to expose this false humility for what it is so we recognize the error in this type of thinking and can learn to reject thoughts like this.

The fourth strategy the enemy will use in a stronghold of poverty is to keep us terrified of loss. He will throw an onslaught of thoughts at our minds full of vain imaginations of tragedies, which will keep us afraid of losing our possessions, our positions, our titles, our jobs, our loved ones, or anything else we esteem as important or as a source of our provision. Have you ever had one of those weird daydreams that feel so real you get emotional, where a loved one suddenly dies, or where you experience some other form of tragedy or loss? If allowed to take root, we get a crop of all kinds of "what if" thoughts that will have us making decisions out of fear. We will then begin to live in a constant state of holding our breath, waiting for the carpet to be pulled out from underneath us, where everything collapses, and we lose it all.

Because of this, we stay in a cycle of being tightfisted, afraid to give or lose what we already have, fearing it will never be replaced. We become stingy instead of generous. We will play it safe out of "wisdom" instead of stepping out whenever or wherever God tells us. We will become too afraid to gather in worship because some disease might get us, rather than walking in our authority over every sickness and disease. This poverty stronghold affects every area of our lives, not just our financial provision. Lacking any good thing, even health, is poverty and is not from God. It is from the one who steals, kills, and destroys. We are the ones who either enforce our cross-given victory or not. We are the ones who either push back the darkness or let it take from us. If Satan can keep us in fear, thus in poverty, he can keep us from using our God-given authority against him to stop the destruction he seeks to cause.

The fifth and final strategy we are going to discuss is that Satan may actually give us great riches, but our lives will be just as empty and full of worries as if we were destitute. Satan is the god of this world's system, and we can see by his exchange with Jesus in the desert that he, too, can give people great riches.

Read Luke 4:1-7.

We see how it ends in that Jesus never succumbs to temptation, and His weapon for defeating the devil was by declaring the entirety of what God's Word said, not the twisted versions Satan was quoting. Here are some other revelations from this passage and how we can see these strategies at work:

"If you are the son of God"—We see Satan using the strategy of trying to get Jesus to doubt or question His identity as a Son and bring His worthiness into question. (Strategy 2)

"Tell this stone to become a loaf of bread"—he tried to get Jesus to focus on His lack (how hungry He was) and use that as motivation to trust in Himself for His provision by seeking to get Jesus to work or perform for His own provision, obtaining provision in a different way other than what God said. (Strategy 1)

"No! The scriptures say…"—Jesus defeated the enemy by knowing and speaking the whole Word of God. (More on this later.)

"Because they are mine to give to anyone I please."—Satan is called the god of this world (John 12:31 and John 16:11). He has control over this world's system and resources and can give them to whomever he desires. (Strategy 5)

"I will give it all to you if you will worship me."—his ultimate goal is to get us to abandon the will of God and our God-given assignments to keep us from fulfilling our God-given destiny.

Satan's motive for using poverty is always to keep us from the plan and purpose of God. This is exactly what Satan was trying to get Jesus to agree to—to turn from God and abandon His mission. When Satan gives wealth, it is always for our destruction. However, when God gives wealth, it is to fund and support His plan and purposes for our lives. Again, having a poverty spirit has very little to do with how much wealth and possessions we own and more to do with how we view those possessions and what or who the source of them is. We see this strategy number five of a poverty spirit manifest in people like many celebrities, for example, who seem to have gained everything by the world's standard of wealth and from a monetary standpoint.

Although they seem to have "everything," it is never enough to keep them from striving for more. They live under constant worry someone is going to cheat them out of or steal their wealth, causing many of their relationships to remain shallow. They don't trust anyone because they think people only like them for their money, and they can't let anyone get too close for fear of being used for their money. Although they seem to have what the world calls "everything," many of them live in constant states of anxiety, depression, and emptiness, causing many of them to turn to drugs, alcohol, and other vices for solace. They may have wealth, but they have no prosperity.

Proverbs 10:22 tells us when the Lord is the source of our riches, He adds no sorrow with it. If we have great wealth, but our lives are full of sorrow, stress, worry, anxiety, depression, fear, and emptiness, it is a good indication the Lord was not the source of that wealth. It is important to note that financial independence or prosperity does not mean we all will be rich enough to buy whatever we want, like mansions and

Ferraris. God doesn't give us more wealth than we can handle. Financial freedom means we will be free of every financial burden, tie, or bondage to money, so we will make decisions based on what the will of the Lord is and not on how much money we do or don't have. Financial freedom means we should be able to fulfill every assignment God puts on our hearts and be able to give into any and every assignment, project, or need into which God tells us to give.

Earth was never designed to be a temporary enslavement camp on the way to heaven or a temporary prison until we die and can finally be free. It was always intended for us to have all the provisions we need on earth to fulfill our mission. Jesus was about, and taught us to be about, bringing heaven to earth, not trying to get the earth into heaven. Jesus taught us to pray, *"Thy kingdom come, thy will be done on earth as it is in heaven."*[2] The gospel is not about getting those on earth into heaven, it is about getting heaven into those on earth. It is supposed to be *"on earth as it is in heaven."*

Do we live in poverty in heaven? Does heaven have streets of potholes? So then why have so many of us adopted the belief that God wants us poor on earth but rich in heaven? If wealth is bad, why did Jesus tell us in Matthew 6:19 to store up treasure in heaven because in heaven it can't be corrupted, stolen, or lost? Why would Jesus want us to have wealth that never disappears if wealth is bad? The difference is earthly riches are perishable, and we should see them for what they are—nothing more than resources to help us fulfill our mission and assignment. It is wiser to amass treasure where it will never decay or be perishable. That should speak to us about God's heart for us. He wants us to invest in treasure that will never disappear, rust, or decay. That means He doesn't want us to be poor. He simply doesn't want us to give the wrong priority to a temporary version of wealth found on the earth; He wants our priority to be storing up eternal wealth.

So again, why has much of the Church adopted a poverty mindset so easily? Part of the reason may lie in the fact that we recognize the falsehood and error of the "name-it-and-claim-it" gospel, so we figure the opposite must be true. It would seem both extremes are what is described in 1 Timothy 4:1 as being teachings that come from demons and deceptive spirits designed to get us either over-focused on wealth, so we hoard it and not fund kingdom assignments or get us to repel wealth, so we don't have it to fund kingdom assignments. The spirit of poverty wants us to adopt the beliefs of either extreme to make us feel like we will never have enough, keep us tight-fisted and afraid to lose what we already have, or repel wealth by believing money is evil. Why?

The enemy doesn't want wealth in the hands of believers because a broke army can't move forward and advance into and take territory. A broke army can't focus on fighting if they are preoccupied with searching for basic provisions. How well could soldiers in natural armies fight if they had to chase basic provisions instead of simply having them supplied by the government for which they were fighting? Soldiers' needs are provided by the government they represent and are fighting on behalf of. Even more, it is the obligation of the government the army represents to make sure the army has all the food, ammunition, and gear to carry out its mission. How can an army focus on tackling their mission and completing their assignment if they must work to provide those basic needs?

The government of God is no different. He will supply everything needed to advance His agenda and His assignments in our lives, not our own personal agendas and desires. If it's God's will, then it's God's bill. It is God's responsibility to supply the provision for every assignment He gives us. However, God is not responsible for, or bound to, provide every little thing we feel like doing or having, even if it's for a good cause. If it's our will, then it's our bill. This is not to say God, in His goodness and mercy, won't still sometimes provide for these things anyway, but He is under no obligation to do so. However, He is obligated to provide for the assignments He sends us on just like any government is obligated to provide for the army they send on assignment.

The problem is, instead of trusting Jesus to supply these basic needs, many of us spend most of our time here on earth consumed with chasing provision on our own to supply the necessities of life, instead of focusing on the assignments and operations God has given us to do and having faith the provision to fulfill those assignments will show up. That is exactly what a poverty spirit keeps us doing. It is impossible to disciple nations without prosperity. It takes money to print and ship Bibles, to send provisions to those in need, to send missionaries on assignment, to build orphanages, to feed the hungry, and to clothe the naked. That money comes from believers who give of their wealth for the cause.

If the enemy can intercept the supply lines, he can render the entire army ineffective and dead in its tracks. If Satan can keep money and provision out of the hands of God's people, he can greatly hinder the gospel from going forth. This is why he has worked so hard to infiltrate the Church with a poverty spirit and poverty thinking. The good news is there is a clear, biblical strategy that will dethrone this stronghold of poverty in our lives. If we follow it, we can demolish this stronghold and help others do the same.

WHAT IS A STRONGHOLD?

Remember a poverty spirit is a stronghold, but in order to know what to do about it, it is important to first know what a stronghold is and how it operates. Once we understand exactly what we're dealing with, we can get into the keys Scripture gives us for demolishing strongholds.

Read 2 Corinthians 10:3-5 AMP.

According to this passage, where are strongholds located? Where are sophisticated arguments located? In the mind! Are strongholds made of bricks, mortar, and stone? No, they are made of thoughts and sophisticated arguments built in our minds. A stronghold is a fortress of wrong thinking built out of lies and can even harbor a demonic entity that continually feeds and reinforces the lies it hides behind. The fortress is built out of beliefs developed from knowledge of a "sophisticated" argument of worldly wisdom, a lie, or both, that erects itself against the true knowledge of God. Notice that these arguments are sophisticated, and they also exalt themselves as truth over the true knowledge of God, or in other words, over what God says is true. Without us even realizing it, it causes us to trade the truth of God for a lie, which means we have now elevated a lie above the truth of what God says. These arguments are so sophisticated we don't even realize we are doing this.

What does sophisticated mean? It means "highly complicated or developed; complex."[3] Satan is crafty and cunning. These arguments must be complex enough to have an appearance of being biblically sound, otherwise, we would easily reject them. A fortress is different in structure than an ordinary house. A fortress is built to withstand an outside force trying to breach it. It's more complex than a regular house. A regular house can be broken into and torn down much easier than a fortress. In the same way, a mental stronghold is tougher to tear down than an average thought that can be easily dismissed. The only weapon strong enough is the truth of God's Word.

HOW DO WE DESTROY STRONGHOLDS?

So how do we destroy a fortress made of thoughts? If we destroy the argument, we destroy the stronghold. How do we destroy a sophisticated argument that has become a mental stronghold? We hold those thoughts up against the Word of God and allow the Holy Spirit to take us through a process of reevaluating them, even ones about money and wealth. We take the false argument and replace it with the truth of God's Word. We take the half-truth and replace it with the whole truth. We use the truth of God's Word like a battering ram, chipping away at the false belief until it finally crumbles.

The human mind is often equated with a computer. If we were to think of our brains like a computer, a stronghold is like a virus made from a program of lies. Reading the Word of God is like running anti-virus software. When we read truth that contradicts something we already believe, the truth works to expose or detect the lie originating in our false belief. Then, just like a bad or corrupt file, the lie can be deleted, and truth can be installed in place of that lie by memorizing God's Word. The only way a lie can be exposed is to compare it against the truth. However, it's not enough to simply read or memorize scriptures (as can be seen by how Satan takes the truth and twists it), it's mostly how we interpret them that gets us in trouble. Many times, we have the Word right, but we have the interpretation wrong. This is why it is so important to be in communion with the Holy Spirit. Without the revelatory insight that the Holy Spirit breathes into what we're reading, we are left to interpret Scripture through the limited filter of human reasoning.

The battle rages in the thinking process of the believer. The battleground to remove strongholds is the same place they are in—the mind. To destroy a stronghold, we must destroy the lie with the sword of the Spirit, but the power behind the sword must come from the Holy Spirit. Freedom is achieved not by might nor by power but by His Spirit.[4] We must make quiet time with the Holy Spirit a regular priority in our lives. Then, when we use the Word of God to resist the devil, he will flee from us just like we are promised in James 4:7 (NLT), which reads, *"So humble yourselves before God. Resist the devil, and he will flee from you."*

However, we can't skip over the humbling ourselves before God part. Before we can defeat lies, we must have the humility to accept the fact that we may be believing incorrect things. It takes humility to admit we could be or are wrong. Once we accept our wrong thinking in humility, we can ingest the Word with fresh revelation, and it will dispel the lies. If we are reading the Word of God with a "know-it-all" attitude, our hearts will be hard, only reinforcing the stronghold. Humility softens our hearts to receive truth and let it do its job.

Satan can only rule where there is darkness or ignorance of the Word of God. This is why Jesus said, *"And you will know the truth, and the truth will set you free."*[5] Freedom comes by knowing the truth in a deep, intimate way and having a relationship with the person of truth, Jesus, who is the Word. Knowing facts about Jesus, or even being able to quote His Word, can, but should never, be a substitute for knowing Him. Without the relationship, Scripture will be nothing more than words on a page. Without knowing Him, we may have money, but we will not have prosperity, and our money might as well be filthy rags.

Satan has memorized Scripture better than most believers! However, it has no positive effect on him because of his hard heart and pride. That's why we must humble ourselves before God before we can resist the devil. He has no relationship with the Living Word. The Pharisees could quote the scriptures faster and better than anyone else. Yet, when the Living Word was staring them in the face, they didn't recognize Him. In the same way, the early Church didn't have the New Testament to study. It was being written. They relied on the guidance of the Holy Spirit. We are so fortunate we have both. Relationship always precedes knowledge. Having vast knowledge of a person and memorizing their life story is never a suitable replacement for being in relationship with them. Knowing them as a person and knowing their life story are nowhere near the same thing.

Since the prison bars of our captivity or strongholds are built out of lies, truth must be the key that unlocks them. Truth neutralizes lies. Any area where we are not free must have an absence of God's truth or is missing the correct interpretation. Again, it is not enough to just know and memorize words on a page. (Remember, strongholds are sophisticated arguments, many times formed out of a half-truth.) Without an intimate relationship with Jesus Christ, we very well may know just enough truth in Scripture to form the very prison bars we seek freedom from.

Once we possess the truth, it can only open the prison by coming into contact with the lie. Just like possessing a physical key does nothing unless we take that key and bring it into contact with the lock; if we are not actively taking truth and putting it in contact with the lies, the lock never opens even though we possess the key. We must insert the key into the lock, turn it around, and release the door. In the same way, we must take the truth, insert it into the lie, turn it around and we will be set free.

When we look at different passages of Scripture where Satan interacts with humans such as in the Garden of Eden or when tempting Jesus in the wilderness, we gain some insight into how he operates[6]. In these instances, we see Satan didn't challenge Eve and Jesus with outright lies, he came at them with the Word of God! Satan used it in a half-truth way, trying to get them to agree with a different meaning and different application of what God said. The bars of his trap were made of parts of God's Word. Comparing the interaction of Satan with Eve in Genesis 3 versus Satan's interaction with Jesus in Matthew 4, we can see how important it is to have a strong and firm understanding of what God says. With Eve, Satan's twisted truth seemed right enough to deceive her. With Jesus, we see His strong knowledge of the Word of God because He is the living, breathing Word of God. That knowledge allowed Him to fight off the deceiver with what God actually said.[7]

FIRST STEP TO FREEDOM: USING TRUTH TO DESTROY LIES

All warfare can be summed up as a battle over what thoughts we agree with. Satan studies us and knows if, where, and how he can infiltrate our minds. If he succeeds, he can infiltrate our lives with his strongholds. Everything in our lives began as a thought. From brushing our teeth to drinking a cup of coffee, nothing becomes our reality or experience without it first being a thought. If Satan can get us to disagree with, break agreement with, or keep us from knowing the Word of God by getting us to agree with a different thought or idea, he has won that territory in our mind and inserts himself securely behind a fortress of lies we agreed with.

The first step to demolishing any stronghold is finding what God's Word says about the subject. We then read it repeatedly, planting those seeds of truth in our minds and hearts, and become so firmly grounded in it that we won't fall for Satan's bait. As we read the Word of God, it may challenge some of the things we believe, so we need to read it with the intention of allowing it to find and flush them out. However, as mentioned before, even more important is having an intimate relationship with the Holy Spirit, the Spirit of Truth, Jesus, because Scripture tells us He will "teach us all things."[8] All things are not just spiritual, biblical, or religious things. For the sake of the discussion here, the subject in question is prosperity, money, and wealth. We must be willing to cast aside what we think we already know of the matter and let the Holy Spirit challenge any sophisticated arguments so we can let truth drive the lies out of our minds, tear down strongholds, and build new beliefs based on truth.

With that in mind, conquering a poverty stronghold begins with our mindset about money. We must examine what we believe about poverty, money, and wealth, hold those beliefs up against the Word of God, and dissect the half-truths until we have the whole truth. This is important because as we come into agreement with the lies of the enemy instead of the truth we are making a trade with the enemy. When we choose to accept the information or lie instead of resisting it with the truth of God's Word, we trade away our true identities as children of the King and take on identities as orphans. We begin to see life through a lens of lack, instead of the abundance of heaven being available to us.

We trade our identities for what is promised by the lie. We begin to believe we're unworthy, wealth is bad, poverty pleases God, and we will never have enough or that the resources we've been given are ours and we are in control of them to do what we wish. We then begin to believe we are excused from fulfilling

God's assignments for us, or we can't fulfill them because we lack the provision to do so, never mind the fact it's largely because we've wasted provision on lifestyle stuff. We play right into the enemy's mission of preventing us from fulfilling the will of God for our lives.

The only way to freedom is to break our agreement with the lies that hold us back. By replacing those beliefs with the truth of what God says in His Word about prosperity, wealth, and provision, we can proactively create a new mindset built on the belief of what God's Word says on the subject.

SECOND STEP TO FREEDOM: CREATING A NEW BONDSLAVE MENTALITY

When we don't know who we are and whose we are, we can't properly discern what can, should, and does belong to us as a kingdom citizen. This is how many of these strongholds form to begin with. In Class 2, we will discuss more about our identity, citizenship, inheritance, and what being a co-heir with Christ is supposed to look like, but until we can fully comprehend and absorb that new identity, we must embrace the truth that when we begin a relationship with Jesus Christ, we are not our own and have been bought with a price.

Read 1 Corinthians 6:19-20.

When we buy something, we own it, and it gets used for the purpose we say it does. We are of such high value to God that Jesus stepped into humanity and purchased us back from the master who held us captive to sin so we could become individual and personal temples for His Spirit. Does God own anything He doesn't take care of? When we allow ourselves to meditate on the truth that we have been purchased with the currency of the highest possible value—the very blood of God Himself, which Jesus shed on the cross—it helps us develop the proper mindset that we no longer belong to ourselves. We have been purchased. Therefore, whoever owns us also owns what belongs to us. This revelation helps our hearts properly take on the posture of a bondslave—one who is the owner of nothing but is only the steward of all their master owns.

We view life and possessions as the temporary things they are. It's like when we stay in a hotel. We know our stay is temporary, and although the amenities have been leased to us for a time, and we are free to use and enjoy all of them during our stay, we don't become attached to any of them because they're not ours. We know that although we paid the money for the right to use these things during our stay, they are only rented for the duration of that visit. When we vacate the room, we aren't sad to leave the microwave, television, or anything else behind because it was never ours to begin with. Those possessions were loaned to us by the real owner. It would not be wrong to enjoy the use of them during our stay. In fact, that's the purpose of those amenities to begin with. We simply don't become improperly attached to these things.

This is how we must treat all possessions and money. We must recognize that God is the owner of it all and not attach our hearts to any of it. The only attachment our hearts should have is to Him. Although allowed to use and enjoy all things during our stay here on earth, ultimately, we own none of it. It all stays behind to be used by someone else when we leave this life. Bondslaves are servants and they know their place. They are not in a power struggle with their master. They treat their master's possessions with respect and care because they know they are not the owner. They also are not caught up in the worry of whether their master will provide for them. They work from rest in the knowledge that they are provided for. When we take on this heart posture, fear of lack has no hold on us.

Adopting this mindset will help dethrone a poverty spirit because we then won't fear losing something, we won't have the temptation to hoard material things, and we won't feel unworthy to have money or possessions when we know none of it belongs to us anyway. A lot of people struggle with the thought that since they worked a job to earn money and to buy stuff, it is theirs by right and not God's. This improper mindset is born from not knowing our place. Even though a bondservant works whatever job or assignment is given to him by his master, he has no money of his own. He can't freely spend what he has been entrusted with because it technically isn't his. Even though the bondservant was the one who "worked" for it, they wouldn't even have that job if it wasn't provided to them by the master.

Let's say my kids needed some money, so I came up with some chores or odd jobs they could do to receive extra cash. Even though they did the job, they wouldn't have even had the opportunity to earn it if I hadn't created it for them. I was the one who created the opportunity to earn the money they wanted and gave them the ability to do so. I wasn't obligated to create such an opportunity for them. I could have just kept my money and left them to their own devices. However, as a good parent, I not only created an opportunity for them to receive what they wanted but I did it in such a way that built their self-esteem and sense of contribution.

Both Psalm 24:1 and 1 Corinthians 10:26 let us know that the earth is the Lord's and everything in it. That means God owns all money and property. It's like life is one big stay at God's hotel, and we are just here visiting. As the owner, God gave stewardship and dominion of the earth and its property to Adam, who then gave it away to Satan. By coming into agreement with Satan instead of God, Adam joined in the rebellion of Satan and the fallen angels, thereby forfeiting his position. Jesus won the position, authority, and stewardship of God's property back.

It's like God made Adam the hotel manager with free use of the hotel and all its amenities. When Adam disobeyed God, he relinquished his title and position as ruler of this world, handing it over to Satan. Jesus came in, kicked Satan out, and gave the management position back to Adam's descendants. Dominion was given to man when God created Adam. That man, Adam, lost it through disobedience; therefore, Jesus had to step into humanity, go to the cross on our behalf, and win dominion back as a man, allowing us to walk in authority again. That position of stewardship and authority is ours only because the owner of it allows us to hold that position.

Even though the scripture above tells us the earth is the Lord's and everything in it, Psalm 115:16 (NKJV) says, *"The heaven, even the heavens, are the LORD's; but the earth He has given to the children of men."* At first glance, these scriptures seem to contradict each other, so perhaps an easy way to understand is the analogy of a landlord. The landlord (God) owns property with a house on it (earth). He chooses to lease this property (earth) to someone else (Adam and his descendants). Just like if I own a piece of property and build a house on it with my own two hands, even though I own it all, I could, of my own free will, choose to limit my own authority and control of that property by leasing it out to someone else. I still own it, but I am bound by the terms of the lease agreement, limiting my authority in certain regards.

When a landlord enters into a lease agreement with a renter, even though he maintains ownership of the property and the final say so on certain decisions, the landlord willfully limits his own control of certain aspects, although he is technically still in charge of the property. Once leased, even though the landlord still owns the property, he no longer maintains full control of the property and legally can no longer enter the property without warning unless invited or without a set appointment time arranged with the tenant ahead of time. The landlord is still in charge but not in control. The landlord willfully chose to transfer stewardship to a tenant. This means that even though the landlord can still control certain aspects, he doesn't control anything that happens in the house or the tenant's free will decisions.

The tenants can come and go as they please, go to bed when they want, have company when they want, decide what kind of furniture to have, etc. The landlord is allowing someone else to steward his property, trusting they will treat the arrangement with respect and not destroy the property, or allow unauthorized tenants to take up residence there. Not only did Adam allow an unauthorized tenant to take up residence, but he also relinquished his authority and dominion over the property to this unauthorized tenant—Satan. Jesus's finished work on the cross retrieved that authority back. Jesus then gave that dominion back to mankind as was originally intended. The only difference is that we still have this unauthorized tenant, Satan, as a roommate. Until Jesus returns and banishes Satan to hell, our assignment is to use the authority Jesus gave back to us to keep Satan in check and enforce heaven's authority over his activities on earth.

Even though this analogy may not be a perfect representation, it gives us a picture of the arrangement God made with mankind regarding stewardship of the earth and who owns what. The things of the earth—property, possessions, wealth, our assignments, and jobs—have been "leased" to us by God. Yet, instead of recognizing that even though God does not control us, He is still in charge. We are merely stewards of His property. Many of us want to maintain full decision-making power over how "our" money is spent and leave God out of the equation—that is unless and until we need or want Him to rescue us from our decisions.

Because God endowed human beings with free will, He does not enforce control of our decisions but instead lets us control our own actions, even with His property. So instead of living in financial victory, we end up in a power struggle with God. We want to decide what house we live in, what car we drive, what clothes we buy, if we tithe, etc. We want full decision-making power over how those resources are used.

How we use these resources and whether we use our free will to invite God into our decisions by humbling ourselves and recognizing who they truly belong to is a test of what is in our hearts.

God, as Creator of all things, is in charge, not in control. This is an important distinction. God oversees the universe and the laws that govern life but does not control anyone. He doesn't even control Satan. He, of course, has the power and ability if He wants to, but that is not how God operates. So what's the difference? Think of children playing on a school playground. There is a yard duty who has the authority and is in charge to make and enforce the rules of the playground and bring justice if a child breaks the rules. However, the yard duty does not control the children. The yard duty doesn't control what the children play or where they play within the playground. The yard duty doesn't control what the children wear or what they bring for lunch. However, the yard duty is still in charge.

This gives us a picture of how God operates in His interactions with mankind. God oversees the rules that govern life. God decided how many resources like gold, silver, precious stones, water, land, etc., are on the earth. He created the animals, vegetation, and all matter, so, therefore, it all belongs to Him. However, He chose to give control of those resources over to mankind. In perfect creation, there is nothing wrong with this. It is no different than an owner of a company delegating certain responsibilities and control over certain decisions to managers. However, mankind messed up and allowed sin to enter, which brought with it a curse of poverty, scarcity, and lack. It brought rebellion against God and His original plan.

If we continue with the analogy of a company owner, this would be like the manager not being content with the power and authority they've been given to both manage and freely use all that is at their disposal and, instead, wanting to be the owner as well because the owner has the authority to override the manager. This is the same sin mankind has fallen for since the Garden of Eden—the temptation to be "like God."[9] The ironic thing is that Adam already was, in a sense. He had been given complete dominion over all of creation. Because of what Jesus did for us, restoring us to our original position, so have we.

1 John 4:17 (NKJV) says, *"...as He is, so are we in this world."* In other words, the same authority and dominion Christ walked in, we also walk in. However, Jesus was in full submission to the Father. Our problem is that we don't want to live in the same submission Christ lives in, to carry the same authority He carries. We want authority and control without paying the price because we don't like someone else telling us what to do, and we don't like going through the character development that only comes through suffering. The irony is that living in total submission, with the attitude of a bondservant, is what gives us the very authority we crave so much.

So why is it so important to understand the difference between God being in control and God being in charge? Why is it important to understand how and why God has chosen to limit his own authority and where the boundaries of our own authority are? The reason is so we can have the partnership with God He desires to have with us. Having this blanket attitude of "God is in control" causes us to be passive Christians, thinking God is just going to wave His magic wand and take care of everything, and we have no part to play because "it's out of our control." Neither should we seek to run with the authority we've been given and just forge ahead, trying to do things in our own strength and power.

Biblically speaking, there are levels of authority. We see this in the encounter between Jesus and the Roman officer recorded in Matthew 8:5-10. Even those who walk in great authority are submitted to someone or something. This is why the greater the authority we seek to carry, the greater the suffering we are going to walk through to get it. That suffering is what keeps our hearts submitted to the one from whom our authority comes.

God works in the earth through people. He is looking for those who are willing to act on His behalf, partnered with, but also submitted to Him. That is exactly how Jesus, the Holy Spirit, and the Father operate together in the earth. Jesus, empowered by the Holy Spirit, walked in His full God-given authority but stayed in constant submission to the Father. Jesus didn't just passively sit around and wait for the Father to do something; Jesus, in submission to the Father and by the Holy Spirit, went about doing good, allowing the Father to work through Him. This is how we must be, and why it's so important to understand true biblical submission and authority and stay permanently anchored between the two.

Think of it this way: let's say we decide we want a fish tank, and we are in control of its creation. We decide its size and how many gallons it will be. We choose to fill it with salt water or fresh water. We control how many fish we start with, what kind of fish, and what the internal habitat will be. We are in control of whether it has a sand bottom or rocks, coral, plants, or all the above. As creator, we are in control of all these things—all conditions the fish live in. However, we do not control any of the fish. We don't decide where they can swim. We control how much we provide for them, but we do not control how much of it they choose to eat. We don't control what friends they make. We decide how many fish to start with, but we don't control their procreation or if they choose to multiply themselves.

We control the rules governing the environment for the fish, but not the actions of any of those fish. Within the parameters we do control, the fish are free to exercise their own free will. One fish can even choose to kill and destroy all the other fish unless another fish rises up to stop it. The fish tank is ours and everything in it, but we choose to limit ourselves to allow the fish to use the resources we gave them; however, they decide. We stay in control and can add or subtract what goes in the tank, but we've limited our own control and have allowed the fish to control what they do with what is in the tank.

How ridiculous would it be for the fish to try and be in a power struggle with us? What if the fish were like, "This is my sand and my rock," or "I don't like this rock. I want to live in a bigger rock!" "These plants aren't pretty enough!" Yet, this is what we do when we act like the stuff God has provided is ours to own rather than for our use during our life journey. God wants us to enjoy the things He provides. He just doesn't want us to give those things the wrong priority in our hearts. Now, again, this analogy isn't necessarily a perfect representation, but it helps us grasp the difference between being in control and in charge. The major difference is the fish do not live in partnership, communion, and relationship with us. They have no ability to invite our presence into what they are doing like we can with Jesus. In fact, offering our lives and all we have as a living sacrifice by inviting our Lord in is one of the greatest acts of worship we can do. When we humble ourselves, turning all we possess over to the Lord, it keeps those possessions from gaining a foothold or wrong priority in our hearts.

This wrong priority can be a doorway to a spirit of poverty. An improper mindset that gives money more rank than it should have gives entrance to the enemy to infest our lives with poverty. When we agree with the lie that we are the owners, not just the managers, instead of recognizing that God is the source of everything and is the one who gave us the skills with which we earn income, we make money an idol. We forget that God is the one who gives us opportunities to even earn money with those skills as well as the one who gave us all our skills and abilities to begin with. We then have the audacity to look at God and demand He provide for all the things we want, which maybe He never even authorized us to have, and demand He give us stewardship of more. We want decision-making power with "our" money rather than turning it back to God and acknowledging His position as Lord of our lives, which thereby also makes Him Lord of our resources.

Recognizing Jesus in this way shows we worship and honor Him with our possessions, not just our mouths, as instructed in Proverbs 3:9 (NLT), which implores us to *"Honor the Lord with your wealth and with the best part of everything you produce."* If we do this, the very next verse promises, *"Then he will fill your barns with grain, and your vats will overflow with good wine."*[10]

We demolish a stronghold of poverty and dethrone money as an idol when, as an act of our own free will, we give up our control and turn it back over to Jesus by recognizing His place as Lord and honoring Him with the possessions and wealth we have. For some of us, that statement immediately sparks a fear of loss because we begin calculating all the things we spend money on, and we know if Jesus was the one truly allowed to be in control of our finances, He would cut them from the budget. Our perception of our provision is usually based on the bank balance we see with our natural eyes. Many times, in Scripture, the abundant provision didn't show up until after the person obeyed God to give up and sow what they already had in their hand.

Isn't it funny how we can call Jesus our Lord, yet we don't give Him full access to the checking account or debit card? If we do give Him some say in our spending, it is usually a really strict budget of what He's allowed to tell us to spend. We are worshipping with our mouths, but our hearts are far from Him, like Jesus refers to in Matthew 15:8. When Jesus says He wants us to give money toward a certain need, project, assignment, or offering, or He wants us to invest in our spiritual growth and education in a certain course, school, or book, and our response is, "But I have bills to pay! I can't do that, or I won't be able to pay my bills." What we are really saying is, "Hey! I'm the one that worked for this paycheck, so I make the financial decisions around here." We are saying, "Jesus, I know I said I want You as my partner but more like a silent partner."

We want all the benefits of having Him as a partner, but truly, it's that we want His investment without giving up any control over that provision and without submitting to what He tells us to do. If Jesus prompts us to give $3,000 to a certain need or assignment, but we only have $2,000 in the bank, most of us will focus on our lack, telling Him what we don't have. We think this lack gives us the right to override His instruction and give only what we think we can instead of what He said. Those who will be granted the ability to steward more are the ones who obey and believe Him to provide despite anything they appear to lack.

This may sound harsh, but we can't change or defeat what we won't confront, so we must confront our poverty thinking because it causes us to live a faithless life. We don't want to be those people who claim Jesus is their Lord, but their hearts are far from Him because they don't love or trust Him enough to put Him before their money. We don't want to have selective obedience because of fear or because we want to be the ones both in charge of and maintaining complete control of how our provision is spent instead of letting Him lead those decisions.

This does not mean Jesus wants to make all the decisions for us. If that were the case, then we might as well just live under a dictatorship and not even have free will. That isn't love and isn't the heart of God. If God sought to control people, He would not have given us free will. He would much rather have people who willingly love Him enough to recognize His ways are far better, and, out of love, include Him in our decisions. He just wants to be brought into a partnership where He has a say. It really is simple. We can't afford anything less than sold-out devotion to our King. If He is King, then at the very least, He should be consulted and invited into the decision-making process. It's not because He wants control but because He wants things to go well for us, and He has information we don't have. He wants to rightfully be acknowledged as our source.

In Luke 5, when Jesus told Peter when and where to let down his nets, it wasn't because He wanted to control Peter or Peter's business. It's because He wanted to bless Peter's business! Jesus wanted things to go well for Peter. Peter needed to be humble and willing to listen to the Lord's direction and obey it! Anyone can acknowledge Jesus with their mouths, but how many truly acknowledge Him by inviting Him into monetary decisions and submitting their wills to His if He gives a specific direction?

What about our personal finances when we feel the Lord leading us to give to a certain ministry, project, or assignment? Do we obey, or do we tell Him we don't have the money? It is not Jesus's fault we have allowed our lifestyles to overextend our finances in such a way that now we must tell Him, "Sorry, I know You want me to do this certain thing, but I've got bills to pay." Jesus didn't sign those contracts that put us in debt or subscribe us to services that can be done without. Jesus didn't rack up those credit card bills because we desired to own things we couldn't afford. We did that. I'm not saying this with condemnation, because we don't live under condemnation, but we can't defeat what we won't confront. I'm not saying any of those things are wrong to have or to do, per se, unless Jesus was never allowed to be part of that decision-making process. The issue is never the property, lifestyle, or stuff. The issue is always the posture of our hearts.

God is not meant to be a silent partner, where He just bankrolls every desire we have. However, the terrifying thing is, most of the time, we don't even realize we're treating Him this way. If we can't change what we won't confront, we certainly can't confront what we're not even aware of. This is why the poverty spirit seeks to work under the radar, ingrained in our thought patterns, behind strongholds of wrong thinking that even seem biblically based. This is why an intimate relationship with the Holy Spirit is so important, so He can shine His light and expose these things in us. That exposure only happens when we sit still in the careful examination of His light.

Many of us sincere Christians still have idolatry in our hearts in relation to money because we trust more in our jobs or bank balance, and we allow them to make our decisions. People will serve or obey whatever master they believe is paying the bills. Who or what rules over us or makes our decisions for us is, in fact, our lord. If God is the one truly telling us to do something, (not just things we want or desire to do—even if what we desire to do appears "right" or "kingdom,") and our response is, "But my job won't let me," or "I don't have the money for that," it indicates who or what our real master is. In a sense, we are telling God "No" because we fear losing our jobs because we falsely think our source of provision is our job and not God Himself.

We say with our mouths, "God is our provider," but if we really believed this, why would we be afraid to lose our jobs? The truth is, we are afraid that if we lose or walk away from our jobs, we will lose the ability to pay for our stuff. If we lose the ability to pay for our stuff, we will then lose our houses, cars, furniture, cable, etc. The degree to which we fear the loss of our possessions or positions is probably the degree to which we are still not dead to these things. Our jobs, business, or other sources of provision are "sacred cows" to us if we fear losing them, or if we will disobey the will of God in our lives to maintain possession of these things. Just because God sometimes provides through a job, doesn't mean a job is the only way He will or wants to provide for us forever. Somewhere along the way, we began to see our job (or business) as our source of provision, instead of it being a vehicle through which God is providing for a season.

It is amazing how easily we can convince ourselves it is God's will for us to have something like a certain house, car, or job, simply because we want it. This is why it is so vitally important to take on the mindset of a bondservant. When Christ is our life and we seek Him and His kingdom first for our provision and decisions, then He can trust us with the earthly possessions we are called to rule over. However, if He isn't first, and we want to maintain full control of how our money is spent without allowing God's input on those decisions, possessions or money will inevitably rule over us.

WHAT CAN WE LEARN FROM THE STORY OF JOSEPH?

Jesus wasn't the only one who walked through great suffering before walking in great authority. As an Old Testament example, we find the story of Joseph.[11] Joseph was Abraham's great-grandson. He was one of the twelve sons of Jacob. These are the twelve sons who later became the twelve tribes of Israel. Joseph's story is so amazing that it takes a full seven chapters of the Bible to tell. It begins with God giving him a dream about his destiny to become a great ruler—even ruling over his older brothers and ultimately ends with him fulfilling that destiny after many years of great suffering and loss.

Even though he had a God-given dream, every circumstance in his life looked the opposite. His brothers were jealous of him because he was their father's favorite and hated the favor of God on his life, so they banded together and tried to kill him. One brother intervened on Joseph's behalf, so instead of killing him, they sold him into slavery and faked his death, so Joseph had no hope of anyone coming to rescue him. While working as a slave, he was falsely accused of rape by his master's wife simply because he was honorable and refused her sexual advances. He did the right thing yet was still thrown into prison for years because of this false accusation. How many of us could endure such things without turning our backs on God? Yet, in all these circumstances, God caused him to prosper and have favor. This eventually led to him interpreting a dream for Pharaoh, and Pharaoh put him in charge of all of Egypt and its resources. He was number two only to Pharaoh himself. That is power. He had authority over an entire nation and all its wealth, resources, and people.

Like Joseph, we must first be trained and prepared to properly manage the level of authority, resources, and abundance God has destined for us, or that abundance will get misused on things with no lasting value. What if Joseph didn't first learn to trust and submit to God and thus didn't manage Egypt's resources correctly? What if Joseph didn't properly ration Egypt's abundant provision at the time and instead just spent it on whatever he wanted, like lavish parties, hoarding it, or giving it to his friends? Nations of people, including the Israelites, would have died in the famine that struck Egypt.

Our abundance always has God's purpose attached to it. In Joseph's case, God needed to ensure the survival of His people, the nation of Israel, during the famine headed for Egypt, or the entire plan of salvation would have been at risk. The Israelites were the lineage through which the Messiah would come. He prepared Joseph and sent him ahead of time for their survival. Joseph's prosperity was not about him living a blessed life. He prospered to fulfill the plan of God. Was it wrong for Joseph to enjoy and partake of the provision and abundance his position afforded him? No! That just wasn't the purpose of Joseph's prosperity.

Joseph had his heart postured right first to be able to recognize the plan of God and the kingdom's purpose of it. Joseph knew his rise to fame and fortune wasn't at all about his own success, position, dreams, or accumulation of wealth. He recognized God gave him those things for kingdom purposes, and as a result, God also gave him those things to enjoy. Joseph, probably due to his extensive time in actual prison, had the mindset of a bondservant. He recognized his prosperity had less to do with God's desire to bless him and more to do with preserving entire nations and the Messiah's lineage.

God always thinks generationally, not just about the here and now. God's plan of salvation needed the Israelites to survive that coming famine, and Joseph's success was part of that plan, but not until Joseph was prepared and transformed from a spoiled, arrogant, and entitled brat to a steward who could handle that type of elevation of status without becoming corrupted by it. That kind of transformation is cultivated in the pit of suffering. Too many of us want the blessing while trying to bypass the pit of suffering. We fail to recognize that for many of us, the wilderness is the most important part of our preparation—where our will is traded for His will, and our mindset changes from being our own master to being a bondslave.

There are many scriptures showing God not only desires us to prosper but He also takes great pleasure in it! Psalm 35:27 (KJV) says, *"...Let them say continually, let the LORD be magnified, which hath pleasure in the prosperity of His servant."* God wants us to prosper, but His Word in Proverbs 1:32 (KJV) says, *"...Prosperity of fools shall destroy them."* We need all foolishness trained out of our hearts before acquiring prosperity or it will destroy us. God's warning is not against prosperity, it is against being foolish. God doesn't want us to abuse prosperity by giving it the wrong priority. There are safety rules. God wants us to prosper, but He doesn't want us to trust in riches or be so afraid of losing them that we hoard them instead of operating in His generosity. He wants us to recognize money, jobs, businesses, etc., is not our source, but instead, He is.

If we are God's servants (bondservants), then He delights in our prosperity, not in our poverty. As parents, we don't want our kids living in poverty, lack, and constant struggle, having just barely enough to get by. On the contrary, it gives us pleasure to see them succeeding and doing well, having all the provisions they need to live life to the fullest. Why do we think our heavenly Father is any different? To think He wants us to be impoverished is a lie attacking His very nature as a giver of good gifts to His children as Jesus tells us in Matthew 7:11 and Luke 11:13. Most of us want our children to have abundance; we just don't want them entitled. If provision has its proper place in our hearts, we won't be corrupted by it. If we are taught the proper truths about provision from the Word of God, we won't be entitled anyway. The difference is in our attitude. Are we God's bondservant, or are we trying to make God our servant where we make all the decisions, and He just foots the bill? Keeping a proper heart posture towards God will keep us from embracing the lies of lack and from being so attached to our possessions that we walk in financial disobedience from our lack of submission.

THIRD STEP TO FREEDOM: BEING DOERS OF THE WORD

So, if it's God's will for every believer to prosper, why are so many experiencing poverty and lack? If we've addressed our false beliefs and our improper mindset, the answer may be found in our actions or inactions. The third step to overcoming and destroying strongholds like poverty, which goes along with knowing the Word of God, is putting the Word of God into action. It's not enough to just have a covenant of financial prosperity with God, as promised in His Word. Many times, the breakthrough results not just from knowing the Word but also from being doers of the Word with a properly postured heart, which releases the blessings.

James 1:21-25 warns us to be doers of the Word, and not hearers only and deceiving ourselves. Often, the promises in God's Word come with conditions to meet in the natural. We can memorize the promises all day long, but until we internalize them to the point where we demonstrate our new beliefs by acting them out to meet those conditions, we will only be deceiving ourselves. We see this all the time in many people who claim to be Christians and can quote more Scripture than anyone else, but the fruit of obeying what they seem to preach never shows up in their lives. They can quote it, but they don't live it.

3 John 1:2 says we will only prosper to the degree our soul prospers, or in other words, we will only prosper in proportion to our understanding and application of the scriptures and the degree to which we allow God's Word to renew our minds. Our covenant with God is based on exchange (which most covenants are), so we must know the terms in order to be faithful and fulfill our part. Faith without works (actions) is dead. In other words, in covenants, something or some action is required of both parties. For us, first and foremost, we must read our contract!

Joshua 1:8 (NLT) says, *"Study this Book of Instruction continually. Meditate on it day and night* (the belief part) *so you will be sure to obey everything that is written in it* (the action part). *Only then will you prosper and succeed in all you do."* (Prosperity again promised as a reward for obedience.) Also, Psalm 1:2-3 (NLT) says, *"But they delight in the law of the LORD, meditating on it day and night. They are like trees planted along the riverbank, bearing fruit each season. Their leaves never wither, and they prosper in all they do."*

It's great to meditate on the Word, but blessings aren't released until we obey. We can see it is God's will for us to prosper after first meeting the conditions of 1) His Word being a priority in our lives, and 2) obeying what is written in it. When these conditions are met, the promised blessings are released into our lives. We also won't need to worry about prosperity being a wrong priority because we will already have our priorities straight.

It is God's will for everybody to be saved, and yet there are still going to be people burning in hell. Why? Either they never heard the gospel regarding salvation so they could then apply those scriptures and act on them, or perhaps they did hear and rejected them instead of acting on them unto salvation. Just because we hear it and can even quote it, doesn't mean we act on it. There is always an action component to faith.

In Romans 10:9, the Bible tells us that if we believe in our hearts (the belief/mind component) and confess with our mouths (the action component) we will be saved. The same is true with prosperity. There are some Christians who don't know anything about financial prosperity as a promise from the Lord. Others have rejected it, thinking it is wrong just because some ministers have abused the prosperity message. Financial prosperity must be seen for what it is: part of our redemption Jesus Christ died and paid for. How unfortunate to leave the gift of that purchase untouched due to our own ignorance! Galatians 3:13-14 (KJV) states, *"Christ hath redeemed us from the curse of the law, being made a curse for us…that the blessing of Abraham might come on the Gentiles…"* To find out what the blessing of Abraham is, we need to read about it.

Read Deuteronomy 28.

It is great to both know and memorize these promises; however, is that enough for heaven to release those blessings? We must also know if the Word says there are any conditions to meet or actions to take for those blessings to be released. According to this chapter, we find there are several conditions to meet for these blessings to be released into our lives:

- if we fully obey and carefully keep all His commands (vs. 1)
- if we obey the commands of the Lord and walk in His ways (vs. 9)
- if we listen to these commands of the Lord and carefully obey them (vs. 13)
- we must not turn away from any of the commands given today nor follow other gods and worship them (vs. 14)

What is the curse we have been redeemed from? This same chapter also tells us the destruction we bring upon ourselves by walking in disobedience to the Word. Our disobedience gives our enemy, the devil, the legal right to devour and bring destruction in our lives, such as:

- our towns and your fields will be cursed
- our fruit baskets and breadboards will be cursed
- our children and crops will be cursed
- the offspring of our herds and flocks will be cursed
- wherever we go and whatever we do will be cursed

One definition of the word cursed or *qalal* is "to bring into contempt." Contempt is a legal term meaning "willful disobedience to or open disrespect of a court, judge, or legislative body."[12] Contempt is disapproval tinged with disgust or a state of being scorned. Our willful disobedience to the Word of God is what gives Satan the legality to devour our provision.

All the curses listed here describe different areas of provision. We must remember this was speaking to an agricultural society, so land, crops, and cattle were their sources of wealth and provision. To have these things produce poorly or not at all is the very description of poverty. The only reasons Jesus ever experienced any poverty in His life were to pay the price for us to be free from it and for us to gain authority over it. 2 Corinthians 8:9 (ESV) states, *"For you know the grace of our Lord Jesus Christ, that though he was rich, yet for your sake he became poor, so that you by his poverty might become rich."*

However, notice in both Galatians 3:13-14 and 2 Corinthians 8:9 that the grammar is past tense. This redemption from the curse is not a future event we are waiting for; it is something Christ has already done. It is finished. Christ made a legal trade—His wealth for our poverty—which means we can trade our poverty for His wealth. Notice this scripture says "might" become rich. It is not automatically guaranteed. It is up to us to both know the promises we've been given and take the necessary action the Bible tells us we must take. We act based on the Word of God.

The Bible calls poverty a curse, and there is nothing blessed about being poor. Poverty can keep us from doing the will of God. It takes finances to move and live and have our being on the earth. It takes finances to fund kingdom assignments. Those finances must come from somewhere—the stewards who faithfully manage God's stuff and who make God and His kingdom priority and not the possessions.

This is why the goal of the poverty spirit is to erect a stronghold made of false beliefs in our minds. Its ultimate endgame is to keep us from being able to do the will of God. Knowledge of the will of God is important if we are going to have faith in our prayers. We can't believe for something if we don't even know it's God's will for us to have it. That's why, in a later class, we are going to outline exactly what is in "the will" for us and what Scripture says is our inheritance. We will never experience the benefits of being the beneficiary of a will if we 1) don't even know we're an heir in the first place, 2) if we don't know what exactly we inherit as laid out in that will, or 3) if we don't know what conditions we need to meet, if any, before harvesting that inheritance. So we must know the scriptures and what the Bible says God desires for us because, like Joseph, our prosperity has less to do with us and more to do with how God desires to use those finances to advance His agenda, plan, and kingdom on the earth.

Ignorance keeps us in bondage. Many of God's people are not prosperous because they have accepted religious lies instead of biblical truth. An example of a religious lie would be: tithing is legalism—or the other extreme—not tithing causes you to be cursed. Both are religious lies rooted in legalism and a wrong heart. This is why the Word of God must be given preeminence in our lives, so it becomes so ingrained in us that our faith gets partnered with our actions.

FOURTH STEP TO FREEDOM: BREAKING A POVERTY STRONGHOLD THROUGH GIVING

To combat how a poverty spirit works to keep us focused on what we lack or feel like we will never have enough is found in giving. Giving is the greatest solution to the hold that greed, hoarding, covetousness, and fear of lack have on us. We can't covet something or fear losing it when we give it away of our own free will. We see this principle in Matthew 16:25 (ESV) when Jesus says, *"For whoever would save his life will lose it, but whoever loses his life for my sake will find it."* We think Jesus is speaking only of our actual life, but when we dig into the word "life" *(psuché),* we find one of the definitions of this word is "the seat of the feelings, desires, or affections," meaning, part of a person's life is the things their affections are set on.[13] In essence, this verse is saying if we lose or give up the things our affections are set on for His sake, we will find them. However, if we try to hold onto or hoard them, we will lose them. Giving is the solution. The world tells us we will lose something if we give it away, but Jesus tells us we gain what we give away.

God wants His children free. He doesn't want us living as slaves to money, jobs, or sources of provision. However, if we don't get our hearts, minds, beliefs, and attitudes right concerning money and its handling, wealth will only corrupt us. Money just makes us more of what we already are. It is merely a tool made of green paper. However, money has a very sneaky way of exposing our hearts. If we are generous, money allows us to advance kingdom assignments and express generosity. If we are stingy or greedy, money will only advance our collection of possessions and feed our desire for more without ever quenching it. The more we have, the more the fear of losing it all increases.

Greed has never been overcome by finally having more money. The very nature of greed is that nothing can or will ever satisfy it, but there is a biblical strategy to destroy it. A lifestyle of generosity will repel hoarding, greed, and a poverty mindset. When we give and are generous, we express the very nature of our Father. So the solution to these soul issues of greed and covetousness is not gaining more but rather giving from our current circumstances. We can overcome fear of lack by giving away the thing we fear losing the most or what we fear the most we will not have enough of.

To summarize, demolishing a stronghold of poverty takes these things:

1. Exposing our minds and what we believe to be the truth of God's Word. We need to be willing to challenge and question some of the things we believe, like if prosperity is wrong or evil, why are there so many scriptures promising it to us, and why does the Bible talk more about money than it does heaven?
2. We must change our mindset about who owns what. Who is the bondslave and who is the owner?
3. We must recognize prosperity is not automatic; it's conditional. We activate the blessings when we act on the conditions God gives us. Who will be prosperous? Those who delight in the law of the Lord and meditate on it day and night so they can obey it.[14] Meditating on the Word of God is how the truth gets activated in our mind, which then sets us free by detecting and deleting lies we believe and replacing them with truth so we can take new and different actions. Not reading "our contract,"—the Word of God—is dangerous because we won't know if we are violating its terms, rendering it void. We also won't know what benefits we are supposed to receive. Getting results takes both knowing the Word and acting on it.
4. We must live a lifestyle of generosity. John 3:16 (NKJV) says, "*God so loved the world that He gave…*" Out of a heart of love for our Father and for our brothers and sisters whom He loves, we should be the most generous people on the planet. A lifestyle of generosity will keep us from becoming too attached to money or possessions.

If we Christians aren't prospering, we may have a low Word level, especially in finances. We don't know what belongs to us in Christ, or worse, we don't believe it or act on it, or our hearts are not yet postured correctly in relation to God and money. As a result, we live far below the provisions God desires us to have. We can't just read about it; we must activate it by acting on it. There are contractual obligations we must fulfill to experience this prosperity. It's like any other contract between two parties; each person must do certain things to fulfill the agreement. If we aren't experiencing the benefits, we may be in violation somewhere because God always honors His side of the deal. He is always faithful, even when we are not. He is even faithful in showing us where or how we have been unfaithful and allows us to repent and get back on track instead of just canceling our contract and writing us off.

Again, prosperity doesn't mean we will all be millionaires. As Jesus explains in the parable of the talents, what we are given is in direct proportion to our ability. We can't expect to be a ten-talent servant with one-talent ability. To gain more stewardship, we must gain more ability. How do we gain ability in any subject? Through education and practice. We must invest in our financial management and spiritual education to learn what the Word of God says about handling money and how the kingdom of God works. If we want to be trusted to manage more, we must grow in the ability to handle more.

Prosperity does mean our needs will be met with some left over, and we will have all the provisions we need to do everything God tells us to do. That doesn't necessarily mean the provision will come from our own bank accounts. The richest person is not the one who has the most, it is the one who needs the least. Prospering means "flourishing, well-off, successfulness, to thrive, to turn out well, to be fortunate, to increase, to bear fruit, bloom/blossom, make money, gain, and (my personal favorite) do wonders!"[15] Success doesn't happen to us; it happens through us. No one is alive for the purpose of making more money. Money is a resource that supports our purpose and assignment. If we want to make more money just to be free, we're missing the whole point. Our goal isn't to get money to get freedom. Freedom is the starting gate. Money is just a resource that allows the generosity of our Father to have full expression on the earth.

Satan can only rule where there is darkness or ignorance of the truth of God. This is why Jesus said in John 8:32 (NKJV), *"And you shall know the truth, and the truth shall make you free."* Any area in which we are not free must have an absence of truth. Truth spoken by the anointing is the most powerful weapon there is. We must function within the principles governing God's economic system (trade and exchange) to activate the promised results. Freedom does not just happen automatically.

We determine our own measure of financial prosperity by the degree to which we use or work within the laws of the kingdom of God. We need to discover how God's kingdom works, and then work within those terms. We are supposed to bring the kingdom of God to earth, not go from earth to the kingdom of God. God's Word promises we will have all sufficiency in all things, the financial freedom, support, and liberty to abound unto every good work (2 Corinthians 9:8). However, we still must ask, which keeps us in a bondslave mentality. A portion of the prayer Jesus prayed in Matthew 6:11 (NKJV) was, *"Give us this day our daily bread."* He was teaching us to pray for our needs to be met, even though He also says, "*...For your Father [in heaven] knows the things you have need of before you ask Him.*"[16]

Going back to our previous landlord and tenant analogy, we must invite the landlord in. This sentiment is repeated in James 4:2, telling us that we do not have because we do not ask. A bondslave will ask his master what he should do, he wouldn't just do it. Along with asking for our provision, we may need to ask the Holy Spirit if and where we might be believing lies on this subject so we can be set free. He may need to train us more to allow Him to lead decisions about provision, money, and spending. There is a reason we don't learn algebra in elementary school. We wouldn't be ready to receive it yet. It must be precept upon precept.[17]

Let Him lead. We must be willing to let go of the reins, stay in process, and be willing to let all our thoughts and beliefs about money be reevaluated and rejudged. We must have no "sacred cows," even if they are in the form of beliefs we already have about money. If we're not living in freedom financially that is a pretty good indication there might be some things that need to be challenged by rightly dividing the Word and letting new beliefs take root. We are transformed by the renewing of our minds.[18]

I've been through this process and had my beliefs challenged. I have allowed and continue to allow the Holy Spirit to expose where I might agree with lies or a spirit of poverty. I allowed Him to lead me into the pit of suffering, whereby sharing in His suffering, I could share in His glory. I allowed the Holy Spirit to train me in financial integrity to keep my heart postured correctly toward both Him and money. I was born in poverty to a single mother, an alcoholic absentee father, and a grandmother who grew up in an orphanage. There is nothing about my history that would foretell of being debt-free with complete and total financial freedom and no attachment to money or possessions. God now allows me to use the authority I have gained from those victories to help others on their journey. Kingdom prosperity is about having the resources to fulfill kingdom assignments, not indulge our desires. God needs us to learn and master the process of obtaining all that we need so we can fulfill every assignment He gives us, and the purpose of this book is to help us do just that.

There is one last thing we must address. As we can see by my own testimony, many times, poverty is generational. Just as wealth can be passed from one generation to the next, so can poverty. Many times, a poverty spirit gains entrance into our lives as the result of one of our ancestors making a demonic trade. In this instance, I am talking about an actual spirit on assignment to steal and who works to create ingrained mindsets in us. Many of us have ancestors who made sacrifices to other gods, usually Baal, in exchange for protection, titles, influence, or provision. As part of this trade, this ancestor dedicated the family wealth, lands, and prosperity of future generations in exchange for their prosperity.

There is a very high probability someone is living under a curse because an ancestor either traded their prosperity away or committed murder, putting the bloodline under the curse of Cain, if someone is:

- experiencing a lack of prosperity and diminished returns no matter how hard they labor
- working hard and being diligent and wise with their finances, and yet continually experiencing lack instead of walking in the prosperity of their inheritance
- working faithfully, doing everything they know to do, and their beliefs are right but never experience abundance and instead experience failure to thrive and continual lack

This curse found in Genesis 4:12 (NLT) states, *"No longer will the ground yield good crops for you, no matter how hard you work…"* Here are some other scriptures (NLT) where the Bible addresses the topic of generational sin:

- Numbers 14:18: *"The Lord is slow to anger and filled with unfailing love, forgiving every kind of sin and rebellion. But he does not excuse the guilty. He lays the sins of the parents upon their children; the entire family is affected—even children in the third and fourth generation."*
- Deuteronomy 5:9: *"...I lay the sins of the parents upon their children; the entire family is affected—even children to the third and fourth generations of those who reject me."*
- Jeremiah 32:18: *"You show unfailing love to thousands, but you also bring the consequences of one generation's sin upon the next. You are the great and powerful God, the Lord of Heaven's Armies."*

Thankfully, because of the blood of Jesus, these trades and covenants can be undone. Before the cross, they were stuck and could not be annulled. We see a record of this in 2 Samuel 21:1 (NKJV), *"Now there was a famine in the days of David for three years, year after year; and David inquired of the Lord. And the Lord answered, 'It is because of Saul and his bloodthirsty house, because he killed Gibeonites.'"*

We see from this scripture that Israel, under the leadership of King David, was experiencing a famine. When David inquired of the Lord, the Lord told David it was because Saul killed some Gibeonites when he was king. Why is this a critical piece of information? When we dig into who the Gibeonites are, we get a clearer picture of what is happening. When the Israelites first crossed over the Jordan to conquer the Promised Land under the leadership of Joshua, they had been given a command by the Lord to destroy all the inhabitants of that land. Shortly thereafter, the Israelites encountered a tribe of people called the Gibeonites, who were part of the nation of the Amorites. These Gibeonites deceived the Israelites into thinking they were from a faraway country and not inhabitants of Canaan. They did this to prevent the Israelites from killing them. They asked to make a covenant with Joshua, which Joshua agreed to, without first inquiring of the Lord. Only after making this agreement did they discover they had been tricked into doing so.

This tribe really was one of the tribes inhabiting the land of Canaan that the Israelites were commanded to wipe out. Even though this agreement had been made through deception and meant the Israelites would have to disobey the direct command of the Lord to honor it, the covenant still stood. Israel now had to both protect and defend these liars. Fast forward many generations later, even though the nation of Israel had sworn not to kill any Gibeonites, Saul broke this covenant by killing some of them and trying to wipe them out.[19] Just because the covenant had been made many generations before didn't mean it was allowed to be broken without consequence. Even though Saul was now dead, the enemy was legally allowed to bring famine against all of Israel because of this broken covenant. It wasn't until David, now as reigning king, armed with this information of the source of the issue, went to the Gibeonites to make amends and repair the breach.

The Gibeonites required that seven of Saul's descendants be turned over to them to be killed as restitution. This created a dilemma for David, who had sworn to protect Mephibosheth, who was Saul's grandson through Jonathan. Because of Jonathan and David's friendship, David swore to protect his friend's son. David had to carefully fix one covenant—giving seven of Saul's descendants to the Gibeonites—without breaking another—the covenant he made to protect some of those descendants. This should speak to us about how seriously covenants are taken in the spirit realm because if broken, they result in very severe natural consequences. We see in 2 Samuel 21 that only after the careful repair of this broken covenant did the famine lift, and the land was healed.

Satan thrives on our ignorance of what has occurred in our bloodlines. This is why it is so important to be in constant, intimate communication with the Holy Spirit so He can guide us through these things. That is exactly how David discovered the source of his own famine and how to deal with it—he inquired of the Lord. David didn't blame or accuse God of not fulfilling His promises to bless them. David knew that if he was failing to see God's promises manifest, there had to be a good reason for it. In humility, David inquired of the Lord, and the Lord revealed the source of the enemy's legal right to afflict him with famine and steal his harvests. We must be diligent to do the same. We need to appreciate and be incredibly grateful for the blood of Jesus that can be applied to these agreements so it can and will annul them.

If this is the case, we simply need to clear the matter up in the courtroom of heaven. These trades created covenants that Satan could stand on to legally make a claim for whatever was dedicated to him when the covenant was made. Satan, being the legalist he is, knows every trade and covenant made with his kingdom, even between different generations and peoples. Even though we have no clue what may have been done even one generation ago. He uses these arrangements to create uncleared accusations against us before the throne of God, as Scripture tells us he does.

Read Revelation 12:9-10.

As long as these accusations remain uncontested, Satan then uses this testimony to secure a verdict allowing him to legally intercept our harvests. It's just like a natural courtroom, if charges are brought against someone and the accused never shows up to contest the charges, the judge has no choice but to rule in favor of the accuser. It isn't that God isn't faithful and isn't sending the answers or the increase He promises, the problem is that those answers are getting intercepted and devoured because Satan can lay claim to what has been traded or pledged to him, even if it was an ancestor who did it and not us.

The same principle allows God to lay claim to our children because we dedicate them to Him. If we are believing and obeying and still not seeing results, then it is highly likely the enemy has laid claim to our finances. Amazingly, unlike a natural courtroom where we must try to prove our own innocence and hope the judge rules in our favor, by claiming the blood of Jesus as our defense, we receive a "not guilty" verdict every single time—even if we really were guilty of the charges! That is the good news. Jesus gave us the power and the defense to have every charge against us thrown out. All we must do is show up to contest the charges and plead the blood as our defense.

We must call Satan before the throne of God's courtroom. We must stand as a representative of not only ourselves but also our family lines and repent for these trades that either we or our ancestors made through sin or covenants. We also must repent for the motives behind these sins and trades, acknowledge our guilt, and plead the blood of Jesus as our defense. Then, ask Colossians 2:13-15 to be applied, nailing the record of the charges against us to the cross.

Once Satan's legal claim to our inheritance has been removed, we can petition the court and make a claim for the complete recovery for everything the enemy took because of these trades. It is important to ask that all recovered wealth, success, influence, and property that had been traded away be turned back over to Jesus. For most of us, if the wealth of many generations suddenly ended up in our hands, we wouldn't even know what to do with it. So request that it be held in trust with Jesus until He can train us to properly handle it. Knowing how to spend it and knowing how to manage it are not the same thing.

It's God's desire for His children to thrive, not just survive. If we aren't experiencing the manifestation of His promises, the problem is never on God's end. We must learn to discern the enemy's tactics and how he uses legal means to steal from us. Hopefully, we are now wiser to his devices, and will begin to walk in the victory that has already been purchased for us and kick poverty to the curb once and for all!

CLASS 1
STUDY GUIDE AND JOURNAL

Always begin by praying and inviting the Holy Spirit into this time. Ask Him to shine His light on anything that needs to be exposed, to speak, reveal, correct, encourage, bring wisdom and revelation, to teach you all things, and remind you of all Jesus has said as promised in John 14:26. Be honest with yourself. Remember, we can't change or defeat what we won't confront.

How do you feel when you see a super wealthy Christian?

How do you feel when you see a super wealthy pastor?

Do you sometimes feel like they should give all their wealth away if they were "true Christians?"

If someone were to give you a ten-million-dollar mansion free and clear, would you be able to sustain its upkeep?

What negative beliefs do you have regarding wealth and wealthy people?

What possessions are you afraid to lose and why?

What, if anything, needs to change about how you view God being in charge versus being in control or who owns what?

What behaviors can you act on to show God that He is the owner and you are the servant steward?

How can you begin to make generosity a lifestyle, not an event?

While standing on the promises of God, are there any conditions you haven't been meeting?

What financial decisions can you ask the Lord about before making them?

Have you inquired of the Lord to see if there are any consequences of generational sin or covenants that are affecting your life? What has He revealed?

Have you repented of these things on behalf of yourself and your bloodline, both past and future?

Have you asked for any prosperity that has been traded away to be returned to your family or returned to Jesus and held in trust until you are ready to steward it?

Find a minimum of five scriptures about what God said about the prosperity of His people to begin meditating on. Begin to declare these scriptures out loud over your life every single day. Take a moment to thank the Lord for all He has revealed and for all He has done through the finished work on the cross.

CLASS 2

WHAT IS OUR INHERITANCE IN CHRIST?

"The eyes of your understanding being enlightened; that you may know what is the hope of His calling, what are the riches of the glory of His inheritance in the saints."

EPHESIANS 1:18 NKJV

As the saints of Jesus Christ, not only do we have an inheritance, but God also deeply desires the eyes of our understanding to be enlightened because He wants us to know the riches contained in that inheritance. The God of the universe went to great and desperate lengths to make that inheritance available to us. He sent His Son, Jesus, in flesh and blood, to live and walk among us, and ultimately endure the cross while carrying our sins upon Himself. Three days later, He rose from the dead and ascended to the Father, all so we could be possessors and partakers of these riches. How tragic for us to never acknowledge or acquire our inheritance after all he suffered, simply out of ignorance. He doesn't want us missing these blessings out of ignorance. He went to great lengths to spell it all out for us in His Testaments by leaving us a written will of His desires as His heirs.

Almost all legal documents, especially those pertaining to contractual agreements or "terms of use," have an entire section devoted to defining said terms. This keeps agreements from being unclear and lets all parties know what the boundaries and expectations are. Therefore, definitions matter! In legal contracts, clearly defined terms are important, especially because the English language, and probably others, have words called contranyms. These are single words that have two contradictory meanings. In other words, these words are their own opposites. For example, let's look at the words in the following list and their contradictory meanings:

Bolt: to secure or to flee
Bound: heading to a destination or restrained from movement
Fast: quick or stuck, made stable
Cleave: to adhere or to separate
Dust: to add fine particles or to remove fine particles

Now, imagine these words are part of a legal contract. Wouldn't it be important to know which definition is being agreed upon? This is one of many reasons why it is important to define terms and have a clear understanding of what a document is saying. A will, also known as a Last Will and Testament, is a legally prepared and binding document that states one's intentions for the distribution of their assets and wealth upon death. For God's will, especially as it pertains to the distribution of His assets, property, and wealth, we have the Bible. In the Bible, we have the Old and New Testaments. To understand what a testament is, we must define it. The word "testament" has several meanings:

1. A person's will, especially relating to personal property.
2. Something that serves as a sign or evidence of a specified fact, event, or quality.
3. (Traditional biblical use) a covenant or dispensation. (Dispensation means "divinely ordained order.")

Biblically speaking, all these definitions apply to what is contained within its pages. As for definition number one, the Bible tells us what God's will is, especially relating to His personal property. Psalm 24:1 tells us that the earth is the Lord's and everything in it. The Bible clearly states the earth and everything in it is God's property and defines God's will for the use and stewardship of that property. As for definition number two, the Bible also serves as the written testament of the historical record and as a sign or evidence of a specified fact, event, or quality. It is a testament to the written and recorded history between God and mankind. When it comes to definition number three, the Bible also is a covenant between God and people, clearly defining the boundaries and expectations of both parties.

To grasp a fuller understanding of what God intends for His heirs to inherit, as spelled out in His written will and testament, it is important to understand the differences between a contract and a covenant. Even though a covenant is a type of contract, it does not work like a contract. A covenant is a relationship between two parties who make binding promises to each other and work together to reach a common goal. A contract is signed; a covenant is sealed and often accompanied by oaths or ceremonies. Listed below are some of the important distinctions between the two.

A contract is a legally binding agreement, mutually beneficial, exchanges one good for another, and can be opted out; it is signed by both parties. If one party does something in violation of the contract, it is considered broken, and the whole contract becomes null and void. In contrast, a covenant is a spiritual agreement, a pledge, a perpetual promise, something one fulfills, or giving of oneself to another. It is about having the strength to hold up our part of the promise. In a covenant, both parties agree to hold up their end, regardless of whether the other party keeps their part of the agreement. It is a trust-based promise.

The fact that God's Last Will and Testament is a covenant between us and God and not a contract is a very important distinction because even if we fail, it never becomes null and void. God always fulfills His promises based on who He is, not based on what we do or don't do. Before we get into the "what" of our inheritance, we must first establish and define "who" is in the will. Who is entitled to the inheritance? Only the children, direct descendants, or someone who was directly and specifically written into the will get the inheritance of the parents or the person who owned the estate. So, how do we have our names included in the will? The inheritance is for the children of God who are born of the Spirit by faith in the finished work of the cross of Jesus Christ.

Read John 1:12-13 and Romans 8:14-17.

The word "if" here suggests it is not automatic. It is up to us whether we want to participate. This is just one of many scriptural promises that come with a condition to meet to release the promised blessing. The Bible contains two types of promises—conditional and unconditional. Previously, we mentioned that many scriptural promises come with conditions for us to meet, and the same is true of any will. Many times, the deceased will have left conditions for the heirs to meet before the inheritance will be released to them, like being of a certain age, obtaining a certain education, taking on a certain role in a family business, etc.

This passage spells out the fact that we who believe have the legal standing of being children of God, and therefore are heirs to the inheritance. It promises that we are heirs of God's glory if we meet the condition of sharing his suffering. In the next class, we will go into detail about what it looks like to share in his suffering. But for now, we will look at some of what is entailed in sharing in God's glory.

There are approximately 8,810 promises contained within the pages of the Bible. It would be impossible to cover all of them in this book, so for the sake of this discussion, we are going to focus mainly on the ones that deal with provision. By this, I don't simply mean financial provision. I mean anything we could possibly need at any given time as we navigate this life.

Going back to Romans 8:14-17, we can see that to become heirs to the inheritance purchased by the blood of Jesus, we must be Spirit-led children of God, having received Jesus Christ as our Savior and Lord. When we do so, we become children of God and joint heirs with the Son of God, Jesus Christ, and get written into the will, thus inheriting all that is His. Part of our inheritance is eternal in that we get to spend eternity in heaven with Jesus instead of hell. We know this because Philippians 4:3, Psalm 69:28, and Revelation 3:5 tell us that believers, who are also referred to as "the righteous," have their names written in the Book of Life. Revelation 20:15 tells us that anyone not found written in the Book of Life will be cast into the lake of fire. This is why the promise of eternal life with Jesus gets the most attention.

John 3:16 (NKJV) tells us, *"For God so loved the world that He gave His only begotten Son, that whoever believes in Him should not perish but have everlasting life."* This is speaking of eternity. Also, notice the description this verse gives of Jesus—the only begotten Son. God has many children, but Jesus is the only offspring produced directly by God as His natural child. We, as adopted children, become co-heirs with the natural child.

Read 2 Corinthians 5:3-4 and Romans 8:23.

As we can see from these passages, part of our inheritance will not be received until we cross into eternity because these scriptures all discuss things we will receive in the future, either after the death of our physical body or the Lord's return. However, what does having access to an inheritance in Christ mean for us while still here on earth? Is any part of our inheritance for this life? Absolutely!

When we look at Isaiah 53, which describes what the Messiah will suffer and why, we gain some insight into some of the things we are promised while we still live in these bodies. Isaiah 53:5 (NLT) says, *"But he was pierced for our rebellion, crushed for our sins. He was beaten so we could be whole. He was whipped so we could be healed."* The NKJV says, *"But He was wounded for our transgressions, He was bruised for our iniquities; the chastisement for our peace was upon Him, and by His stripes we are healed."*

We can see from this passage that not only do we inherit forgiveness of sin and, therefore, eternal life, but we also inherit wholeness and healing. There is no sickness in heaven, so we will not need healing once we are there. Some people believe the passage refers to the new bodies we will receive, but those bodies will be incorruptible. The text does not say, "by His stripes we will receive new bodies," it says that by His stripes we receive healing. When do our bodies need healing? Is it not while living in a world full of sickness?

We also inherit wholeness. When do we need wholeness? Is it not while living in a world full of brokenness? Partaking in the death and resurrection of Jesus by faith, being co-crucified, co-buried, and co-resurrected is what entitles us to receive a new glorified body like Jesus received after his resurrection. Healing is for these corrupted bodies we still live in. That is what Jesus was bruised, beaten, and whipped for—to gain healing for these broken and corrupted bodies because we live in them until we get our glorified bodies. He made sure to give us an inheritance of victory over the things that afflict our physical bodies.

Galatians 3:13 (NLT) tells us, *"But Christ has rescued us from the curse pronounced by the law. When he was hung on the cross, he took upon himself the curse for our wrongdoing. For it is written in the Scriptures, 'Cursed is everyone who is hung on a tree.'"* The first thing we need to notice is the grammar with which this is written. When we look at the tense of the words "has rescued," we see it is past tense. Our salvation, our rescue from the curse by the innocent blood of Christ being shed on our behalf, is something that has already happened, not something we are waiting for as part of a future redemption. Just from the scriptures we have reviewed already, we can see there are definitely portions of our inheritance for this life just as much as there are for the eternal life yet to come with the revealing of the sons of God.

Read Romans 8:23-25.

Again, we can see there are parts of our inheritance for eternity and parts for the here and now. For some reason, many teachings from pulpits seem to only focus on the eternity part and extraordinarily little about the part of our inheritance for this side of eternity. For that reason, I want to spend time on the part of our inheritance pertaining to our time on earth. Here are a few passages for reference:

- rescued from the curse of disobedience (Galatians 3:13)
- rest when we are weary or burdened (Matthew 11:28-29)
- great and precious promises (2 Peter 1:4)
- strength and power to the weak and powerless (Isaiah 40:29-31)
- our needs will be supplied (Philippians 4:19)
- overwhelming victory and eternally remaining in Christ's love (Romans 8:37-39)
- live in peace untroubled by fear of harm (Proverbs 1:33)
- peace of mind and heart (John 14:27)
- good plans for our lives (Jeremiah 29:11)
- our prayers will be rewarded (Matthew 6:6)
- can ask for anything in Jesus's name and it will be given (Matthew 7:7)
- keys to the kingdom of heaven with power to bind and loose (Matthew 16:19)
- angels (ministering spirits) sent to help us heirs (Hebrews 1:14)

As we go through the Word of God to find these promises, it is important to take notice of whether they are conditional or unconditional promises. For example, in Matthew 11:28-29, when promised rest when we are weary, does it mention a condition? Jesus makes the statement, *"Come to Me."* The condition is that we must come to Him with our burdens. When we do, we receive the promise of rest. How about Philippians 4:19, where God promises to supply all our needs? Paul makes the statement, *"And now..."* This was an apostolic declaration of blessing because he was commending them for supplying his ministry when he was in need, and because of that, now God will supply all their need. We need to get in the habit of noticing any conditions that need to be met to release the promises because this is where so many believers are going wrong. They are trying to claim the promises without meeting the conditions, and they don't understand why it isn't working.

WHY DO WE NEED AN INHERITANCE FOR THIS LIFE?

In Galatians 3:13, we see the phrase, *"the curse for our wrongdoing."* What was included in this curse? To find out, we need to go back to where sin first entered the picture and see what curse resulted from it.

Read Genesis 3:17-19.

To know what all this curse entails, we need to look at the original creation before sin entered the picture. When Adam and Eve were first created in the garden, finding provision was not a thought in their minds. Everything they could ever need or want to live already surrounded them. They did not have to hunt or work for food or provision; all they had to do was select it from the abundance around them. That is how God designed mankind to live. This shows His heart regarding how He wanted it to be for us.

Poverty (lack) and working for provision only came about because of the *"curse for our wrongdoing."* The moment sin entered is when the switch happened, and Adam and Eve went from thriving to surviving. God never intended for us to spend the bulk of our lives toiling and chasing provision. Mankind was meant to start from provision, and that provision was meant to be there to support whatever work man wanted or needed to do in carrying out his assignment to rule over creation. When sin entered the scene, the curse came also. This is where hard work in exchange for provision began, where struggling to scratch a living became the new normal.

Let us break down the terms of this curse. In Genesis 3:17 (NLT) it says, "*...the ground is cursed because of you.*" It is the ground that is cursed, not the people. However, because we live in these temporary earthly bodies, which are made from the dust of the earth that became cursed, this is why we need healing while in this body and why the cross provided it, until we get our new uncursed bodies. Scripture never promises we won't get diseases just because we are believers. Our spirits are saved, but we still live in these cursed earthly bodies, which is why Psalm 103:3 promises that He will heal all our diseases. How can He heal something we never get?

While Adam was in his proper estate, in his assignment of rulership and dominion, he worked under God's authority that had been granted him, so everything was submitted to the jurisdiction of the kingdom of heaven. Just like there is no lack in heaven, there was not any lack on the earth either. When Adam sinned, choosing to disobey the voice of God and instead obeyed the voice of Satan, in a sense, he joined the same rebellion that put Satan and one-third of the angels that followed him under a curse. When Adam did this, Satan could legally claim the authority and dominion that had been given to Adam over the earth, causing the earth to now come under Satan's authority, which is why Satan is referred to as the god of this world. [20]When Adam sinned, it caused the earth to change jurisdiction; it changed who was now in charge of it, causing it to fall under the same curse that Satan is under.

We also see that it says the ground is cursed because of *"you."* This is God talking to Adam here. God is not the one cursing anyone or anything; it was Adam who caused the curse to enter. As Adam stayed under the umbrella of God's protective authority, everything contained in that kingdom flowed into the earth, and the earth flourished with all abundant provision. When Adam allowed the jurisdiction to change kingdoms from the kingdom of God to the kingdom of darkness, everything contained in that kingdom now flowed into the earth. This is how disease, sickness, poverty, and death entered and gained dominion here and how they became cursed.

None of that was or is God's plan or design for mankind. This is why the gospel is called the good news! The good news of the Gospel of Jesus Christ is that His finished work of the cross allows the jurisdiction of heaven to flow into the earth again, along with everything within its jurisdiction, as long as we enforce it by commanding it to. Salvation is not just about what we will experience in eternity, although Satan would love to keep us thinking that it is. Salvation is about bringing the jurisdiction of heaven back into the earthly realm, actively walking in that dominion and authority, and taking our territory back from Satan.

Jesus's death on the cross was the legal transaction needed to give us the right to do so. Through it, Jesus did everything necessary to undo Adam's rebellion and its consequences. Now, it is up to us to enforce it. Just like here in America, our founding fathers did all they could to ensure our personal freedoms. They drafted the Constitution as the written word of what those rights are and set up the government structure to preserve those rights and govern our land. However, just because that has all been set up for us, it does not mean we will always enjoy the benefits of living under that jurisdiction. It is up to us to enforce and keep it. Those freedoms are not automatic. There will always be those who seek to overthrow and set up their own rule, so it is up to us to protect and defend the Constitution as the final authority and jurisdiction of our land. The same applies to enforcing heaven's jurisdiction here on earth and in our own lives.

Christ has rescued (past tense) us from that curse.[21] Christ has redeemed us from the curse of the law—the law of sin and death. Just as the curse partly pertains to this life— sickness, poverty, and death—and part of it pertains to the afterlife—hell and eternal separation from God—the same is true for salvation. The curses that result from our disobedience to the Word of God are not God sending punishment. The curses result from Satan's jurisdiction to legally inflict us with those curses because of our disobedience. When we are obedient to God, Satan cannot legally afflict us with his curses, which is why Jesus never suffered illness, and death could not hold him. Only through our disobedience to God can Satan bring poverty, sickness, and death into our lives because we are willfully choosing to give him that jurisdiction.

Satan loves when we slander the character of our Father by blaming God for inflicting the curses resulting from sin on people. When God warns us, it's not because He will be the one to inflict punishment on us. It's because our loving Father will have no legal reason or jurisdiction to be able to disallow Satan from afflicting us. God is not saying that if we disobey, He will punish us; He is warning us that if we disobey, Satan will have the legal right to inflict those punishments on us and that God's hands will be legally tied without a sacrifice providing Him the grounds needed to intervene. The Cross of Christ now gives the Father the permanent legal right to step in for us, redeeming us from the curse through our faith in

Jesus's sacrifice on our behalf. For further description of the curses involved with disobedience, especially pertaining to poverty and lack being big portions of them during this life, review Deuteronomy 28:15.

The amazing, good news of the gospel doesn't just save us from curses of disobedience, it also imparts the blessings of obedience to us! Because of the cross, the blessings of Abraham that were promised to him due to his obedience to God can now legally be imparted to us.[22]

Read Galatians 4:28-31.

Part of our inheritance in Christ is the blessings of Abraham. Isaac, the child born of faith in the promise, inherited the blessing of Abraham. Ishmael, although also Abraham's son, was born of human effort in an attempt to fulfill God's promise and was not heir to the covenant. A "type and shadow" is a prophetic foretelling of a future situation or event. Ishmael's story is a type and shadow, giving us a picture of what happens when we try to achieve righteousness through our own human effort instead of resting in what God accomplished through Jesus Christ on our behalf.

In the same way, Ishmael, the child born of human effort, persecuted his brother, Isaac, the child born of promise; the ruling religious class (also known as the Pharisees) persecuted their brethren by adding their own list of rules and regulations to the law and thought their keeping of these laws is what made them righteous. We see Scripture makes a stark contrast between them and then points out that our inheritance is with Isaac, not Ishmael. Our inheritance is with the children of promise, counted as righteous because of what we believe, not with the illegitimate child produced by human effort.

However, an inheritance we know nothing about does us no good. Genesis tells us that the Lord was with Joseph, and He prospered. Is the Lord with us? Then prosperity should be the default setting for our lives. This is our legal right in the kingdom of God. When we accept the finished work of the cross on our behalf, we become adopted children of God and citizens of His kingdom, changing the jurisdiction of our lives from the god of this earth to the one true God of the universe. We now have the right to live under the jurisdiction of the kingdom of heaven and all that is contained within it, including the abundant provision of our original creation and design.

Read Romans 4:13-16 and Genesis 3:9.

We see clearly from these passages that part of our inheritance in Christ is receiving and sharing in the blessings of Abraham. Abraham received these blessings because of his belief, not because of his obedience to the law. The law didn't even exist yet. So, what exactly are some of the blessings of Abraham that we inherit? Genesis 12 is the first biblically recorded conversation between God and Abram (this was before God changed his name to Abraham in Genesis 17). During this conversation, God initiates a covenant between them by giving Abram a command to obey, with blessings attached if Abram would choose to do so.

Read Genesis 12:1-4, Genesis 15:4, and Genesis 17:1-7.

Here, we see God upping the ante if Abraham will serve Him faithfully and live a blameless life. One question I have is, how did Abraham know how to serve God faithfully and live a blameless life when the law didn't even exist to spell that out for him? What did serving God faithfully look like? There was no temple or ministry. So often, when we think of serving God with our lives, we think of church life or formal ministry of some kind. God would not have asked something impossible for Abraham to achieve, so obviously there is a way to serve God faithfully and live a blameless life not tied to observing the commands of the law or performing ministry duties in any kind of formal setting or way. The answer is found in belief. When we believe the Lord and what He says is true, we are counted righteous because of our faith, just like Abraham.

In Genesis 12, God initially promises to make Abram into a great nation (singular). Now, God is promising to make him the father of multiple nations! That is blessings multiplied. It took twenty-five years for Abraham to see the fulfillment of that promise, and yet Abraham continued to believe what God said. Many generations after Abraham was dead and gone, we see the Lord keeping His promise to confirm the same covenant of blessings with Abraham's descendants when they take possession of the land God promised them.

Read Deuteronomy 28:1-14.

God now becomes even more specific about what and how He will bless them if they do like Abraham did, making the Lord their God and obeying Him. The specific blessings here deal mostly with wealth and earthly provision while they partner with God to take possession of the land. From these scriptures, we can see that in these blessings God was speaking to their prosperity in the natural realm. As an agricultural society, land was their wealth, and the ability to grow and sell their own crops and livestock was their prosperity. Notice, though, that just having the land meant little. It was the work they did on that land—what and how much they chose to grow is what was blessed and where their prosperity came from.

Even though the Israelites are most often equated with the law given through Moses, the Israelites were the original heirs to the promise through Abraham. What promise? The promised child, the Messiah that would save the world from their sins. Abraham's righteousness came from his faith in God that the Messiah would come through him, out of the nation God would form from Abraham's descendants. Abraham believed God would fulfill this promise even though he and Sarah were both well past their reproductive years. (It had to be that way, so there would be no question that the promised child came only because of a direct miracle from God.) There was no natural way it could have happened, and yet Abraham still believed. This was a type and shadow of another promised child that would come through this same lineage. This is why Abraham is called the father of faith. He had the audacity to believe God for the promised child, Isaac, who would be the lineage to the other promised child—Immanuel, the Messiah to come, also through supernatural circumstances. We are co-heirs because they believed the Messiah would come, and we believe the Messiah did come.

Galatians 3:9 (NLT) says, *"So all who put their faith in Christ share the same blessing Abraham received because of his faith."* In addition, Galatians 3:14 (NLT) says, *"Through Christ Jesus, God has blessed the Gentiles with the same blessing he promised to Abraham, so that we who are believers might receive the promised Holy Spirit through faith."* Whether like Abraham looking forward to, or like us looking back on the cross of Calvary, we all receive the blessings that come through Messiah, through faith. We inherit the promises through our belief that what God promised is true. Abraham's faith in God's ability to fulfill His promise was so genuine that when tested, he was willing to sacrifice his promised son because Abraham believed in God's ability to raise Isaac from the dead. This faith is what gave God the legality to insert Himself into the affairs of men, in the form of Jesus Christ, to be born in the flesh and lay down His own life, fully trusting God to raise Him from the dead.

Read Hebrews 11:17-18.

In the lives of Abraham and Jesus Christ, we also see it is not just what they believed but the actions they took because of their faith. Acting based on what we believe about what God said is where the rubber meets the road and is what demonstrates the genuineness of our faith. We see this all throughout Hebrews 11—affectionately called "The Hall of Fame of Faith." However, as we read it, it doesn't just record what these heroes of faith believed, it records the actions they took based upon that belief. Faith is the seed; our actions are the crop produced by that seed. Jesus had faith in the Father, yet He still had to take the action of enduring the cross. Abraham had faith in God's ability to fulfill His promises no matter what, but that faith was demonstrated by the actions he took. Abraham obeyed when God told him to leave his homeland for a new land that his descendants would inherit when he didn't even have his promised child yet. Abraham slept with his wife even though they were well past reproductive years. Abraham put Isaac on the altar and was ready to sacrifice his life until God intervened at the last moment.

Read James 2:21-24.

So, where does the law fit into all this? The law didn't even come into existence until 430 years after the life of Abraham. However, for some reason, we mostly think of the Israelites in terms of being heirs through the law instead of seeing them as the heirs to the promise that they are. Galatians 3 explains this in detail, including explaining why the law was given.

Read Galatians 3:16-29.

The law was not given as a means of making the Israelites holy by following it. As we see by verse 19, it was given to show people what sin is, so we could understand why we even need a Messiah. We would never be able to put our faith in a Messiah if we never even understood why we need to. To see that need, we must understand what sin is and that meeting the standard of perfection would be impossible for us to achieve in our own effort. This is why the law was given—to show people that any attempt at self-righteousness was futile—so they could see why they needed to put faith in the Messiah to come. Also, without the law, there would have been no legal standard by which Christ could have been judged as holy and without sin. If there was no written law explaining what sin is, how would we know Christ was sinless? What would have been the standard by which to declare such a thing? That's why verse 19 tells us that it was only meant to last until Christ came.

In addition, we see from verse 19, that sacrificing animals was meant only as a temporary solution to last only until the coming of the Messiah. Why is that? Hebrews 10 explains that it is because it is not possible for animal blood to take away sins or provide perfect cleansing. If we back up to Hebrews 9:10, the Bible explains the animal sacrifice system was only in effect until a better system could be established.

So if salvation through Messiah is received by faith in the one who was promised, what is the animal sacrifice system a solution for? Galatians 3:24-25 gives us the answer. These verses tell us that the law protected us and that it was our "guardian." Protected us from what? What did it guard us from? Satan's ability to steal, kill, and destroy until Jesus's once-and-for-all perfect sacrifice could do it on a permanent basis for us.

Hebrews 9:22 (NLT) gives us another clue. It says, "*...without the shedding of blood, there is no forgiveness.*" Why is that important? Just like any kingdom, God's kingdom is a kingdom of law, order, and justice. Justice must be satisfied. Rebellion against God's just ways brings consequences in that Satan now has the legal right to steal, kill, and destroy. Because of sin, mankind was no longer under the jurisdiction of heaven, having joined Satan's rebellion, so without some form of legal protection in place, God could not overrule His own judgment against sin and send the enemy packing.

An interesting observation we see from Scripture is that the practice of sacrificing animals for atonement was carried out way before the law. It started all the way back in the Garden of Eden. All throughout the book of Genesis, as well as other places throughout the Old Testament, we see many people such as Abel (Genesis 4:4), Noah (Genesis 8:20), Job (Job 1:5), Abraham (Genesis 22:2), and Jacob (Genesis 31:54), just to name a few, observing this practice of burnt offerings. At this point in history, the law commanding them to do so did not even exist. So, who taught them this? I believe this example was given directly to Adam from God when God sacrificed the lives of animals to make clothing for Adam and Eve and then passed down from there. Another interesting observation is that in every instance where this practice is mentioned in the Bible, it also records that these were all people who directly called on the name of the Lord. They all had a relationship and communication with the Lord. I believe God gave them this practice as a temporary solution to restrain the enemy so His blessings could flow.

Faith and obedience to the direct Word of the Lord is what gave God legal jurisdiction to bless the Israelites, while the rest of the world lived under the legal jurisdiction of Satan due to sin. Until Christ was born in the flesh and went to the cross, there was only a temporary solution to remove Satan's legal claim, and that was the sacrificial system. Now, due to Jesus's once-and-for-all perfect sacrifice, we come back under the jurisdiction of the kingdom of heaven and receive these blessings through faith in Christ.

Because of the ability of the blood of Jesus to cover all sin once and for all, Galatians 3:14 tells us the blessing of Abraham came on the Gentiles as well through Jesus Christ. In the old covenant, the Israelites only had access to these blessings through their obedience to the law, which was a temporary type and shadow of the permanent new covenant to come. Now, as believers in Christ with access to the new covenant, we receive these promised blessings by faith. We have access to them through Christ's obedience on our behalf. Christ fulfilled the righteous requirements of the law for us. In other words, He fulfilled the legal part, allowing God's jurisdiction to bless the Gentiles. This does not mean we do not still have natural conditions to meet. It just means we have access through faith and not the law.

In addition, we are also citizens of His kingdom and made sons and daughters in the family of God.[23] They had the old covenant with promises based on following the law, but according to Hebrews 8:6, we have a new covenant that Jesus mediated for us with better promises we receive by faith and not by works. For example, in Proverbs 28:27 (NKJV), the Bible promises us, *"He who gives to the poor will not lack, but he who hides his eyes will have many curses."* Through Christ, we have access to that same promise. The finished work does not mean Christ gave to the poor for us. We still must give to the poor before the blessing is released to us. Our faith in what God said He would do when we give to the poor, along with our actions, releases the blessing. This is how faith and action work together to bring the harvest of blessings.

The blessings of Abraham dealt mostly with the natural realm and natural prosperity, but now, through Jesus, we also have all the spiritual gifts, promises, and blessings as well. So what do we do if we are not seeing the promises manifest in our lives? Because we have been brought up and trained as slaves under this earth's cursed system of provision, we need our minds renewed. Romans 12:2 tells us we are transformed by the renewing of our minds. It doesn't happen any other way. We will prosper to the degree that our mind is renewed with truth. Our internal mental picture must change to see ourselves living in the state of the promises fulfilled. If we can't see it on the inside, we will never see it on the outside. In addition, we must study the promises of God to see if they are conditional or unconditional. Many times, people have faith, but they are not meeting the conditions the Bible lays out required to unlock the promise.

Satan cannot take away our inheritance. All he can do is take away or keep us from the knowledge of it. If we do not know the promises contained in our inheritance, our life will look no different than an unbeliever. However, as promised in John 8:32, if we know the truth, the truth will set us free. Jesus is the way, the truth, and the life, so if we know the truth (Jesus), the truth (Jesus) will set us free.

One of the promises we inherit when we come to know Jesus, who is truth incarnate, is freedom. What does it mean to be "free?" We know we are free from the curse that includes poverty, but our freedom does not stop there. John 8:36 (NLT) says, "*So if the Son sets you free, you are truly free.*" In the first part of that scripture, the word "free" is *eleutheroó*.[24] In this instance, it is used as a verb, an action word, meaning "to set free or to liberate, or to release from captivity, confinement, or slavery." In the second part of that scripture, the same word is used in a different form, this time as an adjective, as a descriptive word *eleútheros*.[25] As an adjective, it means "unbound, unshackled, one who is not a slave, one who is freeborn, not under the control or power of another, able to act or do as one wishes, or not physically restrained or obstructed," and is also the same word used in Galatians 4:31, which tells us we are children born of the free woman, meaning Sarah.

If we re-read John 8:36 inserting these definitions in place of the word free, it would read, "So if the Son sets you free, liberates you, releases you from captivity, confinement or slavery, you are truly unbound, unshackled, one who is not a slave, one who is freeborn, not under the control or power of another, able to act or do as one wishes, and not physically restrained or obstructed." Wow! We may need to read it repeatedly until it sinks into every fiber of our being. Our freedom in Christ is all-encompassing. It is not just something that happens to us after we die. He came to set us free from anything that shackles us or makes us a prisoner, including poverty, in this life.

HOW DO WE OBTAIN THIS FREEDOM?

What if we are not experiencing freedom in every aspect of life? If Christ shed His blood to make us free, then why are so many of us living lives that more closely resemble slavery? Just because we have an inheritance, does not mean we automatically possess it. If my husband dies, leaving me an insurance policy, that money does not just show up in my bank account upon his death. There are actions I must take to lay claim to and possess it. I would have to contact the insurance company, prove my status as the heir and beneficiary, submit a legal document called a death certificate to prove my claim is not fraudulent, and once they send the check, I would still have to take it to the bank and deposit it. Just because I am the rightful heir and beneficiary does not mean I will automatically or passively possess what belongs to me. My husband did all he could do to make that inheritance mine but taking possession of it is my choice, as well as the responsibility to take the necessary actions to possess it.

The same holds true for every inheritance Christ paid for us to have, whether it is provision, healing, peace, joy, or anything else promised to us in the Word of God. Many of God's kids are not experiencing the promises because they passively wait for God to "poof" those promises into their lives like a genie rather than letting their faith produce the action needed to take possession. Jesus's faith in healing would have meant nothing if it did not cause Him to act by laying hands on people, declaring and enforcing healing over them.

In the verse just before, we are told that knowing the truth, Christ, will make us free. This is where we find what I believe are three keys to taking possession of that freedom. John 8:31-32 (NLT) reads, "*Jesus said to the people who believed in him, 'You are truly my disciples if you remain faithful to my teachings. and you will know the truth, and the truth will set you free.'*" To obtain this freedom, let's focus on three key phrases in that passage. First, *"Jesus said to the people who believed in him…"* Believing in Jesus's finished work on the cross is the first step to walking in freedom. He is talking to believers. He is the narrow gate that leads to freedom. There is no other way. It's not enough to just be believers in Him; we must believe His promises are for us personally before we will ever walk in them.

Second, Jesus says, *"…if you remain faithful to my teachings."* He gives a condition to meet. We must faithfully do what He tells us, living life how He says it should be lived in His Word. We must know what He teaches to remain faithful to do it, and we must know what His teachings say about provision, finances, and everything else included as promises to us. This word *"if"* proves that these things don't automatically or passively show up. It is up to us to remain faithful to the Word by being doers—taking faith-backed action and meeting any specified conditions.

Third, after we believe in Him, and after we remain faithful to His teachings, then *"we will know the truth, and the truth will set us free."* Satan can only rule where there is darkness or ignorance of the truth of God. He does not want us to find out what is written in the will for us, which is why he seeks to keep us distracted from reading the Word of God or developing our relationship with Jesus. Let's break these three keys down in further detail.

KEY 1—OUR BELIEFS

"Jesus said to the people who believed in Him…" deals with our beliefs. We must know what He accomplished for us in the physical realm, not just the spiritual. We cannot break free from the bondage of the enemy's lies unless we know who the truth is and what He accomplished for us. We can't get our inheritance if we don't even know what our Father desires us to have and what He left in His will for us. The absence of the truth of the Word of God is what allows the enemy's lies to infiltrate our minds and build strongholds of false beliefs and sophisticated arguments. Colossians 1:13-14 (NLT) says, "*For he has rescued us from the kingdom of darkness and transferred us into the kingdom of his dear Son, who purchased our freedom and forgave our sins.*"

Salvation includes both purchasing our freedom and forgiving our sins. He purchased our freedom from the curse, and because of that purchase, we get to share in the inheritance that belongs to His people. He also rescued us from the kingdom of darkness and transferred us into the kingdom of His dear Son. Notice the past tense grammar of *"has rescued."* Our lives have already changed jurisdiction. We are born into sin as citizens of the kingdom of darkness, but because of our adoption through Christ, we are transferred out of that kingdom and into the kingdom of God's Son!

Romans 8:16-17 (NKJV) says, *"The Spirit Himself bears witness with our spirit that we are children of God, and if children, then heirs—heirs of God and joint heirs with Christ, if indeed we suffer with Him, that we may also be glorified together."* However, the good news of the gospel does not stop there. There is so much more contained in this inheritance.

Read 2 Corinthians 1:19-20.

This is astounding! According to this verse, any promise God has promised anyone, at any time, all throughout Scripture is ours in Christ. No matter the promise, the answer is found in what Christ accomplished for us, which is free and accessible to any person at any time by faith. We do not have to ask if we can have it—the answer is always "Yes!" We believe it is ours, and it is. If there is a condition on a certain promise, our faith should produce the work or necessary action to meet that condition, believing we will receive possession of the same promise.

Hopefully, we now have our beliefs right concerning all the cross gives us access to and that those promises we inherit absolutely include prosperity in this life. We have explored just a few of those promises—healing, wholeness, abundant provision, freedom, the spiritual gifts of the Holy Spirit, and access to any promise contained in God's Word. All these things are for our use in fulfilling our assignments in this life!

KEYS 2 AND 3—IF WE REMAIN FAITHFUL TO HIS TEACHINGS / WE WILL KNOW THE TRUTH

These last two keys go together. To remain faithful to His teachings, we must know what He teaches. We must know His Word. When we know His Word, we will know the truth, and the truth will make us free. We know from His Word that not only is it God's will for us to prosper, but it also gives Him pleasure to see His servants prosper. I am drilling this in because we will never receive anything out of God's promises if we do not believe, and we can't believe in a promise we don't know about. We cannot recognize a lie unless we know what the truth is.

We obtain the freedom we are promised to inherit in Christ by repenting, which means changing our minds from our old thoughts (lies) and replacing those lies with the truth (God's Word). Once we become citizens of God's kingdom and members of God's family, how does God transform us? By renewing our minds with the truth. We will not have the ability to know God's will for us until we change how we think. God transforms our lives by transforming our minds and changing how we think by replacing the thoughts we grew up with—His truth.

It does not say He transforms our lives by changing our behavior. Our behavior never changes in the long term until we change our minds first. When we renew our minds by filling them with the truth of God's Word, we are transformed into who He originally created us to be. By the renewing of our minds in and through the Word, by replacing lies with truth, and replacing our thoughts with His thoughts, we can know the will of God, and this will change how we think! So many Christians are not prosperous because they have accepted religious lies instead of biblical truths. Freedom begins in the mind before it ever reaches our physical experience.

Just like a smoker who wishes to be free from cigarettes, they first must desire to be free, which gives them the motivation to change. Then, they must believe that they can be free. They must begin to change their mind, then their behavior changes. Until they think differently, they will not experience anything different, and neither will we. Our lives will change when we change how we think. The environment around us becomes like the environment in us. If we work on the environment in us by deleting lies and replacing those lies with truth, the environment around us will change.

We must see it the way we want it on the inside before we ever see it on the outside. Our imagination, our ability to see a picture in our minds, is the very tool God gives us to create life as we would like it to be. Unfortunately, too many of us think imagination is nothing more than child's play. Why? Because, as little children, our use of our imaginations is less restricted. This is what it means when the Bible says in Mark 10:15 (NLT), *"I tell you the truth, anyone who doesn't receive the kingdom of God like a child will never enter it."*

Anything or anyone that exists first existed in the mind of God. He then created with His hands the prototype in His mind. It is the exact same way for us. Nothing becomes our experience without first being a thought. We don't just wake up in the morning and our teeth are automatically brushed. First, we think the thought, *I need to brush my teeth*; then, we see a mental picture of us doing that which coincides with the thought. We then create that experience with our hands. It's how all of life is lived. The problem is that most people do this by default instead of taking charge of the process. This is why Satan works so hard to capture people's imaginations through everything put out through sights and sounds.

It's important to mention that there is always a "lag time" between a thought and its manifestation. That lag time serves us. Could you imagine if every thought we had manifested immediately? That would be total chaos. In the lag time, it gets decided whether that thought gets aborted or planted. The key is when we agree with a thought with certainty, with no doubt or counterthoughts, our actions will follow.

Applying this concept to prosperity, we can't keep money if we are poor in our minds because we will find a way to lose it. We can't spiritualize dysfunction. We can't and won't prosper if we feel unworthy, if we don't believe or are unsure that God wants us to be prosperous, or if we believe money is evil. Again, as 3 John 1:2 (NKJV) says, *"Beloved, I pray that you may prosper in all things and be in health, just as your soul prospers."* Our souls need to be trained in truth.

We will prosper to the degree of our understanding of and obedience to the Word. If we don't know the Word, we can't be a doer of the Word and not a hearer only.[26] If we don't know the Word, we can't obey the Word. We must also remain faithful to do what it says. Faith without works is dead. There is always an action component to faith because our behavior is determined by what we believe. James 2:22 tells us that by action, faith finds its full expression! Faith is not fully expressed until it produces action. Now that we know exactly what some of His promises are, we must know how to access them.

Read 2 Peter 1:3-5.

It doesn't say to "make every effort to believe" in God's promises. We are told to respond to God's promises. We escape the corruption and curse of poverty by responding to God's promises. It's important that we learn how these promises work and to manifest the things and provisions God's Word promises us. We need to understand how faith in the promises of God's Word and action go together. Notice in this verse that God has already done everything He can do to make His promises available to us. It is up to us to respond. "Respond" is an action word. Stop praying and asking God to do what He has already done and start praying and learning about how you can better respond to Him.

To help us understand how this works, Pastor Gary Keesee in Ohio uses a brilliant analogy of having a signed check with the amount left blank. If I gave someone a signed check made out to them but left the amount blank to which they filled in $1,000, would they have $1,000 in cash? Yes, but no. Is this check $1000? Would this person be able to take this check and go to any store, hand them this check, and walk out with $1000 worth of stuff? No. Why? Even though they have this check, which is like having $1000, what they really have is a promissory note. They have a promise of $1000. They do not yet have $1000 in cash. There is a process they must go through to receive and possess it.

For the one the check is made out to, they must first have faith and believe that the promise is good and that the one who promised it has the means to fulfill it. Secondly, they must believe that the promise is meant for them and the person who made the promise by writing the check really wants them to have it. Once they believe the check is good and they know that the person who wrote it wants them to have it, the switch flips in their mind, and it is like they already have it even though there is still a process to obtain and possess the money. Third, they must now put their faith into action by taking the necessary steps to secure the promise and see it fulfilled in their life. Based on the faith that I am not a liar or a fraud and that I have the means in my estate to fulfill this promise, they must:

Step 1) Take the check to a bank. As believers, we must go to the Bible's bank vault and find a promise relative to our situation.

Step 2) Provide the proper identification. What are we basing our belief on that identifies us as a certified recipient of the promise? That would be 2 Corinthians 1:19-20.

Step 3) Request how they want the promised funds delivered so they can then possess them. This is how we pray differently. Matthew 7:7 says we can *"ask and it will be given."* So, when we pray, we don't ask God for what He has already promised, we ask for the promise to be delivered according to His Word and thank Him for already providing it.

Believing the promises changes their preparation. Maybe they weren't planning on taking a trip to the bank this week, but now, because they have received this promise and have faith in my character and ability to fulfill it, they believe they already have the money. In their minds, they can already see themselves spending it. So they alter their plans and take different actions. It will cost a little time and effort, but they change their behavior based on the full expectation to receive what was promised. They will go to the bank, wait in line, and make a deposit. They will behave based on the expectation that the promise is good.

How might their behavior be different if they did not believe the check was good, or if they did not believe the check was really intended for them, or they did not deserve it? They might toss it aside and never prepare to receive it. Based on this negative belief, they would not take the actions necessary to possess it. Or what if they did not even know I had made a check out to them? What if I snuck up behind them at church to surprise them and just tucked this check in their Bible that they never open or read, so they did not know this promise was hiding in there for them all along?

Even though it would be in their possession the whole time, not knowing about it is the same as not having it. What if they found it, believed it, just set the check on their dresser, and never got around to taking it to the bank? Faith without works is dead. Possessing the promise and possessing the fulfillment of the promise is not the same thing. Just because we have the promise does not mean that if we just patiently sit here passively, it will fulfill itself and turn itself into the promised cash.

Hebrews 11:33 (NLT) sums up the entire process by saying, "*By faith these people overthrew kingdoms, ruled with justice, and received what God had promised them...*" First, they believed (by faith), then, they took action on those beliefs (overthrew kingdoms and ruled with justice), fully expecting to receive what God had promised (and they did). When we believe God's promises, we will change what we do. Would the Israelites have dared to face giants if they didn't fully expect God to fulfill the promise He gave them? Did they have the land? No. They had a promissory note for the land, which caused them to invade and conquer that land. In fact, the first generation chose to believe the negative report of spies instead of the Word of God, so they did not take the actions necessary to possess the promise. We will change our routine when we believe in our hearts that we already have the promises.

James 4:2 (NKJV) says, "*You lust and do not have. You murder and covet and cannot obtain. You fight and war. Yet you do not have because you do not ask.*" How we ask is important. Don't ask or beg God for what He has already promised; request its delivery, thanking Him as if it's done, and imagine you already have it. If we had a blank check, would we be lusting after anyone else's stuff? When we are at an all-we-can-eat buffet, are we worried about what is on anyone else's plate? Are we jealous of it? No. When we have all we could want or need, and if we run out, we can go back to the buffet and get more. There is no greed, jealousy, envy, or striving. The promises of God are the same. There is no poverty in the Father's house or in heaven. We are now under the jurisdiction of that kingdom, and as citizens, we have rights to all that the kingdom contains. However, we do not automatically get what is promised. We receive the promises when we have the faith to enforce God's kingdom rule over Satan's to obtain them.

How do we apply this practically? We do so by finding a promise that pertains to our needs or situation. We deposit that promise in our hearts and then fill out the check by praying and asking the Father for it. According to James 4:2, we do not have because we do not ask.

Read Matthew 7:7-8.

Does this sound like a God looking for any reason to deny, withhold, or say no? Quite the opposite! However, this does not mean we have a blank check for whatever we want; however, we do have a blank check for what God has promised in His Word. Matthew 6:33 (NKJV) tells us, "*But seek first the kingdom of God and His righteousness, and all these things shall be added to you.*" Notice that it says "*these things,*" but it doesn't say "all things." What are "*these things?*" To find out, we must back up to verse 31. In Matthew 6:31, Jesus instructs us not to worry about the necessities of life and then goes on to tell us that "*these things,*" these necessities, shall be given to us. What necessities? Food, drink, clothing, and shelter. All these things pertain to our physical body and are necessary to sustain life. What is not being promised here? Lifestyle stuff. Things to make life easier. Jesus tells us that when we put God's kingdom first by living how God says life is supposed to be lived and by enforcing the jurisdiction of his kingdom, all these things will be added to us. We will not have to hunt or search for them.

In 1 John 3:22 (NKJV), we are given a different promise that pertains to all things, and not simply basic provision. It says, "*And whatever we ask we receive from Him, because we keep His commandments and do those things that are pleasing in His sight.*" Here we see that we can have a blank check for "whatever," when we meet the condition of keeping His commandments and doing those things that are pleasing in His sight. Mark 11:24 (NLT) tells us an even more amazing promise, "*I tell you, you can pray for anything, and if you believe that you've received it* (past tense), *it will be yours* (future tense). How can this be? To help us understand the process of receiving provision from the Father out of heaven's kingdom, we can look at an example from our everyday lives: ordering from an online retailer.

If we have need of something, we can go to a website, find what it is we need or want, place it in our cart, pay any required fee, and as soon as we hit that "Place Order" button, the item is as good as ours. We have full faith and expectation that what we request will show up on our doorstep. We have full faith that the retailer can fulfill our requests; either we have paid for it, or someone else has, so we are the owner of that item, even though it is not actually in our possession yet. We have an order confirmation, which is not the actual item ordered but is the promise that the order has been received, is being processed, and is on its way.

Based on our faith in the one we ordered from and their ability to stand behind and fulfill their promises, we simply wait for the requested provision to show up. We do not necessarily know the exact day or hour of its arrival, but that does not shake our faith. We simply wait for it to manifest. If the package does not arrive, we do not think the retailer is a liar or that they did not want us to have it or that they do not fulfill their promises, or that they only fulfill their promises for some people. We know that something must be hindering it, such as being on backorder, or we look for the problem on the delivery line not with the deliverer. Maybe the package was intercepted or stolen? Maybe it was misrouted because of someone's mistake. No matter the case, we do not lose faith in the retailer. We simply make contact, explain the problem, allow them to work on a solution, and we go back to fully expecting our item to show up.

The same is true with how we receive provision from the kingdom of God. We go through the same steps. We look to God's Word to find the promise of what we need. We receive that promise by asking the Father for it. The price for it and all our provisions has already been paid on the cross, putting us back to our original status of creation, having access to all abundant provisions already surrounding us. The cross of Jesus gives us an open line of credit in the kingdom of heaven to obtain all the provisions we need to fulfill our work and mission on earth, so we use our unlimited store credit. We place our request, fully expecting the provision to manifest, even though we do not know the exact day or hour it will show up. If it seems to be taking longer than is normal, we make contact to make sure nothing has intercepted our provision, holding it in delay, or trying to steal it. We allow the Holy Spirit to show us and work on a solution, and we simply go back to fully expecting it to show up. We do not cry and wail and doubt God, His goodness, promises, or ability. The problem is never on God's end. If what we need is not manifesting, we need to see where the glitch is in the delivery.

What if something intercepted the package? Even though Mark 11:24 (NLT) tells us, *"I tell you, you can pray for anything, and if you believe that you've received it* (past tense)*, it will be yours* (future tense). If we keep reading, the next verse tells us what will short-circuit our receiving by causing a glitch in the delivery. *"...If you have anything against anyone, forgive him..."* Mark 11:25 (NKJV).

Unforgiveness will allow the devourer the legal right to intercept our provision from the kingdom of God. Also, even though in James 4:2 (NKJV) we are promised, *"You lust and do not have. You murder and covet and cannot obtain. You fight and war. Yet you do not have because you do not ask."* If we keep reading in James 4:3, we find another thing that can glitch the delivery. It tells us, *"You ask and you do not receive, because you ask amiss, that you may spend it on your pleasures."* It says even when we do ask, we do not get it because our motives are all wrong; we want only what will give us pleasure. This is why the heart matters first.

Read James 1:5-8.

The third thing that will cut off the flow of provision is having a divided mind. What does this mean? Whatever our backup plan is, that's our true plan. Whatever our "Plan B" to fulfill our need, if God does not come through for us, is what we are really trusting in to meet that need. It's like saying, "I'm going to try my faith over here, but just in case nothing happens, I know I can always fall back to this if I have to." For example, someone could believe in God for a natural-born baby but keep a "we can always adopt" Plan B to fall back on. This is not a slam on adoption, especially in those cases where God is the one trying to lead someone down that path. Adoption is great, and sometimes God is saying that it's the route to take, and the desire to adopt will be a heart's desire as confirmation. The difference is when a person is using adoption as a backup plan and abandons hope for the original promise or heart's desire of having their own natural child.

As another example, if we think, *Well, if God doesn't provide me a job, I will just apply for welfare, or move back in with my parents, or take out a loan.* (This is not a slam to people who need government services, or fall on hard times, or who use credit.) In this example, those alternatives seem like the sure thing for their provision. For some people, the thought is, *Well, if I do not receive my healing, at least I will get a new glorified body someday.* Instead of finding the glitch in the delivery, they change their belief in what God says about healing. When we have a backup plan, it means we think it is the sure thing, and the miracle of promises to be manifested that we are hoping for is not for sure. This is not about condemnation, and I am not necessarily saying there is anything wrong with this. I am simply illustrating that our answer, our provision, is always going to come from where our faith is—what our "sure thing" is.

Our backup plan is our fail-safe. It is the sure thing we are willing to settle for if we do not get our miracle. This means our faith is not in God alone as mentioned in the scriptures above, but rather, it is really in whatever alternative we think we can fall back on. Our loyalty is divided between trusting God to fulfill His promises and trusting ourselves with a backup plan. Or, like in the example of healing, we settle for a different promise. When we have divided loyalty, we have a divided mind, which makes us unstable and unable to receive from God. Our answer will come from the place or thing our faith was in.

Again, if we are lacking provision, the problem is always on our side of the equation. Our prosperity has nothing to do with us and everything to do with what type of Father He is. What would it say about us as parents if we sent our children out in a blizzard without the proper provision to keep warm in just a T-shirt and sandals? Would that in any way reflect on the child's worthiness? Of course not, but it would say something about us as parents. The authorities might even throw us in jail for neglect or child endangerment. The law says a child is worthy of a parent's provision based solely on their status as a child, not on a case-by-case basis.

Our provision for our children is not a reflection of the child's worthiness but of our parenting. Why do we think it is any different with God? Are we better parents than God? Do human beings treat each other with better standards than God treats us? Who tells us we're unworthy? It isn't God. So why would we listen to garbage like that? Truth will lead us to freedom, but we can't test what is true until we replace our thoughts with God's thoughts and judge our experiences and lives by the Word of God.

We will only experience freedom to the degree that we are in absolute uncompromising agreement with God's Word, which is what faith really is. Living by faith is not a denial of the facts. Abraham and Sarah did not deny the fact that they were physically incapable of conceiving a child. The difference is that God's truth always supersedes facts. They chose to align their beliefs with what God said rather than what the facts said. So, when the facts tell us we're going to die from that disease, or we're never going to be able to pay that bill, or see our loved ones follow Jesus, or break free from the paycheck-to-paycheck cycle and get out of debt, our response needs to be: "It is written! I have a promise!" We must know what is written. We cannot remain faithful to His teachings if we don't even know what He teaches.

When we are thoroughly convinced of what God says about how life is to be lived, we will then know the truth and will be able to bring heaven to earth in each situation. Until we are completely persuaded about what God says, we are double-minded, and James 1 tells us clearly that being double-minded inhibits our ability to receive. Our freedom has already been bought and paid for, but it is up to us to use and walk in it.

Who is out in the world waiting for us to walk out the truth of our freedom? People need to see us walk out the freedom of addictions broken, sickness turned to health, and poverty turned to abundance. This is not just about blessing us; it is because through blessing us, others can see, know, and experience the goodness of God, and see who God is. Our provision reflects on Him as a parent.

As part of being a good parent, God does not place His promises in our hands, He places them within our reach. When I was teaching my children how to walk—the life skill that would take them almost anywhere they may need to go—how did I transition them from being a baby that had everything given to them, to being a toddler with more ability to do for themselves? I would find something they really wanted, a cookie, toy, or whatever, and place it within just enough reach to entice them to go after it. I would not just hand it to them anymore. Why? Was it because I wanted to be mean and tease them, or I didn't want them to have it? No, of course not. It was because I did not want them to just have the thing, but rather, I wanted them to develop the skill of being able to walk after and possess anything for themselves. The ability to walk was the greater thing.

I needed them to learn the process of going after, taking territory, and possessing what they desire, not just being handed everything. Never developing that skill would handicap them for life. Yes, I wanted them to have good things; it gave me great pleasure to see their happiness when given those things, but the greater thing was the skill. It would serve them their entire life. God needs us to learn and master the process of obtaining all we need so we can fulfill every assignment He gives us. He needs us to know what is in our inheritance He died for us to have, and He needs us to learn how His kingdom operates and how to move provision from His kingdom to this one. Hopefully, we now have a better understanding of how to do so.

CLASS 2
STUDY GUIDE AND JOURNAL

Always begin by praying and inviting the Holy Spirit into this time and shine His light on anything that needs to be seen and exposed. Ask the Holy Spirit to speak, reveal, correct, encourage, bring wisdom and revelation, and to teach you all things and remind you of all Jesus has said, as promised in John 14:26.

Out of all the things God left us in His will, what has the most significance to you right now?

What new promises have you discovered that you didn't know about before?

Explain the difference between a covenant and a contract and how that impacts you as far as what God has promised you.

How can you begin to push back the jurisdiction of Satan and enforce heaven's jurisdiction in your life? What mountains do you need to speak to with a judicial proclamation of what God has said?

Read Deuteronomy 28 and make a list of the blessings there.

What corrupt files in your mind need to be deleted, and what truth from Scripture needs to replace them?

Read the expanded definition of John 8:36, inserting yourself into the scripture: "*So if the Son sets (me) free, liberates (me), releases (me) from captivity, confinement or slavery, (I am) truly unbound, unshackled, one who is not a slave, one who is free-born, not under the control or power of another, able to act or do as I wish, and not physically restrained or obstructed.*" Where have you been passively waiting for God to fulfill His promises instead of meeting any biblical conditions or taking faith-based action? (Faith-based action is like Abraham continuing to sleep with his wife Sarah until seeing the promise fulfilled, not taking matters into his own hands and sleeping with Hagar.)

John 8:32 tells us that knowing the truth (a.k.a. knowing Christ, who is truth incarnate) sets us free. How can you get to know Christ Jesus in a deeper, more intimate way?

Are there any teachings of Jesus you have not remained faithful to?

How is the Holy Spirit prompting you to change how you think?

How is the Holy Spirit prompting you to respond to God's promises?

Do you have any unmanifested promises that may just have a glitch in the delivery? Has your package just been intercepted?

What do you think was responsible for the glitch (unbelief, unforgiveness, double-mindedness, wrong motives)?

What Plan B have you been holding onto "just in case?"

Find and list five unconditional promises God gives in His Word.

1.
2.
3.
4.
5.

Find and list five conditional promises God gave in His Word. What are the conditions?

1.
2.
3.
4.
5.

Make a list of what you would like to change about your life in these key areas:

Spiritually

Family

Destiny

Financially

Physical Body/Health

Fun/Hobbies

Relationships (outside of family)

Take each thing you list in each category and find a few scriptures that speak to that situation and place them where you can memorize them. (note cards, sticky notes, etc.). Ask the Holy Spirit to show you how you need to change to become the person that can sustain those desires.

CLASS 3

THE WILDERNESS OF PREPARATION—DEVELOPING THE RIGHT HEART FOR STEWARDSHIP

"For his Spirit joins with our spirit to affirm that we are God's children. And since we are his children, we are his heirs. In fact, together with Christ we are heirs of God's glory. But if we are to share his glory, we must also share his suffering."

ROMANS 8:16-17 NLT

As we learned in the previous class, a big part of our inheritance in Christ is the blessing of Abraham as described in Deuteronomy 28. The promises given in this passage speak to our natural provision for this life, not heavenly promises we will receive in eternity. These promises are all about living in supernatural abundance where we have more than enough resources and provision to do everything God puts on our hearts to do. As God's heirs, His blessings are always flowing like water through a garden hose. We also learned how certain things like unforgiveness, double-mindedness, and having wrong heart motives can allow the enemy to cause a kink in the hose, intercepting and blocking the flow of those blessings into our lives.

Unfortunately, instead of understanding we have been in violation of God's Word by not meeting a condition or allowing the enemy to steal our answers, many times, we mistakenly blame God by thinking He is not answering. As soon as we remove what is allowing our enemy to step on our hose, the blessings we are promised in God's Word can flow freely again. Although we touched on a few of the most common reasons we do not always walk in the fullness of God's blessings, there could be other reasons as well. As we learned from Romans 8:14-17, not only do we get to share in God's glory, but also part of sharing in the inheritance of God's glory is connected to us sharing in His suffering. We do not get one without the other.

There is always a "wilderness of preparation" between our current comfort zone and where our promises await us. This place is a season of sacrifice. This isn't sacrificing in the sense of loss but rather giving something up willingly. Anyone can have something forcefully taken from them—that is not sacrifice. Anyone can give up something they don't really want or value—also not sacrifice. It is only when we are in a place where we will sacrifice anything and everything in service to our King that our hearts are truly prepared to allow Him to funnel greater amounts of resources to us.

I recently heard pastor Bill Johnson put it this beautiful way, "To navigate loss well means you can be trusted with gain. To navigate disappointment well means you can be trusted with fulfillment. To navigate criticism well means you can be trusted with praise. To navigate betrayal well means you can be trusted with loyal friends. God is always testing us—not for failure or to mock, but to see what measure of glory we can carry. Glory resting on a sanctified life establishes it. Glory resting on an unsanctified life crushes it." That is so accurate. Whatever we desire to have or to steward means we are going to be tested with how well we navigate suffering the opposite to carry the glory of it. If we want great wealth, then we are going to be tested on how well we navigate poverty and lack.

Just like with natural inheritances, simply because we have an inheritance does not necessarily mean we will have free and unrestricted access to it. It also does not mean we get to dictate or demand our right to it. If a parent with a young child dies leaving behind a substantial estate or amount of money, very seldom is that young child given full and immediate access to the entire estate. The estate's assets and money are usually kept in a trust until such time as the child is mature enough to handle it. Even if the heir is "mature" enough, or even if they are already an adult, many times, there are still stipulations to meet before the fulness of the assets are released into the authority, management, and possession of the heir.

Why would a parent put restrictions on access to the estate? Is it because they do not want their children to be cared for? Of course not. Those restrictions are put in place as a safeguard against immaturity or lack of skill or knowledge that could cause the unprepared child to lose their inheritance through poor management. In the same way, we see from the account of the Israelites who left Egypt, that just because God has a Promised Land for us, it does not mean we will possess it. We have a big part to play in whether we enter and occupy those promises. How we handle the wilderness of preparation determines how long it will take us to possess the promise, or if we will even possess it at all.

An entire generation of Israelites were sent back to the wilderness and never possessed their promise because they could not get their beliefs right. The wilderness experience is about preparation. Unfortunately, very few things build our character or our reliance on God like suffering does. Suffering through different trials, adverse circumstances, or the sacrifice of our desires and worldly possessions is how we gain humility, stamina, and dependence on God. This is the very thing that prepares us to handle greatness with the right heart. The Promised Land is not about "arriving;" it is about being able to take God-ordained territory by driving the enemy out.

Do we want the Promised Land? Well, how much do we enjoy fighting giants? The Promised Land is where we fight and slay the giants. In the wilderness, our warfare is against our old slavery mentality and where our thinking and mindsets change. If we cannot slay our old mindsets, we cannot slay giants and possess the promise because we will never have the faith, courage, or stamina to do so. The wilderness is where we transform from slaves into giant slayers. Too many people are trying to possess and occupy the promise without first going through the process of preparation, and they are discovering that they are getting driven back out into the wilderness and living life in circles with no progress. To possess the promise, we must embrace the development process.

Giving an heir vast wealth of any kind, without them being mature and responsible enough to handle it, will, many times, be more harmful than helpful. Proverbs 20:21 (NLT) tells us, *"An inheritance obtained too early in life is not a blessing in the end."* Why is that? I believe we find the answer in Proverbs 1:32 (KJV), which states, *"... The prosperity of fools shall destroy them."* Our good and loving Father is not going to give His children anything that will destroy us, including the blessings He desires for us to have. Timing is everything.

If I were to die leaving a pristine classic car to my five-year-old child, that inheritance is no good and can even be dangerous. At that age and lack of physical development, my child would not have the mental or physical capability to be able to operate that vehicle, not to mention the legal ability. Would that mean my child would not get to inherit it ever? Of course not. There would have to be stipulations put in place for my child to receive that inheritance at the appropriate time, so they do not hurt themselves or others.

That same gift at the age of sixteen or eighteen would be a great blessing to them if they were properly trained in how to operate it. Just because they have reached an appropriate age does not necessarily mean they should receive it if they have never bothered to invest the time and money to be trained in its use. They must take the proper steps to educate themselves on how to drive it and acquire the proper license to do so. If they do not take these necessary actions to grow their ability, they may own the car, but they still cannot use it and it would be of no benefit to them. If they are not able to possess this gift, it would not be because I was the one withholding it from them. I did everything within my power to make sure it was available to them. Fulfilling the requirements necessary to possess it is their choice.

This is how it is with our heavenly Father. Sometimes, before fulfilling a promise to us or giving us access to manage the entirety of the estate, He waits for us to reach a point where we are physically and mentally able to handle it. Or, sometimes, He waits for us to take the proper steps to educate ourselves to be able to operate it. Our Father desires to see us prosper, and His heart is to lavish us with goodness, so if there is something we are not receiving, it is not because He is withholding it from us. He simply waits for the proper timing, or for us to get in gear and get ourselves properly educated and trained. If I have a dream of owning a restaurant, should the Lord give me a restaurant to own if I have absolutely no knowledge of how to operate one?

If prosperity can cause fools to destroy themselves, our Father certainly is not going to give us great prosperity if we are too foolish to steward it because He is kind, not because He is mean or seeking to withhold things from us. He loves us. God promises to meet our needs, and He does. We will be provided for and taken care of as His children. Beyond that, how much we are given depends on us and our demonstrating the ability to handle wealth with the right heart. Salvation puts our name in the will, but we are not given the entirety of the estate unless and until we are able to handle it.

Just like in the natural, the will most often provides for the heir's basic provision and needs (e.g., food, shelter, clothing, education, etc.), but that heir does not get to have the administration of the estate with full access to the abundant provision of all the assets until they have gone through a process of maturing. It is the same with our inheritance in Christ, when it comes to the portion of worldly wealth. God, in His goodness, will always provide everything we need, but only those willing to walk through the process of maturity will gain the position of being allowed to have administration over more.

Read Luke 16:10-12 and Matthew 25:14-15.

We see from these two passages that how much we are given stewardship is in direct proportion to our trustworthiness and abilities. Every servant received something to invest with that went beyond just the basic provision of food, clothing, and shelter—something they could use to grow in skill and ability at the same time. Jesus reveals that we are the ones who determine how much we are trusted with, by demonstrating both trustworthiness with what we have already been given and by increasing our ability to handle more.

If we want to move from just having our needs met and provided for to having unlimited access to the whole estate, there is a process we must go through. God is not going to give us ten talents to steward with one talent ability. We must be willing to invest in and grow our own ability to handle wealth. Vast wealth with no stewardship ability will end up getting lost. We see this all the time with lottery winners who go broke again within a few short years because they have never learned to properly manage money. Spending money and managing money are not the same thing. So, if we want to be trusted with more, what are we doing to grow in our ability to handle it? What type of education are we investing in? More than just consuming knowledge, what are we doing to put that knowledge into practice?

Being doers and not hearers only is true with any kind of knowledge. Knowing something is not enough, we must act on that knowledge and demonstrate our ability if we want the benefit of that knowledge. There are a lot of very overweight people who have knowledge of what to eat and what not to eat and how to exercise, but are they acting according to their knowledge? Having the knowledge is not enough. It must be put into practice to receive the benefit. If I desire to play the guitar, unless it is a God-given gift, I am not going to magically be able to play that guitar. I must invest both the time and the money in learning how to play it, but even more than that, I must pick up a guitar and begin to practice with it. Over time, with both increased learning, knowledge, and practice, I will increase in ability to be able to play songs of greater difficulty.

Learning something is never forced on us. How much we want to grow in ability is always up to us. However, if we do not put in the time and effort to learn a skill, we have no right to complain when we cannot do it. Why would God give me more guitars if I have not even taken the time to learn how to play the one I have? We have no right to expect to be given the privilege of handling more if we are not properly handling what we already have. I am not the one who says that—Jesus is! Go back and read Luke 16:10-12 again. How much we are given depends on how trustworthy we are and what our abilities are, so we determine how much we are given. Again, notice in the parable of the talents that every servant got something. God does not leave anyone out, and it would be unkind to give us more than we can handle. To grow in management, we must grow in ability.

So how do we grow in trustworthiness and ability? The first part of the process, which was covered previously, deals with the condition and posture of our hearts. Most people want the provision but do not want God telling them how to use it. It does not work that way. God is not the silent partner; He is the majority partner with full check-writing privileges. Our hearts must be fully submitted or prosperity may destroy us.

Jesus said in Mark 8:36 (NLT), *"And what do you benefit if you gain the whole world but lose your own soul?"* God is more concerned about our souls than our profit. Remember what we learned in the last class about our soul prospering before we physically prosper. Speaking from personal experience, trusting God is much harder when we have a big, fat bank account because it is way too easy to trust in the provision that can be seen. It is incredibly easier to trust God when we have nothing left to trust in. If we have not gone through a process of training our hearts first, riches may corrupt us. Wealth would own us; we would not own it. If we are not faithful with the little now, we will not be faithful when given much.

People say things like, "When I have millions of dollars, I will start tithing or putting God first with my money." No, they will not, and Jesus tells us why. If we are not faithful when we have very little to be faithful with, we won't be faithful when we have much to be faithful with. If they will not give $0.10 when they have $1, they will not give $1 when they have $10. If they will not give $10 when they have $100, they will not give $100 when they have $1,000. If they will not give $100 when they have $1,000, they will not give God the thousands when they have millions, either. Jesus said that when we are faithful and consistent with the little first, then we will be faithful with the much.

Read Matthew 20:21-23.

To share in Christ's glory, we must also share in His suffering and death. Just as Jesus laid down His will for the Father's will, we must die to our wills and what we want for our lives in exchange for His will for our lives. To share in Christ's glory, the cost is that we must die to our own ambitions and desires. In this passage, we see that even the disciples wanted glory without the process of suffering and self-sacrifice where we put our own wills on the altar. They wanted the prize without paying the cost. People today are no different. We always want success, position, honor, and finances without walking through the wilderness of suffering and discipline that people who have those things walked through to get them. We want the gold medals without the years of sacrifice, discipline, and grueling training it took to get to that level.

There is no honor without first drinking the cup of suffering. Jesus, knowing they would share in His glory, made it clear they would also share in His suffering. Suffering postures our hearts properly before Jesus, so when honor comes, we will not be corrupted by it. Even Jesus did not get the inheritance without first drinking of the cup of suffering and sacrifice. Joseph was not elevated to his position of honor without first spending time in the pit of suffering and being trained and growing in ability.

The Israelites did not go straight from the slavery of Egypt to occupying the Promised Land without first walking through the wilderness of suffering. There is always a wilderness on the way to possessing the promise. Humility and suffering always precede honor in the kingdom. The wilderness is where we learn to let go of comfort in pursuit of something greater and where we learn to trust in God as our provider instead of our "Egyptian slave masters" (our jobs, our businesses, or other sources of income) as our provider.

It is so easy to point our fingers at the Israelites, but how many Christians today are selling out their Promised Land for the "sure thing?" We are so afraid of the unknown that we are willing to forsake doing great exploits with God for the false security of the sure thing. The Israelites, when finally getting the opportunity to possess their promise, did not want to go through the fear of facing the giants who possessed their promise. They would rather have God just "poof" and take their enemy out. However, because they were going to have to put their faith in God's promise to give them the land into action, they chose to turn back. They are the reason they did not receive the promise, not God.

If they knew God, who He is and was with them, in them, around them, and for them, they would have never been afraid to begin with. The real problem is that they did not even know the God they were worshipping. They knew stories and even saw Him do mighty things on their behalf, but they did not know Him. If they did, they would have been thrilled to watch Him put His super on their natural and fight with and for them.

What we do with God and for God can never take the place of knowing God. More than that, God does not just want to do everything for us, He wants to do things through us. This is why God didn't just slay all the inhabitants of the land and let the Israelites move right in. He needed them to learn how to walk in His power and authority, not just sit around complacently while God does everything. God works in partnership with us. He expects us to step out and act based on our faith that He will back us up.

This is why the Israelites had to get up, swing their swords, and take the land. What they did not understand was that making them pick up swords and swing them against those giants was about getting them to face their fears and build their trust in Him and what He wanted to do on their behalf. Joshua 1:9 (NLT) says, *"This is my command—be strong and courageous! Do not be afraid or discouraged, For the LORD your God is with you wherever you go."*

A while back, there was a picture circulating the internet of a lion cub coming up against a larger predator. What the little cub could not see was the adult lion behind him backing him up, but the predator could see it. That is exactly what it is like having God with us wherever we go. We either believe God or we don't. He is either with us wherever we go, or He is not. If we know He is, then why would we ever be afraid to go anywhere or do anything? If we are still afraid, then we need a greater revelation of who God is and that He is with us. While He is with us, He can only act through us; therefore, our participation is a must. If we run away, nothing gets done. The giants got to hold that land an extra forty years because the Israelites refused to participate. They let their fear dictate what they did instead of believing what God said.

Just like the Israelites, we must unlearn the slavery mentality we grew up in and learn to trust, obey, and depend on God before we can conquer and occupy a Promised Land. How long we spend in the wilderness is determined by how obedient we are while we are there. It takes trust to obey. We only obey authorities we trust or fear. Jesus wants our trust! Trust has degrees. It is natural and normal to trust some more than others because trust is developed through situations and circumstances where trust is required. The only way God can develop our trust in Him is to put us in situations where trusting Him is required. Trust is a form of faith; therefore, having faith in someone is synonymous with trusting them.

Read Matthew 16:7-10.

What was Jesus really saying here? Something like, "Come on, guys! Haven't you seen Me create and multiply provision several times over now, and yet, you are still looking at what you lack, not having bread?" In other words, "Haven't we been through enough situations and circumstances where you've watched Me come through for you, and yet, you're still going to look at the facts instead of believing in My truth or trusting My divine nature? I created the entire universe out of nothing, can I not also create any provision you need? Do you still have such little faith, even after seeing Me do this several times now, that you must see it again before you believe it?" Jesus was floored at their lack of understanding, trust, and faith, especially after seeing Him miraculously provide for them several times.

Likewise, the Israelites in the wilderness had to learn to trust God for their very existence. This wilderness had no food, water, clothing stores, shoe stores, or shelters; the only option was to trust God to provide literally everything they needed. What's important to note is when God provided in the wilderness, He did not give more of what they needed. What they already had never ran out or wore out. In the same way, God allows us to experience lack for a season, so we learn to trust Him as our provider. However, even in the wilderness, the Israelites were not even really in lack. They had everything they needed, they just were not yet able to administrate the abundance of the Promised Land. The wilderness is where every luxury gets removed and the true difference between a necessity and a luxury becomes clear. It is amazing what we can convince ourselves is a necessity that is truly a luxury. The wilderness is also where we lose our entitlement and regain our gratitude.

God took the Israelites through this wilderness season of learning to trust Him to provide their food, shelter, clothing, etc., because if they could not even trust Him for those most basic things, how could they ever trust Him to slay giants? Promised lands are where the giants are and where the battles are fought. There was a battle to get out of Egypt and a few skirmishes along the way, but nothing like the opponents they had to defeat and displace to possess their promise. Life's biggest battles are fought in the Promised Land as we learn to take territory and occupy what God is calling us to. We will need to know how to trust and obey Him to fight and slay those giants. We will never develop that kind of trust without first learning to trust Him to provide for the little things like life's basic needs.

The wilderness is where we learn it is God who sustains us before we get to our Promised Land where God advances us. To try and take on conquering the land without first developing a proper heart towards God of trust and obedience would destroy us. Would the Israelites have had enough trust in God to be obedient to a ridiculous battle strategy of marching silently around a city for days if they did not first learn to trust that God would feed them every day? It takes trust and obedience to not lean on our own understanding and try to rush into battle to try and conquer a city in hand-to-hand combat without first going through the testing of learning to trust.

In Joshua 7, we find the story of Achan and the battle of Ai, which is an example of trying to obtain the promise without a fully submitted heart. The very first battle the Israelites fought in the Promised Land was the battle of Jericho, found in Joshua 6. They were commanded not to take and keep any of the gold or spoils. What was not commanded to be burned was to be put into the treasury of the Lord. Unknown to Joshua and the others, Achan disobeyed God and took some of the spoils from Jericho. Talk about failing the test and the very first opportunity. The very next battle was against Ai. Ai was a small town that should have been easily defeated, but instead, they overpowered them and many Israelites died. When Joshua inquired of the Lord, the Lord told him about Achan's disobedience and how, because of it, they could not stand before their enemies. To clean the sin out of Israel, Achan's entire family was swallowed up when the earth opened beneath them.

The wilderness will test our hearts to see if we will complain about the "just enough" provision of the Lord. Are we going to demand quail when He gives manna? We want God to provide for us, yet many times, with prideful hearts, we also want to try and tell Him what and how much. We must first demonstrate obedience in our suffering before we will ever be obedient in our Promised Land. Until we are submitted, we will stay in wilderness level provision of just enough and never move to Promised Land provision where we get to administrate and occupy our inheritance.

We must give up something to gain something greater. Just like the Israelites, we must give up our trust in the seemingly safe and secure position as slaves in Egypt and learn to submit our hearts to God and the way He wants to provide rather than the way we want it. Abraham had to leave what he knew—the comfortable and familiar—and go to a new place. The Israelites had to give up the familiarity of Egypt and set off for an unknown place as well. Jesus had to give up His life to gain us. The disciples had to give up their livelihoods and families to follow Jesus and gain the promise. The economic system of heaven is based on trade. Before God will give us what He has, we must give up what we have. He invites, not forces us, to make this trade. Sacrifice always precedes blessing.

As I shared in my testimony at the beginning of this book, my husband and I went through years of wilderness experiences where God trained us in trustworthiness and financial integrity and grew our ability to administrate before the windows of heaven opened to pour out the blessings we could not even contain. For us, it was about a four-year trek from the point of decision to leave slavery and start doing things God's way and depending on God for our daily manna. Here are some of the things we learned.

LESSON ONE OF THE WILDERNESS: PUT GOD FIRST NO MATTER WHAT, IN ALL AREAS, NOT JUST FINANCES

The first step was learning to put God first in our finances, no matter what. God began to show us principles in His Word that, when made part of who we are, bring great blessing and reward. The first area where God began to challenge our beliefs was on the topic of tithing. We are going to explore this principle on a deeper level in the next class, but for now, we are just going to focus on how tithing is one of the best ways to put faith in action and to posture our hearts correctly toward both God and money. For right now, we are going to discuss tithing from a "belief" point of view and gain a simple understanding of what it is and how it exposes what is in our hearts.

To begin changing our money habits, God had to first change our mindset about what tithing really is and what it is for. The Lord showed us that tithing is not legalism; it's a covenant. Satan doesn't want us to have this revelation, which is why he has worked hard to get the modern-day Church to see it as legalism.

Yes, the practice of tithing was included in the law, but it was not birthed from it. The practice of tithing is first seen with Abraham more than four hundred years before the Law of Moses. The Tabernacle was also not in existence yet and would not be until after the Israelites' exodus from Egypt. So where did this concept of tithing come from? Although the Bible tells us that both Cain and Able gave portions of their wealth to God, it doesn't state an exact amount. Although it mentions the practice of giving a portion of one's wealth to God, one can't consider these instances as tithing because the very nature of the tithe is the specific amount.

With that in mind, the very first biblical mention of tithing is found in Genesis 14:20, when Abram tithed to Melchizedek. The word for tithe in this verse is *maaser,* which means "tenth part" or "one tenth" and is where we get the word tithe from.[27] Why one tenth? Why to this person, Melchizedek? Scripture does not say Abraham was under any legal obligation to do this, and again, the Law of Moses would not even exist another four hundred plus years from this time. To fully understand tithing, it is important to understand who Melchizedek is. Melchizedek is mentioned in only three places in the entire Bible, and each instance gives us unique insight into his identity. These three places are Genesis 14, Psalm 110, and Hebrews 7. When we dig into our concordance to discover the meanings of the original Hebrew words in the text, we are given even more information on Melchizedek's identity.

Melchizedek means "my king is right" and "an early king of Salem."[28] It's a compound of the words melchi *(melek),* meaning "king,"[29] and zedek *(tsedeq),* meaning "righteousness,"[30] making the translation "king of righteousness." Genesis 14:18 offers another clue to Melchizedek's identity as it describes him as the King of Salem. Salem (*shalem*) means "peaceful."[31] Salem is an early name of Jerusalem, so this is the first biblical mention of Jerusalem, although it isn't mentioned by the name Jerusalem until Joshua 10:5, when Joshua and the Israelites go to battle against the Amorites and capture the city.

Psalm 76:2 equates Salem with Jerusalem, and in Genesis 14:17, the description of Salem being in the "valley of the kings" further confirms this is what later becomes known as Jerusalem. So, Melchizedek is the king of the territory that later became known as Jerusalem, God's choice as the capital of Israel, under King David and where the temple was built under David's son King Solomon. Psalm 132:13-14 tells us the Lord has chosen Jerusalem and will dwell there forever, so Jerusalem has eternal significance both historically and prophetically. Melchizedek, being the first biblical mention of the king of this territory shows he is a very significant character and someone worth paying attention to.

In addition to his name and kingdom, Scripture also tells us he was both a king and a priest. What's even more interesting is that this passage also tells us that He prepared a table for Abram of both bread and wine (which we know later as communion when Jesus prepares the same table for his disciples at the Last Supper). Melchizedek is the only king described as also being a priest. There was no Law of Moses yet, no Temple or Tabernacle, and the Levites (Israeli priests who would come from Abraham's great-grandson, Levi) did not exist yet either, yet Melchizedek is described as not just being any priest, but a priest of "God Most High."

This happens to be the God Abraham also serves, and his bloodline becomes the chosen people of this same God. We know what a king is—ruler of a specific kingdom—but what is a priest? A priest is a mediator between God and man. How was it known that Melchizedek was a priest when there was no mention of any temple? Moses, the author of Genesis, doesn't tell us how they knew these things about Melchizedek, so obviously, it was common enough knowledge that it didn't seem necessary to include that bit of information.

The second biblical mention of Melchizedek is Psalm 110:4, where King David is prophesying about the Messiah to come and describes Messiah as *"a priest forever in the order of Melchizedek."* The word "order" or *dibrah,* means "reason, suit or style, cause, estate."[32]

David is saying Messiah will be a priest in the same manner as Melchizedek, meaning not in the manner of Aaron or the Levites, meaning Messiah's priesthood is eternal like Melchizedek, not temporary like the Levites. This is a significant distinction because under the law only Levites could receive tithes, but neither Melchizedek nor Jesus is of the Levitical line. Like Melchizedek, Jesus was not a descendant of Levi and Aaron and thus would not qualify for Jewish priesthood under the Law of Moses! (Isn't that ironic?)

However, in the third and final mention of Melchizedek in Hebrews 7 (written to a Jewish audience), we receive much more context and clues as to who Melchizedek is. Hebrews 7:3 describes Melchizedek as without father, mother, or genealogy, without beginning of days or end of life (a.k.a. eternal), resembling the Son of God, and he remains a priest forever. The only other biblical character matching these descriptions is Jesus. When we put all these clues together, all these clues point to Melchizedek and Jesus being one and the same. We know that Abraham had many visits from the Lord, so why not from pre-incarnate Jesus? Abraham's biblically recorded visits from the Lord are found in Genesis 12:1, 12:7, 13:14, 14:18 (encounter with Melchizedek), 15:1, 17:1.

The fact that Abram tithed to pre-incarnate Jesus is extremely significant, especially when it comes to the much-debated topic of tithing in the New Testament church. A tithe was given to Melchizedek, who we now know was pre-incarnate Jesus, way before tithes were ever given to Levites under the Law of Moses. As a matter of fact, it is the very first mention, biblically speaking, of anyone being given that exact amount and is where we even get the concept and the tithing from. Abraham tithed to an eternal priesthood, meaning it has no beginning and no end. Abraham is also called the father of faith, not the father of the law, which was Moses.[33] In John 8:39, Jesus said, *"The children of Abraham should do the deeds of Abraham."* If Abraham tithed to a priesthood with no beginning and no end, then so should we, according to Jesus.

Even though under Jewish Law, neither Melchizedek nor Jesus would qualify to be a priest, Hebrews 7, goes into great detail as to why the priesthood of Melchizedek is superior to the priesthood of the Levites and Aaron.[34]

- Levite priests were temporary. When they died, their priesthood died. Jesus holds His priesthood permanently.
- Levites were the temporary version of the eternal priesthood of Melchizedek.

- Abraham paid tithes to Melchizedek. Since Aaron was in Abraham's loins when this took place, it was as if the Aaronic priesthood was paying tithes to Melchizedek also, making Melchizedek superior. Side note: this is also why sins are attributed generationally.
- The one who blesses is greater than the one being blessed; thus, Melchizedek is greater than Abraham. Levi was in the loins of Abraham when this took place, making Melchizedek greater than Levi, too.[35]
- If the priesthood of Aaron was effective, God would not have needed to mediate a better covenant and not needed to call a new priest of a different and eternal order.[36]
- The basis of the Aaronic priesthood was ancestry. The basis for Melchizedek is everlasting life. There is no interruption to Melchizedek's priesthood due to a priest's death.[37]
- Christ, being sinless, doesn't need a sacrifice for His own sins, as well as others.[38]
- The priesthood of Melchizedek, offering atonement for sin, is more effective than the priesthood of the Levites because it required a single sacrifice that was once and for all, while the Levites had to continue to present endless sacrifices.[39]
- The Aaronic priests served in an earthly copy of the eternal heavenly temple that Jesus serves in.[40] Hebrews 7:8 tells us that even though mere mortal men are receiving tithes here (in earthly temples), there (in the heavenly temple) Jesus is the one receiving them.

The covenant of Jesus (New Testament) is thereby superior to the covenant the Levitical priests were under (Old Testament). The book of Hebrews, which was written to an audience of Jews, went to great lengths to convince Jewish believers and unbelievers of this truth. Is tithing included in this new covenant and new priestly order? Yes! Because it is eternal, it both predates and outlasts the Levitical version of it, and the Bible goes to great lengths to show us that tithing has always been and always will be about Jesus, not the Old Testament Law.

What does the practice of tithing under this new covenant look like? Abraham was under no obligation, yet he did it as an act of worship to honor the Lord, putting Him first above everything. It looks like a financial covenant we make with God, and needs to be taken as seriously and joyfully as the covenant of marriage. Just like we are not forced or obligated to marry, once we make the commitment, it is a commitment for life.

As if all of this isn't enough to convince us that tithing, although included in the Law of Moses as part of God's economic structure for the nation of Israel, transcends that law, we find other biblical examples of the practice of tithing centuries before the Law of Moses is even in existence. In Genesis 28:22, Jacob, Abraham's grandson, pledges to give God a tenth of all God gives him, making tithing a covenant between God and himself. It shows us that tithing is a covenant one enters with God, not some legalistic rule to follow. Nowhere does Scripture say God asked or required him to do this. It was a covenant he initiated with God. When both Abraham and Jacob did this, there was no temple or priests to give to, making this have nothing to do with the law.

The main point here is that tithing is a timeless principle and has nothing to do with legalism. As New Testament believers, we do not have to practice tithing. However, neither did Cain, Abel, Abraham, or Jacob. Even though their stories are found in the Old Testament, there was no written law compelling them to tithe and yet they did. Who taught them to do this? What did they understand about partnering with God with their wealth?

In John 8:39, Jesus says those who are from Abraham should do the deeds of Abraham or, in other words, should follow his example. We start economically demonstrating we have a Lord over our lives and our finances through the tithe. Tithing keeps us in a "God first" mentality. It shows God we love Him more than money, possessions, and wealth. Tithing also protects us from greed and falling into the love of money. No matter how much provision we do or do not have, giving God the first cut of it is the ultimate demonstration of faith, trust, and loyalty.

It takes faith and trust to give God that first tenth, especially when it means we will not be able to pay our electric bill for doing so. My husband and I know because we lived it. However, we were so desperate that we came to the place where we made the commitment to honor God first, no matter what we had to give up or sacrifice. If we do not stick to that commitment when we have nothing, we will not do it when we have everything because there will always be a reason or excuse not to. Many New Testament believers give way beyond the tithe, but everyone must start somewhere. If we cannot even be consistent with the small amount of ten percent, we will not be consistent with more. It all begins by changing our beliefs about what tithing really is.

As I stated, my husband and I held the false belief that tithing was just an Old Testament law, and instead, we were under "grace." We didn't understand tithing has nothing to do with legalism, like being told not to lie has nothing to do with legalism. Every precept in the law was God trying to show us how to live our best life, but again, tithing did not even start with the law; it began with Abraham who lived by faith not by law.

My husband and I also had a false belief that "churches just want our money," and tithing was a way for them to guilt people into giving it. God then showed us in His Word that the reason the tithe was included in the law was so the tribe of Levi would have an inheritance among their brethren. They were the only tribe without an inheritance of land because their lives were dedicated to the running and managing of the temple. As an agricultural society, land was their wealth because what they could produce on it would meet their own needs, and they would have something to trade or sell from what they grew. The tithe was intended to provide for the priest's needs and maintenance of the temple.

Priests were set apart to oversee the temple and manage the sacrifices of their brethren; they were not allowed to have other jobs or businesses to support themselves. This hardly seems fair. They had to dedicate their lives to serving in the temple on behalf of the people, having no other inheritance. God instituted the tithe amongst the other tribes for the priests' livelihood and provision to care for and maintain the temple.

We used to believe we "couldn't afford to tithe." However, this was nothing more than a justification for the fact that we weren't willing to sacrifice to do it. When we really examined our hearts, those false beliefs really were just our way of justifying our lack of faith and understanding. We did not understand that tithing is more than a law; it is an opportunity to partner with God in our finances. It is an opportunity to enter a financial covenant with God.

God invites us into this financial covenant if we will set aside a tenth of our income to take care of His house and fund kingdom assignments. In return, He promises us many blessings. Some of these promises are found in Malachi 3. We explore the principle and its benefits in greater detail in Kingdom Government and Economics and how tithing is the moat around our financial castle. For now, let's simply grasp the revelation of what tithing really is and dispel the lies that many of God's children believe about it.

Due to not understanding what tithing really is, many of us inconsistently throw a few token dollars in an offering plate, deceiving ourselves into thinking it is the same thing as tithing. Then we want the benefits promised to tithers when we have not lived up to our end of the deal. Giving more than ten percent or giving wherever we want is not tithing either. These individuals do not follow God's instructions in the matter and then have the audacity to get frustrated when those covenant promises do not show up in their lives.

As new covenant believers, we do not have to tithe. We are not required to. However, my question is, why wouldn't we want to? If this is a struggle for us, then we truly don't understand what it is and why we should do it. This is usually an indication that we have an improper view of God and His character. I've heard something along the lines of, "We think God is playing mob boss godfather, demanding ten percent in protection money and will curse us (a.k.a. send His cronies to beat us up) if we do not." Nothing could be further from the truth.

We are not under obligation to tithe, just as we are not obligated to participate in the covenant of marriage. We are not forced to marry, or forced to marry a particular person, or forced to be married by any particular time. God alone, as the designer of marriage, is the only one allowed to define what marriage is and is not, so if we are going to enter the covenant of marriage, then we must abide by His rules for it, or we're going to end up in a mess. The same is true of tithing.

Just like with marriage, if by our own free will we choose to enter that covenant, we must abide by certain parameters. We must forsake all others and not pop in and out when we feel like it or when it's convenient. We are either married or not. Tithing is a covenant because God clearly spells out what it is and goes on to list specific "conditions" or parameters of "when we do ________ (give this specific amount, to this specified place, for this specified purpose)," then He will pour out the specific blessings promised to those who tithe.

Tithing is a specific type of giving that comes with a specific list of benefits. No one in the new covenant is under obligation to do this but can, of their own free will, choose to do so and will reap the specific benefits. If we do not meet the conditions or if we are on-again-off-again covenant breakers, we do not get the benefits. The promises for tithing are some of many biblical promises with natural conditions to meet to release them.

Outside of tithing, there are several other types of giving with distinctly different sets of promises and benefits attached to them. Why do we think God gave the Old Testament Israelites this requirement? Did God need their money? The silver and gold are His, according to Haggai 2:8, so it cannot be because He needed their money. The reason is that Satan is the god of this world and economic system. Tithing was about enacting a covenant, giving God the legal jurisdiction to bless while mankind lived under the curse of the fall. By tithing, the Israelites financially changed governments and entered into a covenant with God. Tithing is and was always about God's desire to bless, not take. However, as part of that covenant, the tithe does acknowledge God's right to say what it is and where it goes.

Although we are under no obligation to tithe in the new covenant, if we are to enter this financial covenant with God, then there are conditions to adhere to. The tithe is set apart. It belongs to God, and He alone gets to decide where it goes, how much it is, and what it is for. The tithe is specifically ten percent of our resources dedicated to a specific purpose. Malachi 3:10 tells us that the purpose of the tithe is so *"there might be food in my house."* The sole purpose of the tithe is to provide for the needs of the temple and the priests. It goes to *"the local storehouse,"* which is the local congregation where one gathers and for that house of worship. It does not go to any other house. It is to support the needs of that local body.

If we really believe everything we have belongs to God, then tithing is not even up for debate. If we do debate it, it means we believe "our" money is really ours, and God should not tell us what to do with it. Tithing is the ultimate put-up-or-shut-up. It has nothing to do with legalism and everything to do with training our hearts in submission to God. Doing things our own way got my husband and me nothing but debt, frustration, and fear of loss, no matter how much money we made. So, we decided we would try things God's way. Why wouldn't we want to, especially when He promises nothing but blessings for doing so? The only reason someone wouldn't is they do not really believe they will receive those blessings.

A major purpose of the tithe continues to be taking care of and financially supporting the priests or modern-day pastors and apostles so they can focus solely on serving God and His people. How effective would they be if most of their time were taken up working for provision? How effective can they be in spending time seeking the Lord on top of tending to their congregation if they also must hold down a full-time job? If we do not want a part-time pastor, then we must pay them a full-time salary so they can focus fully on pastoring rather than on having to secure other means of provision for their family.

Personally, I get angry when I hear ill-informed Christians begrudge pastors for having a nice standard of living. They are God's kids who have dedicated their lives to looking after God's other kids; they should have the best! They are representatives of the kingdom of glory. How does an impoverished lifestyle demonstrate the glory of God to a world needing to see who God is? If an ambassador of another country came here in rags, it would speak volumes of the government that sent them and not in a good way. The same is true of ambassadors of God's kingdom.

Additionally, it is important to note that tithes and offerings are not the same. We are not making an offering until we have returned our tithes. We do not give our tithes; we return them. Tithing is a principle that transcends law, so it will leave our hands one way or another—willingly to the One it belongs to, or the devourer, Satan, will have legal access to take it.[41] It's not about God doing the cursing of anyone; it is about legal jurisdiction, and Satan, as the god of this world, has the legal jurisdiction to take it.

Tithing is just like being in partnership with another person. That is what a covenant is—a partnership—but more than that, it's a relationship. This is why we covered contracts versus covenants in detail previously. To give us an example of what this covenant arrangement looks like when it comes to tithing, let us say I owned a car and saw that a certain person had a need. I decided to partner with them to help them meet that need. (Perhaps they had a bill they could not pay, or maybe they wanted to start a business or had some other need that they did not have the money for.) As an example, say I decided to invest in this person's need, giving them an opportunity to make some money by taking this car of mine and selling it for the cash to pay for that need. However, as part of this arrangement to provide for them, the only stipulation I give them is that when the car is sold to pay for their need, they are to give ten percent of the proceeds back to me. Then, and only then, could they use the other ninety percent to meet their need.

Now, if they sell that car and receive the money from the sale, they would be required to pay me my ten percent share as their partner, per the arrangement. When they give me that ten percent, they would not be giving me an offering, they would simply be returning to me that which was already mine due to my ownership of the item sold. In fact, if they withhold that ten percent from me, not returning to me what is mine, they would be robbing me. When they do return it to me, they would not be doing me any favors. They would simply be returning to me what is already legally mine, and it would be absurd and crazy for them to act like they were generously and righteously giving me an offering. Yet, this is exactly how many Christians behave regarding tithing.

Now, if this person does not act honorably by not abiding by the terms of our covenant, would I continue to partner with them further? Would I owe them any kind of protection over this financial dealing or any other they may have? Would I increase the amount of my property I give them stewardship of? Of course not! Yet, this is exactly how many people treat God and then wonder why their finances are a mess.

I will mention that tithing, just like giving offerings, is different from the principle of sowing and reaping (which we will cover in Kingdom Government and Economics). The tithe is not ours to sow. It already belongs to God. The tithe is for the local storehouse; sowing is for the things we love and the projects we care about. As owner of the earth and everything in it, the Lord gives us a certain amount of property and wealth to steward, and all He asks in return is that we allocate ten percent to the local storehouse so there will be "food" in His house.

Tithing is not a requirement; it is a test. Will we acknowledge God's rights in our finances and obey this most basic principle because we recognize our position as bondservant and not the owner? An entire generation never moved out of the wilderness to occupy and administrate the Promised Land because they would not master the most basic obedience. If we fail to activate this covenant partnership, we are not robbing God of money; we are robbing Him of the ability and the legality to bless us further because we are violating the terms of the covenant. It is no different with our children and us, if they do not even cooperate with basic obedience, we are not going to keep piling on blessings, prizes, and rewards. If they refuse to do what we ask with what we give them, we are not going to give them more and increase their self-indulgence.

Money carries what it has been dedicated to. Tithing, which is faith in action that God is first, brings our finances out of the jurisdiction of the god of this world's system and brings our finances under the jurisdiction of God. This is significant because anything offered into God's kingdom gives Him the legal jurisdiction to multiply it back. We see in Matthew 14 that the boy's lunch was not multiplied into a miracle until it was first sacrificed as an offering into the kingdom. I think this is why Satan has worked so hard to create so many false beliefs and doctrines around money and tithing in particular. He hates us giving to God. Why? Because we are taking money out of his kingdom and moving it over into God's. Among other things, this furthers the gospel throughout the earth. Of course, Satan is going to do everything he can to convince believers not to give to God.

Satan is the god of this world, but he is not the God of the earth. In other words, he is the god of this world's system of provision and finance, which includes money. There is no money in heaven (but there is wealth). In heaven, every need is provided, so there is no need to buy and sell goods for provision. However, heaven is described biblically as having vast wealth where even the streets are made of pure gold.

Throughout time, people traded goods and made exchanges with each other. Although effective, it is a very cumbersome way of doing business because one would have to carry around those goods to make those trades. Money became a universal medium of exchange. It was much easier to carry around a coin purse than crates of furs or vegetables. Therefore, money was invented and is a product of earthly kingdoms with the faces of earthly kings and leaders printed on them. However, money has a clever way of exposing things in our hearts. What we spend it on shows us what we value. When we can show God that we value Him and His kingdom more than anything of our earthly kingdom, it shows He can trust us with more.

If we want full stewardship of our inheritance more quickly, we must allow the Holy Spirit to train us in these new beliefs and actions. The price for success is non-negotiable, and it must be paid in advance. An athlete goes through sacrifice, suffering, discipline, and training upfront. Then, and only then, will they get a shot at the gold medal. They are not given a shot first and then begin training. Those opportunities only come to those who have already paid the price in advance, who have spent time, energy, and resources in the wilderness of preparation. The same is true for us.

Even though we have discovered that tithing started centuries before the law, many still fall into the temptation to argue that "tithing is for the Old Testament." Was *"Thou shall not lie"* or *"Thou shall not murder"* only in the Old Testament?[42] Are we now allowed to lie and murder because we are no longer under the law? We cannot cherry pick certain parts and label them as "legalism." It is either all legalism or it's not. If we are going to say tithing is for the Old Testament just because it was part of the law, then we have to say that all of it is. That would mean keeping the Sabbath as a New Testament believer is legalism and only for the Old Testament.

These principles transcend generations and times. Legalism is an attitude, not an action. I can do anything out of legalistic compulsion. That does not make the action itself legalistic. If I think following these principles makes me more holy and not following them makes me less holy, the problem is the legalistic and religious attitude in my heart. This is the problem the Pharisees had, thinking it was their observance of principles that made them righteous and holy. The problem is not with following the principles; the problem is with the motivation for doing so. Holiness and righteousness (right standing with God) come from faith in Christ alone—faith in His finished work on the cross—which transfers His holiness to us not which principles we do or don't follow.

But what if I told you that Jesus said we should tithe? Luke 11:42 (NLT) says, "*What sorrow awaits you Pharisees! For you are careful to tithe even the tiniest income from your herb gardens, but you ignore justice and the love of God. You should tithe, yes, but do not neglect the more important things."* We can see from this verse that Jesus endorsed the practice of tithing, but tithing does not entitle us to neglect the other things God cares about, like justice and love. Jesus used the topic of tithing to address their attitude.

Tithing is nothing more than a physical demonstration that God is first with our money. Although tithing does not make us more holy or righteous when we honor God in this way, He blesses us back even more. It is important to know that we cannot tithe our way into wealth, but building wealth without tithing will be much harder. (We will learn more about why when we discuss the specific blessings God promises to tithers in Kingdom Government and Economics.)

LESSON TWO OF THE WILDERNESS: STOP USING DEBT FOR PROVISION

The second thing my husband and I had to learn in the wilderness was to break the habit of using debt for provision. As was mentioned before, we have been trained in the world's system of slavery under the curse of Adam in having to work for provision. The old system we fell under due to the curse of sin was *"by the sweat of your brow you will eat."*[43] With this training, if we have a major purchase to make and no money in the bank, many times, instead of asking God for it, we ask a bank to loan us the provision, thereby putting ourselves back into slavery in exchange for that provision. Proverbs 22:7 (NLT) tells us, *"Just as the rich rule the poor, so the borrower is servant to the lender."*

When we take loans from banks, credit cards, or other sources, we then must serve financial institutions who do not give a darn about us. We become enslaved to them until that debt is paid off rather than to God. When we have a need and no money, we immediately calculate how much overtime we can work, how many extra jobs we can take on, or how good our credit is to get a loan to meet that need.

Under the new covenant (redeemed from the curse), the mandate becomes *"Seek the Kingdom of God above all else, and live righteously, and he will give you everything you need."*[44] We must break the habit of borrowing money—taking on debt to meet our needs instead of seeking God's kingdom way of meeting that need—because we are making a vow to work until that debt is paid off. We are selling our time and our lives to pay that debt. This denies our identity. We are not our own to sell—we have been bought with a price.

The Israelites fell into this trap when they began to grumble and complain in the wilderness, desiring to go back to Egypt. They were willing to accept slavery for the false comfort of knowing where their provision would come from instead of trusting God for it. By desiring this, they were denying their identities as children of promise, destined to occupy the Promised Land and produce the lineage of the Messiah.

Initially, we must decide which economic system we are going to live in. Are we going to seek the kingdom of heaven for our provision—God's system of trust and trade (sowing and reaping)—or are we going to trust in the world's system of selling ourselves into debt? We cannot serve two masters. We cannot be double-minded. We cannot live in both Egypt and the Promised Land simultaneously. We must choose. The wilderness is where we learn to do without slavery-based provision and to trust God for provision, so when we do enter our Promised Land, we do not sell ourselves back into slavery.

This is not to say all debt is bad and cannot be used, but only at the leading of the Holy Spirit and after we have mastered basic precepts first. Is driving a car bad? Only if we are ten years old and not twenty. But once we go through a maturing process and master the basic skills, we can then use debt without debt using us. But for now, the further we are in debt, the less free we are. Once in debt, we cannot simply walk away from a job to walk in an assignment God may have for us; thus, we are not free to pursue what God created us for. As a result, we end up living frustrated and stuck lives, striving for mere survival because we are beholden to the taskmaster of that debt.

When we use debt to obtain things we cannot afford, we are selling out our birthright for momentary provision. We sell ourselves into the slavery of debt to support a lifestyle of possessions that we then become afraid to lose to pursue God's kingdom call on our lives. This is not to say that for some of us, our job is the mission field to which we have been called. I am in no way implying that if we have a job, we are not fulfilling God's call on our lives. The problem comes when we are afraid to change or lose our jobs at God's direction because how will we then pay for the lifestyle we've been supporting?

If we are not free to move at God's direction because of too much debt, then we have sold ourselves to another master. Thank God for His grace and mercy that helps us when we truly surrender these things to Him. When we are willing to sacrifice these things to pursue God's best for our lives, He will make a path from slavery to the Promised Land for us. However, we must be willing to forsake Egypt and leave everything behind, including how things are done in Egypt. It is important to clarify that using debt to acquire assets and build our wealth portfolio is a very different thing than using debt for lifestyle basics like food, clothing, and consumer purchases. However, we cannot build financial wealth at this level while we are still using debt to meet our basic needs.

LESSON THREE OF THE WILDERNESS: LEARN TO WALK IN FINANCIAL INTEGRITY

The final area the Lord had to clean up in our lives during our wilderness experience was teaching us to walk in financial integrity according to His Word. The first place He dealt with our integrity was along the same line of creating debts but slightly different. We had to learn that if we borrow money from someone, we must be diligent to pay it back. It seems common sense, but we are so good at justifying our actions. He had to show us that if we spent money on anything that was not a necessity to live, instead of paying that money back to someone we owed, that lacked integrity and was wrong.

Let us say we loaned someone $2,000 when they were in need. Instead of making any effort to pay it back, they have let months or years go by without even an attempt, and suddenly, we see them post photos of being at Disney or some other lavish vacation. How would we feel? Let us say they got a big tax return or some such "windfall," and instead of honoring past vows, they splurge instead. That is an integrity issue. The same is true if they are regularly spending money on luxuries like going out to eat, getting their nails done, cable tv, or going to the movies. If a person has money for these activities, then they have money they could put towards their debt. To not do so lacks integrity.

Now, what if those same people profess to be Christ-followers? How does that behavior reflect on their character and the character of the God they claim to represent? If we have the money to go to Disney, then we have the money to pay our debts. If we have money for even simple luxuries, it should be going to pay back the vows we made when we borrowed.

Ecclesiastes 5:5 (NKJV) says, "[It is*] better not to vow than to vow and not pay*." If we spend money on luxuries instead of paying our debts, we are word-breakers and covenant-breakers, and this gives the devourer, Satan, the right to devour our provisions. When we borrow money from someone, telling them we will have the money to pay them back when we get paid, in a sense, we are selling them a chunk of our future paycheck ahead of time. If we then do not pay that vow when that paycheck comes, choosing instead to spend the money on other things, even bills, that is wrong and reveals a lack of integrity.

Once money has been promised to pay back our loan, that part of our paycheck now belongs to that person. To take what is now another man's and spend it on something else is both lying and stealing. How do we think it reflects on our God when unsaved friends or family members see us do such things? As children of God, we should have the highest standards of integrity in finances as much as any other area and not behave how the world does. Jesus is the one who lays out this principle in Luke 16:12 (NKJV, where He states, *"…if you have not been faithful in what is another man's, who will give you what is your own?"*

Another aspect of walking in integrity is slightly different but follows the same line of thinking. When we have an employer, we agree to sell our employer our time for a certain wage. If we then spend that time that they bought from us doing anything other than company business, we are stealing from them. We are taking the time we sold them and are giving that time to something else like social media, non-work emails, or personal errands rather than company errands. This is stealing because now they are paying us to do these other things instead of what they agreed to pay us for and without their consent or knowledge. This lacks integrity.

If I sold someone a car, I would not then turn around and give that car to someone else. That would be stealing from the person who bought it. I would be taking what they paid for and giving it to another. If we are at work, being paid by an employer, if we spend that time doing anything other than what we are being paid to do, it is stealing. That time was bought and paid for by someone, so that time is now someone else's. If we are not faithful with what is another man's, who will give us what is our own?

We are warned in 1 Peter 5:8 (NLT), *"Stay alert! Watch out for your great enemy, the devil. He prowls around like a roaring lion, looking for someone to devour."* This warning is to the church. If it were not possible for Satan to gain the right to steal our stuff, then we would not be warned to stay sober and vigilant! Satan gains authority to devour our stuff through our lack of integrity and faithfulness. If God does not have these poor choices trained out of our hearts when we are stewards over little, what will the impact of those losses be when the stakes are much higher?

Much of this may seem elementary or common sense, but not everyone is in the same place of maturity, and these foundations must be laid securely. When we allow the Lord to train us in these principles, they will guard us against greed, and the love of money or possessions will not become a wrong priority in our lives.

We must be willing to stay in the wilderness long enough or in the pit of suffering and sacrifice long enough, until our hearts are fully submitted to Him. Before the glory and the honor comes the drinking of the cup. Remember, how long we are there depends on how quickly we learn these lessons, and how quickly we allow our minds to be renewed to truth instead of religion. Money is not evil, or the root of evil.[45] Money is just green paper. The love of money is the root of evil. We can commit that sin without a dime to our name! Going through the wilderness of preparation teaches us how to fall out of love with money and back in love with Jesus. It's about walking through sacrifice so we can be trusted and equipped to carry more of His glory.

CLASS 3
STUDY GUIDE AND JOURNAL

Invite the Holy Spirit into this time of reflection and ask the Lord to reveal anything and everything He wants to reveal. Ask Him to shine His light into every dark place and renew your mind to His truth.

Read Romans 8:16-17. What does it mean to you to share in His suffering?

What area(s) is God having you suffer or sacrifice?

Can you now see that perhaps God has allowed this suffering as preparation to be able to carry His glory in this area?

What does Proverbs 20:21 tell you about an inheritance?

What is a promise you've been standing on, waiting for the fulfillment?

Is it possible that the reason for the delay is that it is simply too early?

Just like the Israelites in the desert, could you be extending your own time in the wilderness by refusing to change your mindset?

In what ways may God be wanting you to submit to the transformation process, so you possess your promise and don't die in the wilderness?

Jesus wants your trust. How is that trust developed?

What does Proverbs 1:32 say about a fool (someone who lacks wisdom) having prosperity?

What area may God be wanting you to grow in wisdom before releasing prosperity?

Read Luke 16:10-12. Is the Holy Spirit bringing anything to mind where you might have behaved in an untrustworthy manner?

Take a moment to repent and ask the Holy Spirit to help you correct anything that may need to be corrected. What are some specific actions you can take to correct these things?

Based on Matthew 25:14-15, everyone receives something, but you determine the amount you are given by the level of your ability. At any time, you can choose to increase and grow in your ability to manage greater levels of finances. How might you need to increase your ability to handle more finances?

Luke 16:10-12 further clarifies that our ability and our trustworthiness are tied together. Do you need to increase in ability, trustworthiness, or both?

Read Joshua 1:9. What area(s) do you need to realize, remember, or recognize that God is with you?

Take a moment to visualize God's Spirit covering you like a shadow as He is there with you in that situation. What does Psalms 91:1 say about this?

How does acknowledging God is with you change how you feel about being in and facing these situations or circumstances?

Read Matthew 16:7-10. Take a moment and remember some of the ways God has already come through for you, answered prayers for you, and provided for you. Testify about these things.

What are some ways you can put faith into action to put God first in any area?

How has the revelation of Melchizedek changed your understanding of what tithing is and what it isn't?

Have you been using debt to pay for lifestyle stuff (not a home mortgage, unless your mortgage is more than twenty-five percent of your income)? If so, this means you are living above your means. What might you have to sacrifice for a season so your lifestyle doesn't exceed your income?

Are you willing to make the sacrifice to downsize your lifestyle or house to bring your finances into a healthy place of balance?

Have you been calling anything a necessity that is actually a luxury? In Ecclesiastes 5:5 (NKJV) the Bible says, *"[it is] better not to vow than to vow and not pay."* Do you have any unpaid vows that the enemy is using as legal grounds to take from you? (If so, take some time to go before the Lord and repent.)

Have you spent time at work doing things other than what your employer is paying you for? (If so, take some time to go before the Lord and repent.)

1 Peter 5:8 (NLT) warns us, *"Stay alert! Watch out for your great enemy, the devil. He prowls around like a roaring lion, looking for someone to devour."* How has the enemy been using any of the situations above or any other situation to devour God's blessings in your life?

The sooner you correct these things, the sooner your season of preparation comes to an end. What are some situations or battles you thought were just warfare but were your bootcamp of preparation? What lessons did you learn or need to learn to bring these seasons to a close so you could begin to occupy your promise?

CLASS 4

KINGDOM GOVERNMENT AND ECONOMICS

"Of the increase of His government and peace there will be no end, upon the throne of David and over His kingdom, to order it and establish it with judgment and justice from that time forward, even forever. The zeal of the Lord of hosts will perform this."

ISAIAH 9:7 NKJV

Hopefully, by now, we are anchored in the truth that we do have an inheritance that includes prosperity through the blessings of Abraham due to the finished work of the cross and Jesus paying the price for the curse of poverty to be broken off us. Prosperity is one of the things that Jesus's life and death paid for us to have. This doesn't mean we have all the money we ever want to have; it means God's blessing is going to be on the work of our hands and will cause it to prosper. Because of this promise, we need to retrain our thinking by removing thought patterns of poverty and exchanging them for thought patterns of prosperity.

2 Corinthians 8:9 (NLT) tells us, "*You know the generous grace of our Lord Jesus Christ. Though he was rich, yet for your sakes he became poor, so that by his poverty he could make you rich.*" The only reason Jesus suffered

anything was to free us from it and that includes poverty. It is important to point out that this verse is not saying that Jesus was poor and homeless while He lived on the earth. Jesus, as the Son of God, had ownership of all the wealth of heaven and the entire universe. He left all of that behind, giving it all up to be born and live as a man so He could go to the cross on our behalf, where He died as a common thief. Crucifixion is how they executed criminals, even though He did nothing to deserve it.

Jesus's heavenly wealth was so vast that even if He lived with all the world's wealth, it would be considered poverty when held up against it. That is what Jesus left behind to pursue us. 2 Corinthians 8:9 is not trying to tell us that Jesus was poor and homeless, so to be righteous and virtuous, we should be the same way. We are going to break that lie right now! The poverty being referred to here is Jesus being stripped of the wealth of His status as God of the universe so He could die as the servant of mankind. He became poor by leaving that wealth behind to be born as a man with nothing. He endured the loss of all things so we could inherit the right to gain all things. We can now become rich in every way because He took away the curse of our poverty. We are now free to be blessed and prosper as children of God.

If poverty is blessed and wealth is cursed, why doesn't God promise to bless us with poverty? Why is wealth not a curse for disobedience? If wealth is bad, why are heaven's streets made of gold instead of pebbles? If poverty is more blessed, why did God bestow wealth on Solomon instead of poverty if poverty is the greater honor? How are we defining wealth? Is it simply owning a lot of stuff? I know a lot of people who have a lot of "stuff" yet can hardly afford their bills, are living paycheck to paycheck, and are continuously dodging calls from the repo man. That used to be me!

On the other side, I also know many people who live a very minimalist lifestyle as far as possessions are concerned, even though they have vast fortunes. Choosing not to own things is quite different than not having the ability to own things. The former is what we see modeled in the life of Jesus. There are many people who have sold most of their possessions, including their home and downsized into an RV. For many people, this is their retirement goal. Why would they do or want such a thing? For freedom! They want to be free to travel anywhere at any time, not anchored down by stuff. This is not because they are poor. On the contrary! They still can own those things but are choosing not to so they can be unhindered.

The ministry of Jesus was mobile. He traveled from place to place, declaring the good news of the kingdom. Jesus was not in one stationary place expecting everyone to come to Him or come to His church. He went to them. Choosing to not be tied down to one physical location is not the same thing as not having the finances to own a home. Just from the gifts Jesus received from the wise men, Jesus would have been wealthy by the world's standards. Jesus choosing to be mobile in a traveling ministry does not mean He was too poor to own a house. He purposely did not want to be tied to one physical location. How could He tell others to leave their homes and follow Him if He was still tied to a house Himself? Matthew 4:13 tells us that immediately following His time in the wilderness, He returned to Nazareth and then moved to Capernaum by the sea.

Mark 2:1 (ESV) also tells us, *"And when he returned to Capernaum after some days, it was reported that he was at home."* Jesus did, in fact, have a home. We do not know if He specifically owned it, rented it, or someone else owned it and let Him stay there. The important thing here is He was not homeless and wandering in the streets. Jesus had material blessings that took care of Him and His disciples as they worked and ministered, as seen in Scripture. God always provides for His assignments when He sends us to do something.

Luke 8:2-3 (HCSB) gives us some insight into where some of this provision came from. It says, *"And some women, who had been healed of evil spirits and infirmities: Mary called Magdalene, from whom seven demons had come out, and Joanna, the wife of Chuza, Herod's steward, and Susana and many others, who supported Him with their possessions."* We can see that Jesus had many people, including wealthy aristocrats, who financially supported His ministry out of grateful hearts for the personal deliverance they received.

From a few other scriptures, we gain even more insight into the financial status of Jesus. John 12:6 (NLT), speaking of Judas, one of the twelve disciples, tells us, *"Not that he cared for the poor—he was a thief, and since he was in charge of the disciples' money, he often stole some for himself."* Also, in John 13:29, we read, *"Since Judas was their treasurer, some thought Jesus was telling him to go and pay for the food or to give some money to the poor."*

We know Judas was the treasurer of Jesus's ministry. If Jesus and the disciples were poor, why did they assume Jesus was telling Judas to go give to the poor? Obviously, they thought "the poor" were people other than themselves. The second thing we need to notice is that Judas often stole from the treasury. He was able to do this without being noticed, or so he thought. Obviously, there was enough money in that treasury to where Judas could take some and think no one would miss it. If there is only $5 in a wallet, it is very easy to notice if one dollar goes missing. However, if there is $500 in a wallet, one dollar gone missing is not easily noticed. Jesus being poor and homeless is a lie Satan has used to get the Church to adopt poverty as being holy and righteous. Hopefully, now, we can see it for the lie that it is.

As we have discussed, everything begins and ends with the attitude of our hearts. Though we cannot serve both God and money, we must serve God with our money. In order to train our hearts to serve God with our money and not ourselves, we must share in Christ's suffering if we also want to share in His glory. One way this is done is in the wilderness experience, where we learn through real life in real time that God is the boss and not us. Even John the Baptist, of whom Jesus said there is none greater than he of those born of women, did not get a pass on the wilderness experience.[46] John lived in the literal wilderness until he began his public ministry to Israel. King David lived in the wilderness experience while being transformed from a shepherd boy into a mighty king of war.

The wilderness is about preparation. As children of God, just like the Israelites, our needs will be met, but moving into the realm of stewarding supernatural abundance comes after embracing this time in the wilderness and being a quick study when it comes to obeying God. The wilderness experience is not about how much wealth or possessions we currently have. It is where we learn to do what God says with it.

Another interesting fact that many people do not realize is that the Israelites actually went into the wilderness wealthy! They plundered the Egyptians and left with the wealth of Egypt. God used this wealth to test them, as He still had to train their mentality. They had the choice to use that wealth for God's kingdom—like when they used it to make the Tabernacle—or, like some, they took that wealth and turned it into a golden calf.

The wilderness is where we learn to depend on God alone and not on the provision we do or do not have. It's where we unlearn how to live under the slavery of Pharoah and learn how to live from God's kingdom. As already mentioned, the wilderness is not necessarily about moving from poverty to wealth but rather about training and conditioning our minds and hearts. The wilderness is different for everybody and has little to do with the amount of wealth we have. It is where we learn to give up our will for God's will, where we learn true surrender, where we learn to give up anything and everything that is already in our hands in service to our King, and where we learn how to live under His government and authority, not just our natural one. This learning process includes a completely different way of looking at provision and how we obtain it.

Read Matthew 6:25-33.

This whole passage has to do with the provision, with Jesus remarkably declaring this new kingdom way of life. We must remember that up until this point, mankind was under the curse of sin, and they had to work for their food, as seen in Genesis 3:17-19. The curse that was pronounced upon mankind stipulated that only by toil and sweat would we eat from the food of the ground. In other words, we now must work for provision instead of simply receiving it. Jesus, knowing He would undo the curse, flipped the script. He gives us a new paradigm in this passage in Matthew 6. He tells us to simply trust God for our provision. Jesus points out the birds and lilies, giving us two different examples that don't work for provision. He then tells us to do the same thing, to receive what we need, by simply seeking God's kingdom and righteousness first, "*and all these things shall be added unto [us].*"[47]

This means we must learn what His kingdom is and how it operates, as well as His righteousness. Righteousness is just a fancy word that means what God says is right. Righteousness is what God says is right about all things, including how He designed life to be lived. To understand living from God's kingdom, we must first learn what it means to live from any kingdom.

A kingdom has a specific territory defined by specific borders. Those borders can expand or contract based on whether that kingdom conquers more territory or is conquered. A kingdom has its own specific ruler, leader, or governing body, with its own specific rules or laws that its citizens live under. In Matthew 6:10 (NIV), before Jesus changes our paradigm on provision, He teaches us to pray, "*Your kingdom come, Your will be done, on earth as it is in heaven.*" Jesus is teaching us to pray that the borders of heaven would expand into all the earth, bringing God's kingdom authority, rules, and laws with it. He is teaching us that we can live under God's kingdom rule and government, not just the earth's.

To experience this, we must know how the kingdom of God works. Just like with America or any other kingdom, we must know the rules and laws we live under as a citizen of that kingdom and work within the rules of that kingdom's economy, if we want to live successful lives. The same is true of God's kingdom, if we are going to pull on provision from God's kingdom and move it into this one, we need to know the rules and laws of operation to use them to be successful. Now, there is most definitely a non-kingdom way to obtain provision and grow wealth. Some people are born into wealth, inherit wealth, or acquire it over a lifetime of work. This does not necessarily mean they have prosperity. Prosperity means that we are thriving financially, at any level, and have peace and joy along with it. Wealth is relative.

Some people in third world countries might think you're wealthy based on the amount of property you have compared to themselves, whereas you might be struggling to pay for the very lifestyle someone else interprets as wealthy. You might not see yourself as wealthy and might only consider those with millions or billions of dollars to be wealthy, but they are miserable, emotionally and spiritually bankrupt, and could be losing money despite their millions. Remember, the blessing of the Lord makes one rich, and He adds no sorrow with it. Prosperity and wealth are not necessarily synonymous.

So how do we ensure that we have prosperity and not just wealth? The system of the world for acquiring provision is the world's cursed system of toil and sweat, where we exchange hard labor for provision. However, as we've just discussed, this is not the kingdom way. Luke 17:21 tells us that the kingdom is within us. The kingdom is in us but moves through us on the currency of our faith. Faith is alive. It has an energy to it. Every answer for every need can be found in this kingdom, which is in us.

How exactly does that work? Mankind was originally created to work from provision, not for provision. We talked about their original state previously, but we are going to cover what that looks like more in-depth in a later class. For now, we are going to focus on how God's kingdom works.

Everything we see in the natural realm comes from the unseen realm—the kingdom of God. God spoke everything seen into existence. The spirit realm existed first, and everything natural manifested out of it and still does. Life never stopped operating that way. So this means the kingdom of God contains within it (thereby within us) every answer we could ever need as it pertains to this realm: provision, healing, wisdom, and guidance. Part of the good news is that we have restored access to this kingdom's authority, rules, and laws.

The laws governing our natural realm, such as gravity, lift, electricity, etc., are no respecter of persons. It does not matter if we are a Christian or an atheist; if we jump off a three-story building or stick a fork in a light socket, we will splat on the ground or suffer electrocution. The same is true for the laws that govern God's kingdom. They are no respecter of persons, and they work the same for all who have access. Once we are restored access by accepting the finished work of the cross on our behalf, we are granted citizenship in God's spiritual kingdom.

The laws of God's kingdom do not negate natural laws; they supersede them. For example, gravity is an undeniable, unseen law governing our natural world, and yet, a multi-ton jumbo jet flies utilizing the law of lift. How is this possible? The law of lift doesn't negate gravity or deny gravity; it supersedes it working despite gravity. Gravity is still in operation the entire time, so if one fails to properly utilize the laws that govern lift, gravity will default and take over. Lift occurs when a moving flow of gas is turned by a solid object. The flow is turned in one direction, and the lift is generated in the opposite direction, according to Newton's third law of action and reaction. Because air is a gas and the molecules are free to move about, any solid surface can deflect a flow.

For an aircraft wing, both the upper and lower surfaces contribute to the flow turning. Neglecting the upper surface's part in turning the flow leads to an incorrect theory of lift. No fluid, no lift. No motion, no lift. Trying to put the law of lift into operation improperly is going to be ineffective, and the aircraft will never get off the ground because gravity is still in operation the entire time. We must have every component required in operation for the law of lift to work properly and move the aircraft off the ground. Leaving out even one part means we stay stuck on the ground and do not achieve the desired result.

The laws of God's kingdom relate similarly to the laws of the natural kingdom. The laws of the natural kingdom are always in operation, but we can simultaneously tap into and utilize the higher laws of God's kingdom. So what does this look like in a practical sense? How do these laws of God's kingdom operate to supersede the natural? For example, when the facts of the earth realm give us a diagnosis, saying we are going to die of cancer, the laws of the kingdom of God do not deny that. However, the kingdom of God does not allow or contain sickness, so instead, the laws of God's kingdom supersede our natural kingdom with the facts of *"by His stripes [I am] healed,"*[48] *"[He] heals all my diseases,"*[49] and *"I am the healed of the Lord."*[50]

Notice that the Bible does not say we will not get diseases, and it also does not promise that God will keep us from getting diseases. As part of the natural world operating under the jurisdiction of Satan, we are going to encounter dangerous things. Jesus warns us of this in Mark 16 when He tells us He is sending us out into the world on a rescue mission to bring the good news to the captives—people living under the enslavement of Satan. In this rescue mission, we are going to encounter dangerous things.

Read Mark 16:17-18 and Luke 10:19.

To rescue people, we are going to have to get our hands dirty, which is why Jesus gave us these promises providing us the ability to tap into a higher law. He does not remove the danger or keep us away from it; He gives us the ability to supersede any danger the enemy can come up with. Jesus needs to be able to send us to touch and heal lepers. He cannot do that if we are afraid we will contract it. He reminds us to not worry, to stand on His promises, and enforce them against the enemy. Satan will try and get away with some stuff but do not allow it. It's up to us. However, if we don't know we can do this, it does us no good.

So how do we tap into the higher laws of God's kingdom? We simply choose to align our agreement and faith with the higher law instead of the lower. This changes our confession to scriptures claiming our healing instead of confessing our diagnosis. What God says always supersedes what the natural says. It all comes down to which one we are going to put our faith in. If we have more faith in the law of gravity than the law of lift, we are not going to get on an airplane. Our decisions and actions stem from which one we believe in most. If we have more faith in what a doctor of the natural world says than what God's Word says, that is the law that will be in operation and be what we reap from.

The same holds true for provision. Jesus never freaked out about money, or lack of money, because He knew He could call on the provision of God in every circumstance. He was completely secure in the love of the Father and His identity as a beloved Son. If we do not first have our identities right and what we are entitled to as being dual citizens, then nothing else matters. As long as we identify as abandoned orphans instead of beloved sons and daughters, we won't be able to receive all our Father is trying to put in our hands. We will reject it, feeling unworthy, or we will reject the knowledge of what He even wants us to have in the first place. When we can understand our true identity first, our minds will be ready to uproot the false beliefs and make room for the truth in all areas, including salvation, healing, provision, etc. That is why we have spent so much time laying these foundations first.

Just like citizens of our earthly countries, if we are not secure in our citizenship, or we do not know what rights and privileges our citizenship entitles us to, we will never experience the benefits of those rights and privileges. We can have freedom of speech all day long, but if we do not know it is a right we are entitled to as a citizen of our country, we are not going to operate in it or use it. That right will be of no benefit to us, even though it has been ours all along.

In the same way, if we are going to travel to a distant country, we better take the time to research the laws of that country, or we could end up in trouble. Not knowing the laws does not give us an excuse for violating them. It is our responsibility to know them before traveling and trying to operate our lives within that kingdom. If we violate the law, even if we do not know better, we can be subject to severe consequences, fines, and even prison. Satan gets away with so much theft and destruction because of our lack of knowledge. He knows how God's kingdom works inside and out, and he thrives on our lack of understanding these things. He loves it even more when he is able to exploit us by stealing our provision and then watch as we get mad at God, thinking God has not answered our prayers, or He does not hold true to His promises.

In Daniel 10, God sent the answer immediately from the very moment Daniel began to fast and pray, but those answers were met with spiritual interference and interception. What if Daniel had given up and assumed God chose not to answer? How many of us do that instead of discerning where the blame really goes and contending until we see the provision manifest?

Just like we have attorneys in our natural world who help us know and understand what our rights are and enforce the benefits of what the law entitles us to, God is raising us up to know what we are entitled to according to our identities as kingdom citizens in the spiritual world. This is so we can help others know, too. As we learn how the laws of His kingdom operate, it becomes our responsibility to teach others. This is also why heart posture is so important because, with our hearts properly postured toward God and provision, we will not come from a spirit or attitude of entitlement. Instead, we will have the attitudes of grateful sons and daughters who know our kingdom rights and authority because we are well aware of the price paid for us to have these benefits.

How many of God's children are living in poverty, sickness, or bondage simply because they don't know they don't have to? This legal matter was settled in a court case over two thousand years ago with judgment rendered in our favor—citizenship granted. Yet so many of us have an uncollected settlement and rights we do not walk in because we either do not understand what our inheritance is, we do not understand that we even have an inheritance for this life (not just in heaven), or we do not know how to access it and birth it from the spiritual realm to the natural. We do not know how the laws governing God's kingdom operate. The laws of gravity and lift have been present since the beginning, accessible at any time, but airplanes have only been around for the last century or so because these laws were not understood. In the same way, we are missing so many freedoms and benefits due to our lack of understanding. The key to access all of it is faith, but how can we have faith in something we don't even know about?

These answers and promises flow from the spirit realm's kingdom of God into the earth's natural realm on the current of our faith. Romans 4:20-21 (NIV) explains this principle of using faith in kingdom promises instead of focusing on what the facts of the natural realm say. This scripture tells us that although Abraham saw what the facts said about both his and Sarah's bodies being dead to reproduction, *"Yet he did not waver through unbelief regarding the promise of God, but was strengthened in his faith and gave glory to God, being fully persuaded that God had power to do what he had promised."* Can we give glory to God now as if we already have our promise?

When we are fully persuaded about something (which is what it really means to be in faith), that has an energy, a passion to it. Let someone try and argue with us that grass is not green or the sky is not seen as blue. We would laugh in their face and stand our ground on the subject because we are fully persuaded, and no one or nothing can convince us otherwise. That is exactly how we must be with the Word of God and His promises.

Not having faith in what God says will short circuit the flow of those promises from the spiritual into the natural realm. Unbelief will keep the promises from manifesting because unbelief gives the enemy the legal right to resist and intercept God's answers. When Jesus spoke, "Be healed!" over someone, He was moving provision from God's realm into this one. It always manifested because Jesus was fully persuaded it would happen. He didn't walk around merely hoping God would back Him up, Jesus was fully convinced, so the provision moved from that realm to this one on the current of Jesus's faith.

We must remain fully persuaded and not allow the enemy to divide our minds. How do we stay in faith? According to Romans 10:17 (NKJV), *"Faith comes by hearing, and hearing by the word of God,"* so we must remain in the Word of God, meditating on His promises until we become fully convinced. How can we believe God for something if we have not heard or even know what God says? Remember, we already learned that we will only prosper to the degree that our souls prosper, and our souls only prosper by being fed soul food.

We must make feasting on the Word of God as much a part of our daily lives as feasting on natural food is. A prosperous soul is one that makes experiencing God in private intimacy a priority. When we are intimate with God internally, in our unseen parts, it will find expression in the external parts of our lives. We cannot have a low Word level in our lives and expect to be prosperous. (Again, as previously discussed, prosperity and wealth are not necessarily the same thing. Many celebrities are wealthy, but they are not prosperous.) Prosperity is wealth or abundance without sorrow. We must know the will and Word of God to have the necessary faith to see God's promises made manifest in our lives.

Read James 1:6-7.

This explains how unbelief can intercept the flow and short-circuit the manifestation of God's promises. If we are not fully persuaded, we are not in faith but rather double-minded—two visions—di-vision. The vision is divided between two possible outcomes. One that believes and one that is unsure it will receive. A plan "A" and a plan "B." If our hearts are not fully persuaded, then mountains will not move. Jesus said the only way a mountain will not move, the only thing that could stop it, is doubt or unbelief. This is why Satan works so hard to keep us in a divided mind. Our own lack of self-discipline in taking dominion over our thought life allows Satan to accomplish this easily.

In Matthew 13:3-23, Jesus explains how this process works through the parable of the farmer scattering seed. This parable explains how we can be diligent in planting the promises of the Word of God in our minds, and yet Satan will come along and try to equally plant an alternate story or narrative. Satan will come after those seeds planted in our hearts, seeking to dig them up and get us to allow him to plant a different seed in the form of a thought contrary to what the Word of God says. For example, we could be meditating on promises of healing, and Satan will come along with thoughts like, "Yeah, well, look at so and so…They prayed and believed God for healing, and it never came, and that person died. God sometimes chooses not to heal people."

If we are not diligent enough to immediately recognize those thoughts as seeds of weeds and reject them, those weeds will take root and choke out the seeds of promise. The landscape of our minds will be divided trying to grow two different crops, and James 1:6-7 tells us what the result of a double-minded person is. They should not expect to receive anything from the Lord. That is how Satan gets us.

Now, what Satan planted might seem true. We all know believers who have not received healing and may have even died prematurely, but is that the whole truth? Remember, many times Satan works in half-truths, not outright lies. So, in this scenario, often, there is way more to the story. Maybe this believer believed that God could heal them but not necessarily would? Maybe they did not understand they already had healing, and it was up to them to enforce it against the enemy? Maybe they had a divided mind preventing them from receiving from the kingdom? Maybe this believer had an unresolved accusation against them, allowing Satan to legally resist the healing anointing and kink the hose?

If someone tried to give us a package we knew was not ours, we would not just take it anyway. We would resist them and say, "No way! That is not mine. I do not want it. Take it back!" That is exactly how we should be dealing with the enemy when he tries to bring us junk from his kingdom.

Just because someone appears to have strong faith to us, we are not God and never really know what is going on in the hidden part of that person's heart and mind. Satan uses our lack of knowledge to try and build alternate narratives that will divide our faith and our minds. The Bible gives many reasons as to why believers can fail to walk in healing and even die prematurely. This could be the subject of a whole other book, but for the sake of staying on topic, I will just briefly touch on one of the reasons the Bible gives for believers failing to receive healing.

1 Corinthians 11:30 (NLT) states, *"That is why many of you are weak and sick and some have even died."* Paul is speaking to the believers in Corinth here. The phrase *"that is why"* tells us he is explaining to them exactly why many of them were weak, sick, and even died. To find out why, we must back up a little bit to verse 17. Here, the subject matter in Paul's letter changes and he begins instructing the Corinthian church about order at the Lord's Supper. Paul begins to chastise them because there are "*divisions among*" them when they meet.[51] If we keep reading, in verses 20-21, Paul then begins rebuking them for their attitudes (not really being interested in the Lord's Supper but there to satisfy their own appetites and, in so doing, being selfish and not sharing with others). They were disgracing God's church and dishonoring the body of Christ.[52]

Because of their attitudes, this congregation was observing Communion in an unworthy manner and therefore, guilty of sinning against the body and blood of the Lord.[53] Verse 29 states they were eating and drinking judgment on themselves, and verse 30 explains why "*many of you are weak and sick and some have even died.*" Paul is letting this group of believers know exactly what the problem is so they can repent and turn it around. However, whenever we fail to see the promised provision manifest, instead of digging into the Word of God to what is kinking the hose, how often do many of us instead change our doctrine to something along the lines of "God chose not to answer our prayer," or "Sometimes God just chooses not to heal or to provide."

The Cross of Christ was a class-action legal judgment against Satan and sickness. When we become believers, we get to "opt-in" to that judgment, which allows the record of the charges against us to be canceled, and as part of that settlement, we get a restraining order against Satan[54]. It is up to us to enforce that restraining order. We are the ones carrying Christ's authority to do so. If we do not do it, no one will. We are no longer under Satan's jurisdiction, and we secure the legal right to evict his kingdom from our lives, which includes sickness and poverty.

However, when we are in violation of what God says, Satan is allowed to "appeal" this verdict. He cannot appeal our salvation, which is secured.[55] Yet, Satan can secure the right to devour. What does he devour? Anything he can. This includes our health and provision. Again, this could be the subject of a whole other book, so I won't go much further into this at this time. I simply want to illustrate that there can be reasons why a believer fails to receive their promise of healing, provision, or whatever they are hoping for. It is important that we know that the problem is never on God's end or that He simply chose not to heal someone or to provide. We must know these things so Satan does not have the opportunity to divide our minds.

For some reason, instead of seeking the Word for answers and to see if we may be in violation of these principles somewhere, we simply brush it off and develop a false belief that God arbitrarily chooses who to heal and who not to. We allow our minds to agree with a narrative other than what the Word of God says; therefore, we never receive the promises. This is an extremely sick and twisted view of God. If our children were sick or in need, would we pick and choose who to help while leaving our other kids without help? That would make us a monster. Yet, we assault God's character with this kind of trash all the time.

Why are we going over faith and healing on the topic of kingdom government and economics? Because healing is just another form of provision, and faith is how we access anything from God's kingdom. Provision is provision; it does not matter what the need is. Faith is the current that moves any provision we need from heaven to earth, from the unseen realm to the realm we see with our eyes.

In Mark 4, Jesus tells His disciples that if they do not understand faith and how to get it, they will not understand anything else about the kingdom. We cannot understand any kingdom principle, including all the economic principles, without first understanding how faith operates, how to get it, and how to use it. Secondly, we can't have faith for something if we don't know it's our right to have it as a kingdom citizen. Once we understand that God's government can override our earthly government, we can be empowered by our rights as citizens to take actions that have both spiritual and natural results.

BIBLICAL PRINCIPLES OF GIVING

When we sacrifice our provision to see the kingdom advance or by meeting a need, there are certain promised rewards for doing so. The Bible gives us three very distinct and different ways of taking our natural provision and trading it spiritually, all with their own unique promised rewards. The three different areas of trading with our finances are sowing, tithing, and giving to the poor. Each of these areas of stewarding provision is different and comes with a different set of promises and benefits. Sowing is not tithing; tithing is not sowing. Even though giving to the poor can be a type of sowing, the promised rewards are different, so we need to make sure we utilize these three economic activities appropriately to receive the right desired outcome. New Testament believers should do all three.

Let's break down the differences between each one as it is important to know how they differ from each other and from giving to the poor. These are three distinct and different types of trades in the spirit realm, having different stipulations that govern what they are and different promised blessings from each. Many believers incorrectly use these terms interchangeably, when they are in fact quite different, and then get frustrated when the promised blessings do not manifest.

NUMBER ONE: SOWING AND REAPING

Now that we know how God's government works, what our rights are as kingdom citizens, and how we can have the laws of His government supersede our natural lives, we need to understand how to work within the economy of that government. The principle of sowing and reaping is one of the most basic of both God's kingdom and the earth's. It is the foundational economic principle for receiving any promise, both in the kingdom and in the natural. Anytime we sow something into the kingdom of God, we are making a trade, whether we know it or not.

Sowing and reaping governs all of life, including finances. Many times, people are sowing and mistaking it as tithing or tithing and mistaking it as sowing. These practices have different guidelines and rewards as established by God, which explains why when those aren't followed, people get frustrated from not seeing the promises they thought they would receive. The biblical promise attached to sowing is a harvest from what is sown, both naturally and spiritually. What type of harvest we get depends on the type of seed sown. Seed reproduces after its own kind. Just like in farming, watermelon seeds will produce watermelons. Apple seeds will produce apples. Seed reproduces after its own kind.

Job 4:8 tells us that those who sow trouble will reap the same. The principle of sowing and reaping governs all areas of life. It shows us that when we put something into any soil, we get something back—good or bad—tangible, natural things as well as intangible things such as forgiveness, mercy, or even trouble. Even these bodies we live in are a seed that will be sown into the ground one day and will produce a harvest of the new bodies we will get. We sow this body in death and reap a new one in resurrection We always reap a harvest from what is sown. So, with that in mind, if we have a need beyond our basic provision, we can sow a seed.

Starting in John 6:8, there is an account where Jesus and His disciples wanted to feed a vast multitude of people, but they did not have nearly enough provision to do so. However, when what they did have was sown into the kingdom, the law of multiplication took over, and a harvest was multiplied back that was more than enough to meet the need (with basketfuls left over). Where did this seed come from? When there was a need to feed the crowd of people, a boy first sowed his lunch (food) into the kingdom. What he had was not enough to meet the need, but he sowed it anyway. That food, sown as seed, gave God something to multiply back, as food, or the very thing that was sown. Anything can be seed, but keep in mind that seed reproduces after its own kind.

What we sow is what will be multiplied back to us and comes from where it was sown. That is why when we take natural seed and sow it into the kingdom of God, provision comes back to us from the kingdom of God. We do not sow in one field and harvest from another. To receive from the kingdom, we sow into the field of the kingdom. That kingdom produces a harvest that shows back up to us. The cool thing about sowing money is that money can be anything. If I take money to a grocery store, it becomes groceries. If I take money to a car dealership, money becomes a car. So, when we sow money into the kingdom, we can receive anything that we need back.

Psalm 126:5 (ESV) tells us, *"Those who sow in tears shall reap with shouts of joy!"* Why would we sow in tears? The reason is that sowing requires us to give up the seed we have in our hands now, which can many times be a real sacrifice. However, we will have joy when the harvest comes because multiplication will give us many more times the number of seeds we had to begin with. This is how we begin to transform our finances. How much we get depends on what we sow to God for kingdom purpose.

Sowing is the only area of giving where seed gets multiplied. Multiplication is exciting; however, zero times one hundred is still zero. This is why we are told that he who sows sparingly will reap sparingly. Why is that? The reason is simple multiplication. Zero multiplied is still zero. One times ten is still just ten. However, ten times one hundred becomes one thousand. The more sown, the larger the multiplication. How much of our finances we sow into kingdom assignments is how much gets multiplied back to us, and we end up with even more than what we gave away.

Sowing is where we get to choose how much or how little we put in the soil of the kingdom to have multiplied back to us. This is also where we get to partner with kingdom assignments and tap into the powerful principle of partnership that will cause us to reap exponentially. Jesus teaches us the principle of partnership to reap great harvests in several places in Scripture. The first passage is found in Luke 5, which is right after Simon Peter gave Jesus his fishing boat to use for Jesus to be able to preach the gospel from (kingdom purpose). We have already touched on this story from the aspect of Peter giving Jesus his source of income—his fishing boat—for kingdom use. However, there is so much more we can unpack from this story. This time, let's focus on the part where Jesus is using this to teach us the power of partnering with kingdom assignments.

Read Luke 5:4-7.

Here, we see Simon Peter was not in business by himself; he had partners in another boat. Even though these partners had nothing to do with Peter's decision to give Jesus the boat, because of their partnership, they shared in the same reward for obedience that Peter received. Partners are viewed as one entity, so it would have been unjust to bless one without the other. The partners in the other boat were blessed simply because of the partnership they had with Peter. This is why Jesus instructed Peter to let down his nets (plural). Jesus meant for both Peter and his partners to do it.

Not understanding, Peter responds that he will let down just his net (singular). However, the harvest was too much for that one net because it was also for his partners, which is why they had to be called over to reap as well. Why did this happen? The partners did not exercise any faith or obedience. They are not the ones who first obeyed a request from the Lord to use the boat or heard and obeyed the word of the Lord as to where to fish and let down their net. So why were they blessed as well?

Read Matthew 10:40-42.

What is Jesus talking about here? What does Jesus mean by *"receive?"* He gives us the answer in verse 42. Jesus says, *"If you give even a cup of cold water…"* We can see that Jesus is speaking of sharing provision with a prophet or righteous person—someone on kingdom assignment. Jesus is telling us that when we receive them, it means we are providing for them. In other words, we are financially backing their assignment. When we do this, we are taking their assignment on as if it were our own. In so doing, we receive the same reward they do simply because we are in partnership. Whatever blessing falls on them will now also fall on us! We will store up treasure in heaven and simultaneously tap into kingdom provision here on earth.

When Simon Peter gave Jesus his boat, he partnered with Jesus's assignment to preach the good news of the kingdom, and his boat became seed sown into the kingdom for kingdom purpose. This caused Peter to share in Jesus's reward as prophet and released kingdom provision to Peter on earth. This is where life gets exciting! It is way more fun to find kingdom assignments to partner with than it is to spend money on any other thing because every dollar becomes seed sown into the kingdom and multiplies a great harvest in the natural. We also share in all the spiritual rewards of that ministry.

HOW DO SEEDS WORK?

To gain a deeper understanding of how this principle operates, it is important to first understand how seeds work. If we were to buy a package of seeds, how can we tell what type of seed we are buying? There is usually a picture on the outside of the package that gives us a future glimpse into what the seed is to become. This is important because before we do anything, we must know what kind of crop we want so we can make sure to plant the correct type of seed. A seed, by its nature, carries within itself a specific promise of a specific plant.

If we were to open the package and take out one of those tiny little seeds, would that seed be the same thing as the picture? Yes! An apple seed is an apple; it is just at a different stage of development. A seed's identity and value are not based on what stage of development it is in. Part of its value is in what it has the potential to become. For example, every human life starts as a seed planted within the womb of the mother. That seed is a human being on day one of conception and has the same amount of "humanness" as it does at full-term. Human life has the exact same identity and value no matter what stage of development: pre-born, newborn, toddler, teenager, middle age, or geriatric. Its identity and value as a human never changes as it ages, only its capability.

The same is true for any type of seed. Whether it is in seed or crop form, the identity and value are not different; it is just at a different stage of development. There is a process the seed must go through to mature into its full glory and promised picture. Just because we possess this seed, does it mean it will become the promised picture? No! We have a part to play in that process. It cannot plant itself; we must choose to plant it. A seed by itself is just a seed. Seed by itself produces nothing. Soil by itself produces nothing. However, when the two are put together, the seed can mature into its full picture, and we can get a crop. Nothing happens until someone decides to take that seed and plant it. Only then does it begin the process to produce the intended outcome.

This is exactly how it is with every promise within the Word of God. From the parable Jesus tells us of the seed and the sower, we see the seed is God's Word and the soil is the human heart.[56] Jesus explains how the whole process works. First, we find a promise in the Word of God that pertains to our situation. Just like with natural seed, it does nothing while in the package. We must purposely take that promise in the Word of God, which is in seed form, and plant it in the soil of our hearts. When watered with our prayers, the seed will produce the intended outcome on its own.

Just because we planted it, does not mean our work is done. We must water it and tend it, while holding onto the picture we intend to see manifest. It is important to note that we do not work on the seed itself. We work on the environment the seed is in. If we do our part, the seed does its part on its own. We cannot do anything to make that seed shift shape other than water it properly and protectively guard against the pests that seek to either destroy or consume it. We must know Satan will try to come after that seed. When planted in good soil, watered, and guarded, the seed will always produce the promised picture it carries within itself.

WHAT CAN INTERFERE WITH OUR CROP?

Now that we know how seeds work to produce what was promised, we need to know what, if anything, can mess with our crop. Through a parable found in Luke 8, Jesus gives us a breakdown of what causes us to either experience harvest or crop failure through different types of soil and conditions. What is it about the soil that makes a seed grow or not grow? Soil provides a base to which the roots hold on to, as well as the nutrients and water. It is important for soil to be loose and not overly packed down. This is why farmers plow before planting—to break up the soil and keep it from being compacted. Compact soil makes it harder for roots to spread out, which limits the seed's or plant's access to nutrients and weakens the plant's hold on the ground. The more room the roots have, the more soil the plant can hold in place so it does not wash away during a storm.

As mentioned, Jesus tells us that the soil is the human heart and the seed is the Word of God. This is why a hardened heart does not receive the promises of God—because the seed can't take root. We must plow our ground and dig up lies we have been believing so that when we plant truth seeds, they can take root, spread out, and grow. With that in mind, let us look at how Jesus uses this parable to teach us how soil condition affects the kingdom law of sowing and reaping.

Read Luke 8:5-8.

Right away, we see the farmer is the one responsible for planting his seed in his field. No one can plant the Word of God in our hearts for us; we must plant it ourselves. Notice also that he plants his own seed. In other words, he had to know what type of crop he wanted and plant that specific kind of seed. We must find a seed promise that produces the type of crop we need in the form of scripture containing that promise, and that is the seed we must plant into the soil of our hearts. When explaining the different outcomes, Jesus tells us that it was different types of soil that created the different outcomes.

The first type of soil Jesus describes here is a footpath—dry and compacted. The hard crust keeps the seed from being able to penetrate, so the enemy can immediately come after that seed and snatch it away like a bird. Satan is immediately going to test our agreement with the Word to see if we will hold on to it or let it go. If Satan can get us to agree with a different idea, dividing our minds with a different picture or doubting the picture we are holding out for, then the seed of that different idea is the crop we will get instead of the seed we let go of.

The second type of soil is the rocky soil. It is dry and crusty but not as much as the footpath. The seed can just barely penetrate the surface. It is too shallow to form deep roots. These are people who live the Word on the surface but give up quickly when the heat of persecution comes. They can quote the Word, but in many areas, they do not live it. They have a shallow and surface relationship with the Word of God, and because of that, the soil of their hearts is unable to properly incubate the seeds of God's promises long enough for the results to show up. How many Christians have we heard profess they believe in healing, but then a pandemic shows up, and instead of heading into the danger to set people free, they are just as afraid as the unbelievers?

The third type of soil has thorns in it. Seeds get planted and begin to grow, but then they get choked and strangled by thorns. In Luke 8:14 (and Matthew 13:22), Jesus describes the thorns as the worries of this life (our responsibilities) and the lure of wealth (pursuing career or business success at the sake of all else). These things act like thorns that we allow to take our attention off the seed in our pursuit of other interests.

We begin neglecting the seed by failing to tend the garden of our hearts. We stop watering the seed and stop pulling the weeds, which are then allowed to overgrow and choke out our precious seed. These people planted the seed, but they did not do the work to uproot lies because they are too busy doing other things, so those weeds choke out their crop before it can bear fruit.

The last type of soil Jesus speaks about is good, fertile soil. This soil is soft because someone did the hard work of breaking up the crust before trying to plant. This soil is receptive because it has been watered through prayer. It provides the perfect environment to let the seed do what it is naturally made to do—grow itself into the crop of the promised picture. A seed reaching its full potential requires healthy soil, which provides several key nutrients in balance—sunlight, clean air, and water, all working together. If any of these components is out of balance, it will affect the quality of the crop.

- With sunlight, plants use the sun's energy and warmth. Not enough sun will slow down a plant's growth and even kill it. In the same way, we need to take the time to sit in the Son's light and let Him expose things in our soil. Too much sun can be a problem if the plant and the soil are drying out too quickly. We see this with soil types one and two. The soil is too hard and compacted, so there's not enough water. Too much time spent praying about something out of worry is like too much sun on the soil, which dries it out.
- Just as importantly, plants need air. Plants take in carbon dioxide and release oxygen as they make their own food energy. The wind, which is moving air, carries pollen and seeds to help spread them around. This is the plant's way of making more of its own kind. Air and wind bring multiplication. When we simply plant the seed and let the Holy Spirit breathe His life into it, it will multiply. The spoken word travels on our air. We need to make sure our confession matches our picture as if we already have it. Polluted air can be harmful, poisoning the plant. We need to watch what we say about the crop we are believing for, or we can be polluting the air with our doubt. Ideal soil allows air to flow through it, not just into it.

- The last component is water. Water flows on top of or through the soil and is particularly important to growth. It is what moves the nutrients from the soil into the plant through its roots. Water keeps the plant vibrant and flexible and helps the plant make its own food. If the ground gets over-saturated, then there is no room in the soil for air, which can also cause stagnation and root rot.

These different nutrients need to stay in balance. Too much or too little of either one and it can kill the crop. We can also see it is the soil's ability to hold these nutrients that affects if or how well the plant grows. The life of the plant depends on the life of the soil. If the soil is lacking, the plant will not grow, will grow poorly, or will die. In this parable, Jesus is giving us an especially important key: if the seed is not producing the picture promised, we need to inspect the soil, not the seed. The problem always lies within the soil.

In this parable, the soil is the human heart, and the seed is the Word of God. Jesus is showing us that soil matters! As with natural seeds, where we plant them is just as important as what we plant. In fact, the type of soil is so important that it determines whether the seed ever develops into its full picture. The number one thing that will disappoint or frustrate a gardener is working with soil that is difficult to manage or is just plain unproductive.

We are not to be passive bystanders because we have a continually active role to play in this process. Did we inspect and prepare the ground before planting the seed? If we choose to sow into hard soil instead of doing the necessary prep work of plowing up the crust and making sure we have good soil ready to receive the seed, we cannot get angry with God or assume the false belief that He has His reasons for not wanting to answer our prayers.

God's Word cannot return void, so if the seed of the Word does not produce what it promised, the problem is never on God's end. Did we inspect and prepare the ground before sowing? Are we intentionally planting the seed instead of just holding onto the package? Did we fail to water the seed, or did we water it too much? Did it begin to grow, but we failed to guard it? Did we not recognize when Satan came after it or when he sowed a different picture for us to agree with?

A seed will always produce. We can invite or encounter crop killers, which are things that ruin our crop, like frost, famine, drought, or pests; however, the seed itself always produces. There are several things that can kill a crop—unforgiveness, unbelief, unconfessed sin, and being double-minded, to name a few. Were we diligent to keep these locusts from consuming our promises? Did we take any necessary action to harvest the crop, or did we let that fruit go uncollected? Many times, instead of taking personal responsibility for the things we fail to do, we blame God or develop false beliefs about Him to explain away why our answers did not show up.

God does not give us crops; He gives us the opportunity to actively partner with Him to produce crops. Once the crop is grown, we still must harvest it. In the same way, God does not give us wealth; He gives us opportunities to capture wealth in Deuteronomy 8:18 (NLT), "*He is the one who gives you power to be successful."* To be successful, we first must actively be doing something. If we are not actively participating in its capture, we will not have it or harvest it.

We see an example of this in Luke 5, when Jesus brought Peter the greatest harvest of fish he had ever seen. This harvest was so astounding that Peter recognized immediately that something supernatural had occurred. However, it is important to note that Jesus did not just give Peter fish. Jesus brought Peter the opportunity to participate in capturing fish; the fish did not show up in Peter's boat. Peter still had to let down his net and haul it in.

If Peter had chosen not to, did it mean Jesus did not bring the answer? One of our biggest mistakes is expecting the fish to show up in our boats, instead of looking for where Jesus is bringing us the opportunity to capture and harvest our provision. Proverbs 6:9-11 tells us that laziness will cause poverty to steal from us. Proverbs 14:23 tells us that work brings profit, but mere talk leads to poverty. It is great to be given words of knowledge from God like Peter received, but if we fail to act on that knowledge or put the labor in, we will miss the harvest. Our faith is not in the work we do. The work we do is based on the faith we have in what He said. From this story, we can see that fishing was not Peter's provider; Jesus was. However, that does not mean that Peter did not have work to do to capture that provision, and the same is true for us.

WHAT PART DOES FAITH PLAY IN THE SEED PROCESS?

Now that we understand how the soil and the seed work together, where does faith come into the equation? We already learned that faith is how we access God's promises in Scripture that come in seed form and knowing how God's kingdom laws work gives us the faith to believe Him for the promise. We also learned how unbelief acts as a crop killer to those seeds planted in our hearts. But what part does faith play when it comes to sowing natural seed that we can see with our eyes?

There is a reason faith is the foundation of sowing and reaping with both natural seed and spiritual seed. Faith is foundational because it takes faith for a farmer to put a seed in the ground. A farmer would not go through all the trouble, hard work, the sacrifice of preparing the ground, planting the seed, and watching over the crop if he did not have faith that a harvest would result from that effort. If a farmer did not have faith in the seed's ability to produce the crop it promises, he would not even bother to put forth all that work.

Sowing requires sacrifice upfront—giving up instant gratification for a future result. We must first give up the seed we have in our hands and do something with it before we ever see the manifestation of what it promises to become. We don't eat the seed; we eat the harvest after sowing the seed. If we eat the seed, we destroy our future. It would be just as foolish to try and plant bread. Bread is the part of the harvest we are allowed to enjoy and partake in. It is the promise in hand.

This sowing and reaping principle transcends all areas of life, not just provision, and it is how we access any promise, which is why it is not only important to understand this principle but also how seeds work and how faith interplays with this law. Galatians 6:7-8 (NKJV) says, *"Do not be deceived, God is not mocked; for whatever a man sows, that he will also reap. For he who sows to his flesh will of the flesh reap corruption, but he who sows to the Spirit will of the Spirit reap everlasting life."*

First, we can see that we can sow both spiritually and naturally. This is why where we sow matters just as much as what we sow. Where do we want our harvest to come from? When we sow the spiritual seed of God's promises into the soil of our hearts, we will reap from that place if we guard the soil and the crop. When we sow natural seed in natural places that is where we will harvest a crop from. For this reason, we need to make sure the soil we sow into has the capability of producing, or we are just wasting seed. Remember, if a seed does not produce, the problem is with the soil, not the seed. The real power comes when we sow natural seeds for spiritual purposes. We reap from both simultaneously, and it multiplies exponentially.

Second, we can see that we cannot cherry-pick what we want to focus on (i.e. just sowing or just reaping). The two go hand-in-hand. We cannot separate sowing and reaping because seeds always produce a harvest. In the same way, it is impossible to separate giving and receiving. Scripture often equates these activities as being the same concept or principle in action. They are inseparable. In Scripture, many times, the act of giving and receiving is equated with sowing and reaping because they work the same way. When we sow, we will reap. When we give, we will receive.[57] When we give something, we are sowing into something: a need, a project, or an assignment. We are giving the soil something to work with. This is why they are interchangeable.

On the flip side, if we want or need to receive, we must give. We must sacrifice seed up front to get the harvest that fulfills our needs. This seems backward. If we are in need, why do we have to sow first? Why don't we get our needs met and then sow? Many aspects of the kingdom of God seem backward according to our natural kingdom. For example, if we want to be exalted, we must humble ourselves. If we want to become great, we must become the least. If we want to lead, we must serve. To go up, we must come down. The same is true with finances and provision. If we want to receive, first, we must give.

We must learn to give out of our poverty before having the opportunity to give out of our abundance. Jesus tells us that if we give, we will receive. He does not say, "First you receive, then you give." Even a farmer knows there is no harvest unless and until there is first a seed sown in the ground, not kept in his hand. Having a seed means nothing until we do something with it. Anything sown multiplies, so for the law of multiplication to take effect, the seed must be let go of and sown. A farmer also knows that the size of the harvest is directly proportionate to the number of seeds in the ground. If a farmer needs or wants a bigger harvest, he must plant more seeds up front. He must take all the risk up-front.

Now, I just want to clarify my use of the word "need." I am not talking about food, clothing, or shelter—the necessities to sustain life. We have already looked at Matthew 6:26, where Jesus promises those needs will be met. I am speaking of things we have need of that go beyond these basics. In this passage, we see the birds have "just enough" and not abundant stores. They have no wealth built up. However, with this principle of sowing and reaping, we can tap into abundant provision instead of just enough provision because whatever is sown multiplies.

When God wants to do more than just meet our needs, when He is seeking to put the law of multiplication into effect on our behalf, it will require us to sow something upfront. Sowing is about what will come to us in the future, not necessarily our immediate provision, although it can impact both. Remember we discussed John 6, where the boy sowed his lunch into Jesus's ministry to help meet the need; it did not just meet the need, abundance was multiplied back. The law of multiplication took effect, which both met the immediate need and multiplied a harvest back. What is interesting is that Matthew 14, Mark 6, and Luke 9 all mention this story where Jesus feeds over five thousand people with only two fish and five barley loaves, but only John records that it was a boy who first sowed his lunch.

In Luke 6:38 (NLT), Jesus gives us an especially important key to how we receive provision out of the kingdom of God and explains why this happened with the boy's lunch. He says, *"Give, and you will receive. Your gift will return to you in full—pressed down, shaken together to make room for more, running over, and poured into your lap. The amount you give will determine the amount you get back."* There are several important things we can glean from this scripture. First is when speaking of giving here, Jesus never says "at church" or "to the temple." It does not mention anything about a specific location, unlike the tithe. Jesus is explaining a principle that governs everything, including but not limited to the church and the giving of finances. It is a principle that is all encompassing.

In the verse immediately before (Luke 6:37), Jesus speaks of the giving of anything, good or bad. He mentions giving judgment, condemnation, and forgiveness. This principle governs the giving of anything and everything, natural and spiritual things. He tells us that when we give something, we will receive it. The second thing we can glean from this verse is that it is important to note the word *"amount"* is relative. It is not the actual amount, as much as it is the percentage of what we have. Jesus explains this in both Mark 12 and Luke 21 when He commends the poor widow. Jesus tells us that her two small coins were all she had to live on, which was greater than those who gave large sums that were a ridiculously small percentage of their total abundance.

The third important thing is Jesus says, *"your gift."* He is not speaking of the tithe. If we choose to participate in the covenant of tithing, the tithe is not a gift we are giving God. It already belongs to Him. We are not sowing it. I do not care if we give ten percent to a ministry; it is not tithing unless we are following all the parameters of tithing by also giving *where* God says to give it, so it can be used for the purpose God says it is for. We will cover more on this in a moment. The fourth thing we need to notice is that Jesus says, *"... pressed down, shaken together to make room for more, running over, and poured into your lap."* This speaks of multiplication. Seed sown always produces more than what was sown. This is how we can use the law of sowing and reaping to multiply what we must create an abundance of.

When it comes to this principle of giving and receiving or sowing and reaping, if we look at the story of Elijah and the widow found in 1 Kings 17, her circumstances were so bad, she was in such poverty that she was literally down to her last little bit of provision. She had nothing left but to die. If anyone should be justified to receive without first giving, it should be her. However, even she did not get a break from how the system works. Out of her poverty, she had to give to Elijah first before a harvest was multiplied back to her.

What if she held on to that provision and had not sown it because she did not have enough? To most people, she would have been justified in her decision, but she also would have missed the miracle of multiplication by choosing to believe the facts instead of having faith that God would come through. God did not just bring her provision like manna. Manna was always just enough and never multiplied. Instead, He brought her the opportunity to capture multiplied provision by sowing first into the kingdom so He could multiply her seed back to her. He wanted to do more than just meet her needs. He wanted to multiply her provision by having the law of multiplication enacted on her behalf, which required sowing of what little she had. A seed must be sacrificed up front before it can be multiplied.

We see another example of this principle in the Gospels, in the same story we just discussed, when Jesus brings Peter the opportunity to capture wealth. Peter lent Jesus his boat so Jesus could use it to preach to the people. What was Peter's boat? It was his income! It was his business. It was how he made his living as a fisherman. Peter gave control of his livelihood to Jesus first, sowing it into the kingdom, and then a harvest of multiplication resulted. Peter was willing to give up his source of income to further the gospel; then he received his harvest.

What if Peter's attitude was, "Who does this Jesus guy think he is? I'm the professional fisherman here, and this teacher proceeds to tell me how to fish?" Peter also could have very easily said to Jesus, "Sorry, dude. I worked all day, and my business made nothing, so I must go back out and keep fishing. I cannot afford to give you my boat right now; I need it to make some money. When I make what I need, then I will let you borrow my boat." What if that had been Peter's response? Peter would have missed the opportunity to partner with God in his finances, and he would have missed the biggest harvest of his life. Yet, how many of us do that to God with our paychecks?

Peter first gave out of his poverty, and then the abundance came. Because Scripture so often associates the sowing and reaping with giving and receiving, we tend to think of this principle only in terms of natural provision. However, it is the same principle by which the Word of God produces anything in our lives, such as faith, healing, and provision. It is how the entire kingdom works. However, again, we see God did not just give Peter the provision; He gave Peter the opportunity to capture it.

At its core, sowing and reaping is closely related to another economic principle called trading. Trading is an activity of the spirit realm and was so before it was ever a principle in the natural. Trading is an economic activity. Before the institution of currency or money for trading, things were traded outright. One person might have fur and could trade that fur for another resource like knives. One person could accept or reject an offer to trade merchandise based on the need. Trading requires sacrificing something you already have to gain something someone else has. It's giving up one thing to gain another. Currency (or money) is just a neutral way of trading. Even though there is no money in heaven, there is definitely trading. Trading has been around since before the beginning of time and is what led to Satan's fall and removal from the trading floors of heaven.

Read Ezekiel 28:14-18.

The *"stones of fire"* speak to the burning coals of the altar before the throne of God. An altar is where trades happen, where we trade with the spirit world. "Commerce" is an interchange of goods or commodities, especially on a large scale...trade or business.[58] It was during this activity of trading or commerce in heaven when Satan became filled with violence and sinned through dishonest trading. An altar is a structure on which something of value is sacrificed in worship to God. Sacrifices are the medium of exchange.

The cross of Jesus was the greatest exchange or trade of all time, where something of value (Jesus) was traded for something else of value (us). During this trade, Jesus became sin for us so we might become the righteousness of God. Because of this trade, we have salvation and everything else included with that trade. The Cross was an altar where something (someone) of value was sacrificed as an act of worship to God. We sow our faith into that finished work, and we reap the promise of salvation. Sowing and reaping still take place.

We must understand trading to understand what we do whenever we sow, give, or sacrifice. All these activities involve trading. Sacrifice triggers trading. Biblically, whenever someone sacrifices something of great value to God in worship, it always produces a response from God to give back something greater to them. Receiving that response was not their motivation for giving. Worship was their motivation, and that type of worship always moves the heart of God so much that He responds with even greater blessing.

Sacrifice is something we do in the natural realm that releases the supernatural realm to intervene and change the outcome of natural events. A sacrifice is always a seed sown, but a seed is not always a sacrifice. Something we sacrifice in worship to God is a seed we plant in His kingdom, and some kind of blessing comes back to us. Jesus says when we give, we will receive, whether we like it or not. He does not say we might receive. Therefore, receiving can be our expectation without it being our motivation. Our motivation is worship, but our expectation is receiving only because Jesus is the one who said it.

There are also times we sow a seed, and it really is not a sacrifice for us. That is okay and we will still reap. It is a principle that is always in operation like gravity is. It does not matter how we feel about it, what our opinion of it is, or whether we even want to receive. The law is going to operate like gravity will always operate. For both a spiritual and natural example of this, let us look at fasting. Fasting is trading. We sacrifice natural food and mealtimes to spend time with the Lord. We are trading earthly food for spiritual food. As a result of this trade, not only do we receive greater revelation and strategy from the Lord, but that sacrifice moves the heart of God to intervene in circumstances that require supernatural intervention.

There are also times we fast in ways that are not really a sacrifice. Our sacrifice is our worship, and our worship is our sacrifice, so it must come from a true heart of worship and not be for a religious show or religious duty, or we should not even bother. The same is true when we sow anything. The heart motive is what God looks at. We see this in Genesis 4 in the story of Cain and Abel. The heart motive behind each offering is what caused it to be accepted or rejected by God.

As with fasting, finances can be another expression of spiritual trading. We are not trading, sowing, or giving to promote ourselves or get something for ourselves. We trade to see the kingdom of God expand and advance. More than having our needs met, our goal should be to see the full expression of heaven on earth so others can see God as a good Father who provides. When people see God manifest in that way, it draws others to Him.

WHERE YOUR TREASURE IS

When we spend money, we are trading. This is also sowing, and sowing always produces a crop. We tend to think of financial sowing only as it relates to the spiritual things we support financially; however, Galatians 6:7 (NLT) makes it clear that we can sow to both the flesh and the spirit, and we will reap either way. It states, *"Don't be misled—you cannot mock the justice of God. You will always harvest what you plant."*

Harvesting what we plant is tied to the justice of God. God would consider it unjust if we planted an apple seed and got an avocado instead. So, if we are sowing money into supporting Hollywood via movie tickets, cable TV, etc., the crop that seed is producing in our lives could be false beliefs and ideas about relationships that can produce sexual immorality and relationship issues. If we are watching horror movies, it can produce a crop of fear or fear-based thinking. It is not necessarily a sin, per se, to watch movies or television; we must know the human heart is an incubator for seed, and we need to be aware of what we are sowing into it that creates a different picture than what God says.

Are we getting a crop of stress, anxiety, fear, immorality, or mixed messages on what is right and wrong? That coffee and donut habit we sow finances into, what is the crop there? Along with the momentary pleasure of that sugary snack, what else are we getting with that trade that maybe we ignore? We could be reaping sugar-related medical conditions like diabetes, gout, and obesity. It does not matter if it is natural sowing or spiritual sowing. Sowing always reaps a crop from what is sown, and it will reap from where it was sown.

Many times, when trading, we get more than we bargained for. What are we sowing finances into that is producing a crop we do not really want? Jesus tells us in Matthew 6:21 that where our treasure is, there our hearts will be also. Jesus is saying that what we spend money on shows what is important to us. We only spend money on things we value. Making a pie graph of all the things we spend money on can be a real eye-opening experience about what we value most. Remember, we only spend money on what we want or what is important to us. Where is our treasure going? It will show us where our heart is. Now, these things are not necessarily wrong—unless they are wrong. If God tells us to allocate funds to a certain area and we are not doing it because we have used up all our seed on things with no eternal value, then we have a problem. The problem is not what we are spending money on; it is with where our heart is. What are we valuing in our hearts more than what God says to do?

NUMBER TWO: TITHING

Although we have covered tithing previously, it was from the aspect of understanding that it is an eternal covenant having nothing to do with legalism. Even though we have already discussed what tithing is and what it is not to some degree previously, we were focusing on how it does or does not relate to the Law of Moses and whether it has a place in the lives of New Testament believers. Now let's delve a little deeper into this principle and the spiritual trade we are enacting when we put it into operation, and how God designed tithing to be a part of His people's economy.

As we have already established, tithing is not legalism, and although included in the law as to ensure an inheritance for the Levitical priests, it is a principle, not a law. What is most important for us to understand is that tithing is an opportunity to enter a financial covenant relationship with God. Just like marriage, tithing is a covenant we can choose to enter with God or not. Even though people are legally married, marriage has nothing to do with living under legalism or law; it is a legally recognized covenant between two parties. A covenant is a promise to be in a relationship the way God is in a relationship. A covenant is different from a contract. Covenants are more focused on the personal relationship, whereas contracts focus more on expected behaviors. Covenants are usually mutual but not necessarily equal. However, as with the marriage covenant, we do not get to partake of the blessings and claim the benefits of that covenant without being in it; the same is true for tithing.

Tithing is a struggle for so many because it requires absolute submission of our will to the will of God. The tithe belongs to the Lord. It is set apart specifically for His house, and He says it goes to the local storehouse, or what is known as our local church or ministry, where we get spiritually fed. Giving ten percent somewhere else is not tithing, just like living together is not marriage. The tithe is specifically so there will be food in His house, which is a provision for the priests. God is the one who designates the tithe to provide for the workings of the temple and to provide for the pastors so they can be devoted full-time to pastoring and teaching, not having to work outside the church for provision.

Read Deuteronomy 14:22-29.

We find regulations or stipulations the Lord puts on the practice of tithing, but more than that, we also find insight as to why the Lord puts those regulations into the "contract," and it has more to do with blessing us than Him. In verse 22, we see a tithe is specifically ten percent or one-tenth. Anything less is not a tithe. Anything above and beyond becomes sowing. This tenth comes from what we are actively participating in capturing and encompasses all we are given. It comes from our crops. (Remember as an agricultural society their crops were their wealth and were traded like money.)

Verse 23 reveals three important points: 1) We shall eat of the tithe because it goes to the place we get spiritually fed. 2) Tithing acknowledges God's right to say where provision goes, not where we want it to go. Tithing blesses the place where we are fed and eat. This means it goes to the local church alone, no other charity. When speaking of giving or sowing in Luke 6:38, Jesus never specifies that it must be to the church. Tithing, however, must be given to the church and, even more specifically, to our own local church where we meet. The Lord is very specific about this. 3) Tithing is for the purpose of teaching us to honor, reverence, and stand in awe of the Lord. It teaches us to fear and honor the Lord and gives us a proper heart posture towards both God and money. Verse 23 tells us tithing is about learning to respect God's place as King and acknowledge His right to say where the tithe goes.

In verses 24 through 26, we see that God is not a hard taskmaster. Tithing does not place a heavy burden on us. Rather, setting the tithe apart allows for feasting in the presence of the Lord and rejoicing over His provision. It could be spent on any type of feasting, whatever the heart's desire, if it was done with thankfulness and gratitude. This is why it baffles me when some churches are so stingy over how that provision is used. What is also interesting is Scripture clearly tells us that tithing absolutely does have to do with money.

How many times have we heard someone say the tithe has nothing to do with money, that it was about their crops, as a way of justifying themselves for not doing so as a modern-day believer? These verses clearly distinguish crops as their wealth, and those crops could be exchanged for money, which could be brought if it was too much of a burden to carry large amounts of crops long distances.

Verses 27 and 28 remind us of our responsibility to give the tithe to take care of our local area—our local pastors within our gates. The tithe is about taking care of those whose lives are devoted to full-time ministry and for the needs of the temple. God is asking us to use our money to value what He values. The command to *"not neglect the Levite in your town"* tells us it is our responsibility to return the tithe and take care of our own local houses of worship. It is not to be sent to another town.

The tithe is the provision God has planned for those who dedicate their lives to temple work. They *"don't have an inheritance among us,"* which means they do not have the ability or time to work their own land to capture their own wealth and provision. I have heard some people argue that the apostles worked to support themselves and ministered. However, what they fail to realize is that the apostles, although they had a right to claim financial support according to 1 Corinthians 9:11-13, sometimes worked to help support themselves because they were not tied to being full-time ministers in any one place. They would get a local body of believers built up and set a pastor over them, and then they would move on to the next assignment. Their full-time work was not in any one place.

According to verses 27 and 28, the tithe is also supposed to be used to take care of the *foreigners*. The foreigners are those who were not God's people, but who lived among them. Like the Levites, the foreigners also did not have access to own their own land in Israel. Land was a person's wealth, and the land belonged to God's people. Even still, God made a way for His people to care for the foreigners living legally among them, too, along with the widows and orphans.

God has ordained and set apart the tithe from those He has given wealth to care for others. If we have anything, we have wealth, and it is God's right to declare what the tithe of that wealth is to be used for. Notice God's economy had these groups of people cared for through the temple, and the tithe was specifically dedicated to those purposes. This is why we bless unbelievers with great acts of generosity. It helps them encounter God's love for them when they see His people use their wealth to bless them.

We understand from verse 29 that the tithe is about using a specific percentage of our money to take care of the things God cares about. In addition to taking care of our local ministers and houses of worship, the tithe is also to be used for taking care of the needs of the strangers, orphans, and widows of our local communities. If we all do this in our own local areas, every area is covered, and no place will be without. It is the Church's responsibility, not the government's. So why do we not even bat an eye at the government taking up to thirty percent of our income for these types of things, but we want to fight tithing a measly ten percent? Why are we okay with offloading the Church's responsibility for this care and denying how God wanted our economy set up?

We want to control where it goes by giving it to whatever ministry we want instead of where God said, or worse, we want to create doctrinal wars with other believers trying to justify our not doing it. When we fully obey Him, we show God that we care about what He cares about, that like King David, we are men after God's heart. This verse also shows us that through this covenant of trading with God, He then will bless us in all our work. If we do not work at something that produces wealth or income, then we are not giving God anything to bless.

We must participate in capturing provision. With the tithe, God does not take from us but rather invites us into partnership with Him. Verse 29 tells us that the tithe is about God's desire to bless us, not to take from us. For a trade to be a trade, both parties give something and both parties gain something. If only one gives and the other gains, that is a dictatorship.

Now, as we have touched on a little bit, tithing is different from sowing. We can sow into many different things, causes, ministries, or charities. Literally, anything can be seed, and seed can be any amount that we choose. After the designated ten percent goes to our local church for tithe, sowing is where we get to decide where our money goes. We have already established that tithing is trading with God, where both parties get something. God ensures that provision is set aside for the things He cares about, but what do we get other than what we are told in Deuteronomy 14:29, that all the work of our hands will be blessed? Tithing, when practiced following all the guidelines God says, comes with a certain set of benefits described in Malachi 3.

- The windows of heaven will open (It says the windows of heaven will open but does not say when they will open—it could be weeks, months, or years of God testing our faithfulness)
- Pour out uncontainable blessing; not enough room to even receive it
- Allowed to test God—this is the only area where we are both invited and encouraged to test God
- God will rebuke the devourer for our sakes, so that he (Satan) will not destroy the fruit of our ground (i.e., the crops from the things we sow into)—God Himself will rebuke Satan for us
- Our grapes will not fall from the vine before they are ripe—we won't experience crop failure
- All nations will call us blessed

Tithing acts as a protective fence around our domain, like a moat around a castle. The windows of heaven will open above our domain and pour out blessings upon all we put our hand to within that domain, but we still must grow something on that land. What we plant on our land is what will be blessed and protected. What are we growing? We decide what and how much to grow. Are we growing one apple tree or a hundred? Are we growing nothing? If we are growing from zero to one, then we cannot complain when the harvest is small.

The more we grow, the more work will be involved in harvesting those apples once they have grown. This is why financial blessing and work ethic are tied together. We cannot tithe our way into wealth, but without tithing our wealth, what we grow gets devoured by pests and does not have the open window of heaven over it. The benefits listed in Malachi 3 are promised specifically to tithers and only when all three requirements governing tithing are followed.

As New Testament believers, we are not required to tithe to be part of this new covenant. It is a free-will choice. However, Hebrews 7:8 (NKJV) says, *"Here mortal men receive tithes, but there he receives them, of whom it is witnessed that he lives."* This scripture tells us that while mortal men receive our tithes here, Jesus receives them in heaven. This was written to New Testament believers. When we bring our finances to the Lord in this manner in the natural, Jesus, who is our High Priest, receives them "there" directly, as an act of our worship. That should make us want to run to the altar with our everything!

We do not tithe to get or earn something; we tithe because He has already blessed us so abundantly with grace, mercy, and forgiveness. In this way, the tithe is freely given as an act of worship for having been set free, not because we are trying to avoid some Old Testament curse. Tithing is an outward display of the inward devotion of our hearts. When the tithe is given in this manner, we are choosing to honor Him. As in the marriage covenant, we do not enter that covenant out of our desire to have those blessings. Even though we get those blessings in marriage, we marry because of our love and devotion to the one we marry. If we marry for any other reason, we should not even bother, and the same is true with tithing. If we are going to do it out of duty or obligation, do not even bother.

God wants our devotion, not our money unless that money is simply an expression of our devotion. If we are going to enter this covenant relationship of tithing with Him, it must be out of love and devotion to Him only from a heart seeking to honor Him with our possessions. Also, just like marriage, once we are in it, we are in it. If we are going to enter this covenant, we enter it for life. We do not want to commit financial adultery or financial divorce. Doing so gives the devourer the legal right to devour our crops. If we have done so, we must repent and either renew our vows or choose to stay out of the covenant if we cannot remain faithful to it.

One last important distinction regarding the tithe is that the tithe is not given; it is brought. Scripture doesn't tell us to "give" the tithe; it tells us to "bring" the tithe. This is very important language. We don't give the tithe; we return it. If I have a business partner, when they are paid their appropriate percentage of ownership, I am not giving them a gift. I am returning to them what *is already theirs*. In the same way, if we choose to enter the covenantal relationship of tithing with the Lord, thereby making Him our partner, when we tithe, we are simply returning what already belongs to Him, which is His by right; it is not an offering we are making. If my child brings me ten dollars out of my own wallet, they aren't giving me a gift or an offering; they are returning what is already mine, and it would be absurd for them to behave as if they were giving me a gift. Yet so many Christians act like they are the ones doing God a favor by "giving" Him the tithe. Again, it isn't given, it is returned because it's already His.

NUMBER THREE:
GIVING TO THE POOR (ALMS)

The last type of giving mentioned in the Bible is a specific type of sowing called giving to the poor. Both the practices of tithing and sowing and reaping are different than giving to the poor. Giving to the poor is a specific type of sowing and is a completely different aspect of giving that comes with its own benefits and rewards. Some of these verses (NLT) are as follows:

- Proverbs 11:24-25: *"Give freely and become more wealthy; be stingy and lose everything. The generous will prosper; those who refresh others will themselves be refreshed."*
- Proverbs 19:17: *"If you help the poor, you are lending to the Lord—and he will repay you!"*

- Proverbs 14:21: *"It is a sin to belittle one's neighbor; blessed are those who help the poor."*
- Proverbs 14:31: *"Those who oppress the poor insult their Maker, but helping the poor honors him."*
- Proverbs 28:27: *"Whoever gives to the poor will lack nothing, but those who close their eyes to poverty will be cursed."*
- Deuteronomy 15:10: *"Give generously to the poor, not grudgingly, for the* LORD *your God will bless you in everything you do."*
- 2 Corinthians 9:9: *"... They share freely and give generously to the poor. Their good deeds will be remembered forever."*

Read 2 Corinthians 9:6-8.

A lot of modern-day Christians use this passage to try and justify not tithing or to try and say that the tithe does not have to be ten percent specifically, but that is not what is happening here. This passage does not discuss the tithe. It is a discussion about taking up a collection for the believers in Jerusalem who were experiencing great persecution and poverty, then leads right into verse 9, which confirms they are talking about sharing freely and giving generously to the poor, not tithing. This is why it tells us not to do so out of guilt or compulsion.

Imagine how we would feel if we were the ones experiencing a need, and other believers gave but had an attitude and did not really want to or gave only out of guilt. This shames and dishonors the poor, which is why we are told that if we cannot give cheerfully to not even bother. If we have so little understanding that what we give is going to come back to us because God promises it as a personal debt, then we should keep our gift. Who wants a gift someone does not even want to give?

This is also why Paul reminds them of the principle of sowing and reaping and how seed gets multiplied, producing a harvest for the one who sowed it, so we should not be afraid to give to the poor. When we cheerfully give of our provision to meet a need for someone else, it comes with the promise that God will generously provide everything we need with plenty left over.

Read Philippians 4:15-19.

This is another passage many believers take out of context when talking about receiving the provision of God. When read in context, we see it was because they supplied Paul's needs that God will supply their need. Because they first sowed into Paul's need, they will reap God supplying all their needs, not just a single need. This is another passage showing us the power of partnership. They supplied Paul's need (singular) and got all their needs (plural) met. Just like Peter supplied Jesus's need with his boat (singular) and had provisions (multiple nets and boats) multiplied back to him.

This is the exact same concept. However, instead of understanding what is happening here, too many believers try to cherry pick verse 19 as a catch-all that God will provide everything they want without acknowledging that this only comes after partnering with a kingdom assignment. Paul is not making a generic promise here; he is making an apostolic declaration based on these believers partnering with his assignment and receiving his assignment as their own.

The promise given by Jesus in Luke 6:38 also applies to giving to the poor as well as supporting other kingdom assignments. Jesus lets us know that it is silly to withhold giving gifts to those who are in need because kingdom law says it will be returned to us along with more than we gave in the first place. If I were out of town and one of my children needed money for something, I would ask one of their siblings to cover the need, assuring them I would pay them back. How silly would it be for them to have a bad attitude about it or withhold from their sibling, unless, of course, they do not trust that I would honor my word?

Having an attitude about giving to those in need exposes the real issue in our hearts of not trusting that our Father is good for it and will keep His word. Otherwise, we would not even hesitate. These scriptures try to communicate that by encouraging us to go ahead and give generously to those in need. Again, this isn't tithing whatsoever; it is a form of sowing called giving to the poor.

When we sow, we can sow into any field, into any assignment, into any need that arises, or whatever things are important to us, but we must look for good soil. One last thing that needs to be mentioned is when we look for assignments to partner with, a ministry "begging" for money, claiming they have this need or that need, and seeking to make people feel sorry for them is not good soil. These completely lack faith, so we want to ensure we are not partnering with lack.

It is completely different than a ministry with a need in full expectation of God meeting that need and merely inviting people to partner with them and share the reward. In faith, they are seeking kingdom-minded investors. This is completely different from ministries that do not operate in faith and feel the need to resort to manipulation and guilt tactics to extract finances from people. They do not actually believe God for anything; they just want the hand-outs and are too lazy to do the deep heart work to discover why they are merely playing church and not operating in faith at all. If we are looking for an assignment to sow into, especially with a specific harvest, we do not want to partner with a poverty spirit here. It will kill our crops.

It is okay to give to those needs should we want to, but that is not a ministry where we would want to sow seed for the purpose of a specific harvest. When choosing where to sow, it is important to be aligned with a ministry that operates in faith. We want to partner where they fully expect and trust God to meet their needs, and if they happen to mention their need, it is not for the purpose of soliciting donations, manipulation, or trying to guilt people into paying their bills for them, but rather for finding people of faith to partner with them on that assignment. When we sow, we come into agreement and partner with that ministry. If we are partnering with a ministry that is always crying poor, always crying about what they lack, then we are agreeing with lack, and it will kill our harvest.

If we know we are giving to the poor, our gift will still come back to us, but we need to find different soil to sow into when we are believing for a big and abundant harvest of something specific. A side note on giving to the poor: I have heard many well-meaning Christians say they will not give money to homeless people because "they will just spend it on alcohol." I would like to challenge those who think this way to read Proverbs 3:6-7.

If we were living in those conditions, we may drink to forget our poverty as well. Our job is not to judge what they do with it; our job is for our hearts to be moved with compassion for them. If drinking to forget their poverty provides comfort, let them drink. We need to quit being so religious and quit hiding behind that religion as an excuse not to take care of someone in such poverty.

GROWING IN LEVELS OF PROSPERITY

Now that we have the types of giving and their benefits clarified, I want to dial in specifically on sowing and reaping a little more and how we can begin to put this principle into practice to grow in levels of prosperity. Again, this principle of sowing and reaping governs every single area of life, not just finances, and it is one of the most basic laws of the kingdom of God and how to receive. It is a powerful principle that we can tap into to grow in greater and greater levels of prosperity.

If we look at 2 Corinthians 9:10 (NKJV), we find a pattern within this principle of sowing that we can begin to use to transform us financially. It says: "*Now may He who supplies seed to the sower, and bread for food, supply and multiply the seed you have sown and increase the fruits of your righteousness.*"

Hidden within this scripture, there are progressive levels of operating within God's system. It is like playing a video game where we master one level and then move on up to the next. We level up. There are levels to God's prosperity plan. Which level we live in depends on mastering and overcoming the one we are in. Some people never do and remain impoverished or continuously stuck at a certain level. It is also important to clarify that some people are born into wealth, but it does not mean they serve God. There is absolutely an earthly way to gain wealth, but that way comes with sorrow.

Why did Jesus say it was difficult for rich people to enter the kingdom of heaven? Many people mistake this to mean salvation, but that is not what He is talking about. He is saying it is much harder for them to seek first the kingdom for their provision because they have provision right in front of them that is much easier to trust in. Many people have riches, but do not live kingdom life. If we want to grow in prosperity the kingdom way, 2 Corinthians 9:10 gives us an outline for doing so.

The first level of prosperity is God gives *"seed to the sower."* God gives seed to the one already sowing. He gives to one who sows first, not to the one who will sow or who intends to sow. Also notice it does not say He gives seed to the one who has sown. This is present tense, meaning He gives seed to the one who is in constant sowing mode who knows sowing is a lifestyle, not an event. Again, this is not tithing. Sowing does not begin until after tithes have been returned. As we are faithful in the tithe, the windows of heaven open, and we can grow more and more in what we sow. As we are faithful to sow, He will give us more seed, which may be in many forms, not just money.

The second level is after He gives seed to the sower, *"then bread for food."* He does not give the food, then the seed to sow. We can only eat of a harvest already sown. God wants our needs met, and we are allowed to eat from the harvests we get. This is where lifestyle comes in. It is okay to have nice things, enjoy nice things, and increase in property. However, first things first—our foundation must be strong. We must be obedient to sow, giving Jesus full check-writing privileges to tell us to sow any amount into any assignment. At this level of prosperity, we are sowing and growing. We have seed to sow, and our needs are met.

The third level of prosperity in 2 Corinthians 9:10 is where God "*then multiplies the seed*" we have sown. He not only gives us seed to provide for our needs, but He multiplies the seeds that are sown. (Notice, the only seeds that are being multiplied are the ones that have been sown, not the seeds we intended to sow but ate for bread instead.) How much lag time in the wilderness we experience between sowing and harvesting depends on how obedient and faithful we have dealt with our trust and integrity issues. Until those weeds are out of our soil, our crop will not thrive and multiply. Only a healthy crop can multiply, and this is the stage where things get really exciting!

Look at one apple seed. How many apple trees can that one seed produce? At first, just one tree. But as soon as that one tree produces apples, how many more seeds, thereby how many more apple trees, can each of those seeds contain? The number is endless, all from just one seed! One seed sown into good soil, taken care of, properly watered, and pruned in season can do all that. Now apply that to every seed sown! We cannot even wrap our minds around the limitlessness contained in one single seed. God will multiply what we sow.

In Luke 6:38, Jesus is literally saying to us, "For every dollar you sow, you will get it back in full, plus, pressed down, shaken together to make room for more, running over, dollars will be poured back into your lap." If people really believed this, they would be rushing down the aisle, climbing over each other, shoving others out of the way, waiting in line for hours for a chance to put their money into the kingdom. Could you imagine if a casino made a promise like this for every dollar put into their kingdom? People would be shoving each other out of the way for their chance there as well.

So why don't we see this in the church at offering time? We have this promise from King Jesus Himself, and yet, how many people empty their wallets, pockets, etc., at every offering? The only conclusion I can draw is because maybe they do not actually believe this promise? If they did, they would throw every possible dollar they could into the offering for that kind of return! We must decide: Jesus is either a liar, or He is not. This is either the truth, or it is not. I empty my wallet almost every time I come into God's house. Why? Because I believe what Jesus says, and no investment on earth will give me that kind of return!

I do not say that to impress you; I say it to impress upon you the fact that actions demonstrate beliefs. I would rather invest in the offering plate than in stocks. That does not mean I don't do both. Both are important. My natural investments give me additional seed for spiritual ones. I am just more interested in spiritual investments than natural ones because they are the types of investments no recession can touch. They never rust or decay. I know the power of this truth and what it has done in my life, and I know God is faithful and a rewarder of those who seek Him, especially in finances, because it takes faith and trust that His Word is true to do that. I can say I have faith all day long, but my faith is shown by what I do with that belief in the Word, not just what I say about it. Faith without action is dead[59].

Now, what if we are sowing into something hazardous? Remember, this is a principle. When we sow, we get that crop, good and bad! When the Bible says "whatever" we sow, it means whatever! We must be careful what we sow our time, talent, and treasure into. This third level seems to be where most sincere, dedicated Christians stop. They are sowing, their lifestyle has increased, and they are harvesting what has been multiplied back so they have abundance. They then reach a plateau, thinking they are on top or they have "arrived" financially speaking, when all the time God has a higher level.

The fourth level of prosperity is God "*will increase the fruit of our righteousness*." This is where we break through to supernatural abundance, referred to as "increasing the fruit of our righteousness." Righteousness is a life of obedience, listening to God, and obeying what He says to do. This is the level of supernatural abundance so few reach because of the level of trust and obedience required to get here. In Genesis 26, we find the story where Isaac, who was Abraham's promised child, was now a grown man living in a particular land where there was a famine. Isaac planned to leave, but God interrupted his plan and initiated a trade with Isaac. Starting in verses 2-3 (NLT) it says, "*The Lord appeared to Isaac and said, "Do not go down to Egypt, but do as I tell you. Live here as a foreigner in this land, and I will be with you and bless you. I hereby confirm that I will give all these lands to you and your descendants, just as I solemnly promised Abraham, your father.*" In verses 12-13 (NLT), we see the result of Isaac's obedience, "*When Isaac planted his crops that year, he harvested a hundred times more grain than he planted, for the LORD blessed him. He became a very rich man, and his wealth continued to grow.*"

Notice that this whole scenario was initiated by God, not Isaac. After living in blessing for quite some time, the Lord will test our allegiance again and usually invite us into a trade, asking us to do something specific that will appear to have an immediate negative impact on our financial situation. In this case, God asked Isaac to take a direct financial hit by staying in a land experiencing famine. God will usually ask us to sacrifice the very thing that was our blessing. We saw this same pattern with God and Abraham, Isaac's father. God promised Abraham a son. Not just any son but an heir to his blessing. After many years of waiting, Abraham finally had his son Isaac and was raising him. Abraham finally had his promised blessing.

Right about that time, God asked Abraham to sacrifice that very blessing as an act of worship back to Him, which would have been an immediate lifestyle change. It also would have meant no heir to pass his wealth to and the death of every other promise God had given Abraham. He would have no descendants to inherit the Promised Land. Even knowing the great cost, Abraham did not withhold what God requested. As a result, Abraham passed the test, moved into the realm of supernatural abundance, and kept his son. This one act of faith is the very thing that gave God the legality to create His son in human form and sacrifice Him on the Cross.

Just like with his father, because of Isaac's obedience to God's request to stay in a famine-infested land, Isaac was able to experience hundredfold returns on every investment he made. Ironically, the very land where God asked Isaac to stay was the very land God promised to give Abraham and his descendants. Even though it was not yet time for those descendants to drive out the inhabitants and possess the land, Isaac's staying was a prophetic act of what was to come and that the Israelites would experience blessing even in a famine experienced by everyone else.

Why was Isaac able to experience one-hundred-fold blessings on his crops while planting them in a famine? Because Isaac did not just sow seeds, he made a sacrifice. Every seed he sowed into this famine-infested land was a sacrifice. His sacrifice was also in doing what God wanted instead of what He wanted. He sacrificed his own will to move somewhere else in submission to God's will. That is what brings the breakthrough. Sacrifice is the offering of anything to God in worship, the giving up of something valuable for the sake of gaining something greater. It is looking beyond today and seeing tomorrow even when it looks like we will be experiencing the death of our very blessing. It is planting into the kingdom of God by faith, not what we will but what He wills. This is not something we can initiate but rather comes to us by direct ask from God.

Read Matthew 10:29-30.

A sacrifice is always a seed, but a seed is not always a sacrifice. When we make a sacrifice, it always becomes a seed planted into God's kingdom, but we can also sow seed without it really being a sacrifice. A seed is what we determine in our hearts and will take us all the way to level three, but it takes sacrifice to move to the next level. Sacrifice requires an immediate lifestyle change and is given by the bidding of the Lord. This comes only after living at level three. Notice we cannot use our will to get our way in on this. The cover charge is whatever He asks us to give.

A seed is what we give voluntarily based on our own will. A sacrifice is what God asks us to do, requiring total obedience and the absolute submission of our will or plans to the will of God. This is where great prosperity lies—not just in tithes and offerings or sowing of seeds—in the increase of the fruits of our righteousness as we obey what God says, like Abraham and Isaac.

As long as the earth exists, there shall always be seedtime and harvest. If we want to flow in the kingdom of God on this earth, we must operate on this principle of sowing and reaping but not in the religious terms we have been taught. Get in covenant partnership with God and ditch the legalism mindset. It will be life-changing.

CLASS 4
STUDY GUIDE AND JOURNAL

Invite the Holy Spirit into this time of reflection and ask the Lord to reveal anything and everything He wants to reveal. Ask Him to shine His light into every dark place and to renew your mind to His truth.

Key Scripture: *Of the increase of His government and peace there will be no end, upon the throne of David and over His kingdom, to order it and establish it with judgment and justice from that time forward, even forever. The zeal of the Lord of hosts will perform this."* Isaiah 9:7 NKJV

Was Jesus poor and homeless? Why or why not?

According to Matthew 6:25-33, what type of provision does Jesus promise to always provide?

In Matthew 6:10, Jesus lets us know we can pray and invite God's kingdom rule into our lives here on earth. What area or situation are you facing that you can invite God's kingdom law and promises to override the laws of the earth?

What promise in Scripture relating to your situation can you find and begin to plant in your heart?

What does Mark 16:17-18 promise?

What does Luke 10:19 promise?

Based on these promises, write out a verbal decree taking authority over the enemy and kicking him out of any area you see Him at work.

Find a minimum of three Scripture promises regarding the provision, prosperity, and health of God's children. Then read these promises repeatedly, at least five days per week to plant the seed in your heart.

At the time it's planted, a seed looks like a seed, not the picture on the package of what it is promised to develop into. Now that you have planted the seeds, spend at least five minutes every morning imagining the picture of what it looks like to have the promise fulfilled. Feel what it would feel like. As you imagine and feel your desired outcome, thank the Lord out loud that the seed is growing, sprouting, and producing to bring the picture to life. You must be able to see it on the inside before ever seeing it on the outside. Write a "thank you" note to God.

What does Proverbs 6:31 promise you can do to the thief?

According to this promise, use your words to issue a decree of judgment against the enemy and demand his repayment and recompense according to Scripture.

What promise have you been waiting for the Lord to fulfill?

Are you fully persuaded that He has already sent the answer? If not, what keeps you from being fully persuaded that you will have it?

What does James 1:6-7 tell us about what happens when we are not fully persuaded?

Read Matthew 13:3-23. What type of soil best describes the current condition of your heart?

Does the soil of your heart need more sunlight, air, water, or perhaps to be plowed to break up the hard, crusty places? Explain.

Has Satan planted weeds of alternative outcomes in your heart? If so, what has he planted to keep you from being fully persuaded that God's promise is yours?

Write Galatians 6:7.

What are some unwanted harvests you've been reaping?

Based on these unwanted harvests, what do you need to stop sowing?

Seed reproduces after its own kind. What can you sow to bring about a harvest of something you need or desire?

In Malachi 3, what promises does God give to tithers?

What are some of God's promises to those who give to the poor? (See Deuteronomy 15:10-11, Proverbs 10:24-25, 14:21,31, Matthew 6:4, and Acts 10:31 for some examples.)

Have you been mistakenly doing one type of giving and expecting the benefits of another? Explain.

Write 2 Corinthians 9:10.

What are the four levels of prosperity described in 2 Corinthians 9:10?

1.

2.

3.

4.

What level of prosperity do you think you're at right now?

How can you become more sacrificial when it comes to giving?

To receive a prophet's reward, what kingdom assignments can you partner with to create both natural and spiritual rewards?

CLASS 5

BUILDING GOD'S KINGDOM, NOT OURS

"For he has rescued us from the kingdom of darkness and transferred us into the Kingdom of his dear Son."

COLOSSIANS 1:13 NLT

We have spent a lot of time in the first few classes laying a scriptural foundation for understanding who we are in Christ and what we are entitled to as co-heirs and citizens of the kingdom of heaven. From Colossians 1:13, we see it is of utmost importance to remember we now belong to a different kingdom. Every kingdom has a king who rules it, so as citizens of this kingdom, our allegiance, obedience, and duty is to this King. This means it is now our reasonable act of worship and service to spend our lives building and advancing His kingdom for His glory, and we should lay aside all desire to build up our lives for our own sake. We must think of everything we own or manage as kingdom property.

Doing this helps us overcome the lies of a poverty spirit and proves scripturally how God views the prosperity of His children. His kingdom is prosperous, multiplies, and grows; therefore, everything under the domain of His children should do the same. Hopefully, by now, we all are convinced from a biblical perspective of the reasons why God's children should want prosperity: because every dollar is used to advance God's kingdom, not for Satan. The harvest that awaits will take a tremendous sum of finances to reap it. It takes money to send missionaries, build orphanages, and train and equip new believers. Where is all this money going to come from? It comes from kingdom people willing to do what it takes to possess it, without becoming possessed by it, and who are willing to give it up for the kingdom's sake once they have it.

It will also take effort to create enough money so this work gets done by strong, diligent, aggressive, and militant people of faith willing to see their paychecks spread the gospel instead of just paying their bills. It is living too small to be so focused on our own provision or just our own families. God has a mission to reach the whole world with the good news of His kingdom. He is looking for believers who will partner with Him in that mission by seeing beyond the provision of their own needs and being willing to grow and be trusted with the wealth it will take to reap the end time harvest. In fact, Jesus told us believers not to worry about our basic needs at all, that those kinds of thoughts consume the minds of non-children or unbelievers.[60]

Our source of income, whatever it may be, is often the master on which we usually base our life decisions. We let our jobs, businesses, and bank balances tell us what we can and cannot do with our lives more than we let the Spirit of God tell us. Because of the fear of losing our lifestyles, we trust or rely on the provision we already have from these sources, instead of obeying and then receiving the provision yet to come for those who obey. This would be like Abraham waiting to see the ram in the thicket before putting Isaac on the altar. Isaac was the literal and tangible fulfillment of God's promise to Abraham. Until Abraham was not only ready and willing to obey but also taking the step to let go of Isaac—his promise—the supernatural provision of God did not show up.

It is no different with believers today. We all want the supernatural provision of God, yet few of us are willing to fully release into the kingdom the provision in our hands. Why? I believe it is fear of loss. We fear losing our possessions, money, homes, cars, and comfort. Even though most people are hanging onto these things by a thread, we want to hold on to what we have and ask God to send us more. We often use the false excuse that once we have "more" we will sacrifice it all for God's kingdom. However, if we are not willing to part with what is already in our hands, we won't part with the "more" either. The only way to overcome this fear is to make Jesus the Master of our money, no matter the cost. Money is nothing but a tool we trade with.

Read Luke 16:9-13.

What did Jesus say money is to be used for? To meet people's needs (benefit others) and to "*make friends.*" [61]Why does He say this? Because success gives us a platform! The world is looking for answers, for results, not for people who quote scriptures at them. Why is the information industry such a big deal? Because people are looking for other people who have gotten the results they want or need and are begging to be shown how to achieve those same results. Demonstrating success in any given area gives us a platform, causing other people to listen because they want to know our "secret" of how to achieve the results they desire.

Why do so many people follow celebrities? Their success gives them a platform because they seem to have achieved the impossible, and other people want to know their secret to success. They look up to these celebrities for the financial success they have achieved, allowing these celebrities they do not even know to have influence over them. These celebrities influence how their followers behave, dress, what they listen to or watch, the things they buy, and even certain medical decisions. Success makes other people want to listen to us. Would we take diet and exercise advice from someone who weighs five hundred pounds? No, because they have not been successful in achieving healthy results. We find someone who has been where we are and who has overcome the same problem we have, hoping to learn how we can overcome it, too. Success gives us a platform of influence.

The same is true with finances. We look for gurus or teachers we hope can give us the answers to our struggles. People followed Jesus because He demonstrated results. John 2:23 (NLT) tells us, *"Because of the miraculous signs Jesus did in Jerusalem at the Passover celebration, many began to trust in Him."* In Matthew 11 and Luke 7, when John the Baptist sent his disciples to Jesus asking if He was the Messiah they had been expecting, or should they keep looking for someone else, Jesus doesn't respond with, "Tell John how I can perfectly quote and explain the scriptures." Jesus says, *"Go back to John and tell him…the blind see, the lame walk, those with leprosy are cured, the deaf hear, the dead are raised to life, and the Good News is being preached to the poor."*[62]

Jesus did not just give people platitudes, nice sayings, or simply quote Scripture at them. Jesus demonstrated and lived out the results of the very scriptures He quoted. Jesus did not just talk about what God can do; He demonstrated it. He produced the results people were looking for, which gave Him the platform to share the good news. He did not preach a sermon to them and then have a prayer line for healing. He healed them and met their need, and then shared the good news of the kingdom with them. Getting the results of the kingdom in action first made them more willing to listen. He addressed physical needs with as much attention as spiritual ones. Notice that preaching is mentioned last by Jesus on the list in Matthew 11:5. The good news is preached after producing physical results that changed people's lives.

As kingdom people, when we go from a life of poverty and struggling to pay our bills, to being able to pay cash for things like cars and houses, people will notice. We better believe they are going to ask us how we did it! Then, we will have a platform to share the kingdom with them. The problem is that we are trying to share the kingdom in theory, getting people to "buy in" to Jesus and how His kingdom should work; meanwhile, we have no results in our own lives. Do we think people want to share in our poverty, illness, or whatever? Do we think they want our Jesus when our lives look as bad or worse than theirs do? When we can demonstrate how we overcame the same struggles they have, then not only are they willing to listen, but they will also come begging us to share how we did it.

Our lives will preach far more than our words ever will. This is why testimonies are so powerful and why almost every successful company uses testimonials in their marketing efforts. When someone testifies to having already achieved the desired results, that builds belief in others that they can and will achieve it, too. They then demonstrate that belief by "buying in" and ordering that product or service. The same holds true for the kingdom of God. We are attempting to give away Jesus without first building people's belief by demonstrating testimonies of what Jesus has already done in our lives and how the kingdom has already produced results.

In Luke 16, Jesus tells us plainly that if we are not faithful with what is His, we will not be given what is our own. If we are not faithful with how we handle worldly wealth (the lowest benchmark), we will not be trusted with true riches—people He wants us to lead into the kingdom. We duplicate what we are, so if we are not trustworthy with our relationship with money, we could damage the crop by reproducing that same tendency. Matthew 24:45 (NLT) tells us, "*A faithful, sensible servant is one to whom the master can give the responsibility of managing his other household servants and feeding them.*" That is the true riches.

In the parable of the talents found in Matthew 25, we see God expects us to take the talents we are given, trade with them in the marketplace, and convert them into income. The master expected the servant to build his kingdom with the talents he gave them. The parable ends with this warning in verse 29 (NLT), "*To those who use well what they are given, even more will be given, and they will have an abundance. But from those who do nothing, even what little they have will be taken away.*"

Jesus is telling us again how the principle of sowing and reaping governs everything in our lives—those who use well what they are given will reap even more. Those who sow nothing reap nothing. Every servant is provided for, but only those who use well what they have will be given abundance. What is the seed being sown here? Faith-based action. The seed is taking the talents we have been given and trading with them. Those who are lazy and sit on their talents will experience even what little they have being taken away. So this is not a "bless me" prosperity gospel used to justify greed. There is nothing passive about this. The lazy servant can try and claim a harvest all they want, but without the work of putting seed in the ground, their claims mean nothing.

On the other hand, it is our duty to use every resource we are given to build our Master's kingdom, not our own personal kingdom. However, without amassing those resources and instead continuing to accept poverty as some sort of virtue instead of the curse that it is, we will be extremely limited in our ability to contribute to building the kingdom. That is why we have spent so much time learning about getting our hearts and minds right first because being trusted to steward a vast amount of wealth requires total obedience and submission to what God says.

People say, "Well, I don't have much of anything right now, but if God ever blesses me, then I will give." These people have it backward. If God tells us to hand over our car keys to someone in need while we are driving a junky old car, do we think that decision is easier when we are driving a Mercedes? If our hearts are not trained in obedience first, we will use wealth to build our kingdom instead of His, amassing wealth, property, and stuff to feed our greed instead of advancing His kingdom. It is not wrong to own or possess nice things as long as those things do not own and possess us. Kingdom purpose comes first.

Read Luke 12:15-20.

Proverbs 10:16 (NLT) says, "*The earnings of the godly enhance their lives, but evil people squander their money on sin.*" It is okay for money to enhance our lives, but it is not okay to squander it on sin or to use it to amass vast amounts of earthly possessions that have no eternal significance. Notice that it says "*earnings,*" not "winnings" or "freebies." This means to either invest our time for working income or to invest our money for earned income on those investments or both. Nowhere does the Bible advocate for laziness or hoping to strike it rich in one fell swoop like the lottery. That person has not learned how to earn and manage, so quick riches will grow wings and fly away. Proverbs 23:5 (NLT) says, "*In the blink of an eye wealth disappears, for it will sprout wings and fly away like an eagle.*"

The more we amass, the more someone else will get when we die. Every time we buy something, all we are doing is borrowing it until we die. What if we used all those dollars to invest in expanding God's kingdom instead? We can buy possessions; however, if spending money on possessions causes us to be unable to fund kingdom assignments, we are unfaithful servants. It's all about our priorities. This is not a warning against owning or having nice things, but rather of wealth and possessions having the wrong priority in our hearts. How do we have a rich relationship with God? By caring about what He cares about. That is what it means to be a man after God's own heart—care for the things He cares for—people!

As kingdom builders, it is our responsibility to use wealth to harvest people, not possessions. Amassing wealth is the means, not the end. If our hearts are not trained in obedience first, we will build our own kingdoms, like the rich man, storing up our own stuff and amassing possessions that ultimately profit nothing.

Read Luke 12:33 and Matthew 19:21-24.

What does Jesus mean? He means it is much harder for rich people to trust God as their source instead of trusting in their money for their answers. It is easy to trust God when we have nothing left to trust in, but how easy is it to trust God when we have plenty? This is why preparing for abundance has more to do with renewing our hearts and minds to the Word of God and obedience through developing a spirit of excellence, tithing, sowing seeds, and giving to the poor.

There is no way around it; there is no magic formula. We can apply worldly wisdom to amass wealth, too, but that is not the same as true riches. People can certainly become wealthy outside of the kingdom and principles of God, but they are generally stressed out and fear losing their money or someone stealing it from them. No matter how much they have, it is never enough. There is a difference between being rich and being blessed. I will take being blessed over being rich because it does not come with sorrow. If I am blessed, I am blessed. My emotions are not tied to the ebb and flow of the financial tide. I can be rich without being blessed. Pharoah was rich; Solomon was blessed.

We have covered in previous classes that in Christ, we have an inheritance. However, there is a difference between an heir who simply benefits from the provision (just having their needs provided for) and an heir who gets administration of the estate. As with heirs to any estate, the inheritance does not just impart power and provision; it can also impart position. Many can be beneficiaries, but not many get to hold the position of administrator. By the time my husband and I pass away, we could have many grandchildren who will be beneficiaries of our estate and will be provided for. However, they will not all inherit the position of managing the companies, assets, and money we leave behind and have the administration of dispersing it and caring for the other heirs. Only our children who have demonstrated faithfulness, obedience, and a strong work ethic will inherit the position of CEO. Those who have been lazy, greedy, or foolish with money will still be provided for, but they will not inherit authority to manage the abundance of the estate. To leave someone like that in charge would jeopardize the estate and the well-being of all the other heirs.

Position involves promotion. Only those who have proven trustworthy enough to handle the magnitude of authority that comes with holding the position get promoted to the position of becoming the one in charge of the estate. They become responsible for managing, protecting, and growing what was left to them (the stuff), but just as importantly, they are also responsible for caring for, providing for, or taking in any persons associated with the estate—the family members, the household servants, or those left behind as orphans.

They have the responsibility of caring for and raising the orphans. The one holding the position of administrator does not get one without the other. He does not get the authority over how the provision is used without acquiring the responsibility to care for the people. There is an entire planet of orphaned people who have been kidnapped by sin, waiting (even unknowingly) for the heirs of freedom to not only let them know they can be free too but to prove it to them by first demonstrating the freedom we proclaim in our own lives.

As children of God, we should be the healthiest, most energetic, most joyful, and most financially free people on the planet. So we can just have fun? No! Because people need to see us live out what our inheritance says we are entitled to. As mentioned before, people are drawn to success stories. They give them hope that maybe it could one day happen for them, too. People are in famine, looking for answers. They crave a way out of the rat race of constantly chasing provision—a way to "beat the system." They do not know it is a cursed system brought on us all by Adam that comes with sin, death, decay, sickness, and painful toil for provision.

In addition, they certainly do not know Jesus bought us out of that. Heck, most Christians do not even know it! If the very children of God cannot even break out of this bankrupt, poverty-stricken way of life, why on earth would lost people want a powerless version of the salvation and gospel we proclaim?! Think of any cultural icon. Did anyone listen to them or care what they had to say before they were successful?

Our financial success provides a platform that makes others want to listen. Our success in all that we do makes others take notice and see God! When average, everyday, normal people suddenly demonstrate significant results, it causes the world to note that surely God must have done something. People think of promotion in terms of money, but what we are really being promoted to is more responsibility. Greater responsibility is what brings bigger paychecks. The world pays people to handle responsibility, to handle authority properly, and to solve problems. The bigger the problems we solve and the more responsibility we can handle, the bigger the income we receive.

There is a reason that brain surgeons are paid more than grocery clerks. I am not saying one job is more honorable than the other, but they differ greatly in the severity of problems they are required to solve. How we handle responsibility determines promotion, both naturally and spiritually. The favor, blessing, and prosperity of God in our lives means we make a difference to others to the effect that they see God. By handling every aspect of life with a spirit of excellence and by demonstrating kingdom results, people see there is something different in us—God.

This prosperity is not just for the benefit of the believer. Pastor Bill Johnson said, "The Holy Spirit is in me for my sake, but upon me for yours."[63] In Potiphar's house, Joseph was a slave, and yet God still gave him success in all that he did, even though Joseph did not own any of it. Joseph was continuously promoted wherever he was because of his ability to solve problems no one else could. Joseph's success was not for his own benefit, other than learning and growing in how to administrate and handle more and more responsibility. Joseph had to learn administration with excellence with someone else's stuff before he was ever given his own. So the success God gave Joseph in his assignment in Potiphar's house was not for Joseph's benefit but for Potiphar's. Pagan Potiphar! Joseph was trained to handle Potiphar's prosperity as his slave before he was given his own prosperity as a free man in the palace.

How responsible are we with what belongs to our boss, both naturally and spiritually? What attitude do we have about increasing our boss's wealth? Do we grumble and complain? Do we work as little as possible? Or, like Joseph, do we show ourselves faithful by using our talents to make our boss prosper and successful? Do we do all things with excellence to ensure our boss prospers? Luke 16:12 (NKJV) tells us, *"And if you have not been faithful in what is another man's, who will give you what is your own?"* Speaking of being faithful with what belongs to someone else, how responsible are we with the portion of our finances God says belongs to Him? As we make sure to grow the prosperity of the leaders or companies we serve in our jobs, the benefit to us is that we build a reputation God can use to promote us later. Proverbs 22:1 (KJV) says, *"A good name is more desirable than great riches."*

Ask any business owner what it would mean to them to have an employee who cared about the company's prosperity more than their own. That is exactly who a business owner would promote as far as possible. No matter where Joseph is—prison or the palace—he prospers. Our prosperity is not dependent on our location or position. Joseph prospered as unto the Lord. Even though it was not even Joseph's stuff, he served the Lord with his entire heart in whatever responsibility he was given. Joseph honors and serves the authority and master over him in the natural world while simultaneously serving his spiritual Master. His service to one is his service to another.

Joseph's life serves as an example that no matter what dark place we are in, we need to light it up with the light of Christ. For light to even be noticed or effective, it must encounter darkness. The darker the room, the more obvious the light becomes. How willing are we to go to dark and uncomfortable places so we can light it up? Even more, can we do this when we are not the ones who financially benefit? Joseph had eleven brothers, and although they had the provision of their father's house, none were promoted to the position of authority Joseph was. Their jealousy kept them from ever being able to achieve more and kept God from being able to put them in strategic positions of influence.

Matthew 5:16 (NKJV) tells us, *"Let your light so shine before men, that they may see your good works and glorify [God]!"* Who do they see by letting the light of excellence shine? God! Who will they glorify by seeing our good works? God! By the time Joseph got to stand before Pharaoh, Joseph was told, *"I have heard it said of you..."*[64] What is being said of us? Are we building a reputation that shines so bright it causes people of power and position to discuss us? It does not matter if we are cleaning toilets—Joseph was a slave, remember? The reason people continuously miss God's promotions is because they discount menial tasks. They think menial tasks are beneath them. If we are never willing to lower ourselves, we will never be raised higher.

People do not understand that it is in the menial tasks that God develops within them a spirit of excellence and integrity where they learn to be faithful with little. It all happens underground, when no one knows our names and we receive no recognition. That is where God trains our hearts not to be set on those things but to be set on Him. Then, He will show up with sudden promotion because we have been tested in loyalty and faithfulness to make prosperity happen where we are, even though our bank account is not necessarily the one that benefits. How can we expect to have employees who seek to prosper our company one day if we have not first been that employee for someone else?

With our freedom, we have responsibility. We should respond with our abilities (responsibility) and use that platform to first show them who God is. When that successful platform prepares them to listen, we then lead them to the same freedom. We are set free to set others free. We are set free to build His kingdom, not our personal kingdoms. How do we build His kingdom? By the assignments He gives us. We are invited to work with Him (not for Him) to bring others into the kingdom.

Read Galatians 6:2-5.

We do not work for freedom but walking in freedom does require action. It requires administrating areas of responsibility. Determine to walk in freedom in every area of life if for no other reason than someone else needs to see it happen. They need to see us be living testimonies of the kingdom of God. Joseph never preached a single sermon; he worked his entire life in the secular sector of society, yet his life impacted nations and generations. We see this same concept in the life of Daniel, who, although he served the pagan king Nebuchadnezzar in the natural, his motivation was to serve the God of the universe through his work with a spirit of excellence. We are called to serve a lost world, not just those already found. Anything and everything we do should be as unto the Lord. We just need to put our hands to something, and let God show us the problems and solutions, and then be willing to administer and manage those solutions.

HOW TO KNOW WHERE WE ARE CALLED TO SERVE

Our gifts, talents, and abilities are clues to what sector of society our assignments will be in. There seems to be much confusion in the Church regarding the difference between our purpose, our gifts, and our calling. So many Christians needlessly stress over "finding their purpose," as if it is something that alludes them. We are never called to pursue purpose; we are called to pursue Jesus. Anything and everything we do should express this. While we each have an individual purpose or unique things we can do, we all share the same calling—to expand the kingdom of God by sharing the good news with others. This is the calling that Jesus gave every disciple—sharing the freedom we have received with others and bringing other people into the kingdom.

Read Mark 16:15-20.

We all seem to get hung up on terms like "calling" and "purpose," not realizing that every gift, assignment, call, or purpose boils down to what Jesus told us to do—go into all the world to bring others to Jesus and build them up in the kingdom. Period. Every single thing people think they are "called" to do is really just a means to achieve the actual calling or outcome of reaching people for the kingdom. This passage does not say they all became pastors and preached. They went into all the world, not just into churches. All the world includes every sector of society. No matter what we call ourselves—pastor, teacher, apostle, evangelist, prophet, businessman, stay-at-home mom, etc., these are simply different assignments. They are ways we all achieve the same calling.

Every disciple has been given the same calling, power, and ability to demonstrate results of providing kingdom answers to people's problems. Notice it says, "*the disciples went everywhere,*" and they both preached the kingdom and demonstrated the results of the kingdom as "*the Lord worked through them, confirming what they said by many miraculous signs.*"[65]God only worked through those doing the work. This is not works-based salvation. They were not working for salvation; they were working from salvation. Their faith caused them to be obedient and do what Jesus told them to. So many people try to "find their calling" instead of just doing what Jesus said to do. They overcomplicate it. Even worse, there are many who sit around doing nothing until their ever-elusive calling just shows up in their lap. There is no passive or idle Christianity. We are told to follow Christ. We cannot follow someone sitting in a chair or on a couch. To follow anyone or anything, we must get up and move.

We all have the same collective purpose and calling—to worship God with our lives by being an expression of Him on earth and to go into every part of society and demonstrate the kingdom, giving us the open door to share the gospel with others. These two things are the same for all of us. We differ in the gifts, talents, abilities, and assignments we are given. Assignments vary from person to person and can even change individually at different times. The things that make us different are the things God gave us to make a difference.

Let us take a good friend of mine as an example. He founded an online ministry school that disciples and trains believers to go out and make more disciples. He has a talent for music and has served his local church as a worship pastor. He is a traveling minister, school starter, business owner, and author. Any of these assignments could be mistaken as the call on his life or his purpose. However, if examined more closely, we see these are simply different ways of manifesting our shared purpose.

Within these assignments, his gifts and talents all come into play and support how he fulfills his purpose and calling. What if he thought his seasonal assignment of worship pastor was his calling or purpose in life? He would miss out on the other assignments the Lord wants to give him. Some people may be given life-long assignments while others have designated time spans. This is why we must stay sensitive to the leading of the Holy Spirit and not get caught up in comparing ourselves to others.

We must not mistake assignments or talents as our purpose or calling. We can have many different assignments that can change throughout our lifetimes, yet in each of them, our call and purpose remain the same. Both things advance God's kingdom and push back the kingdom of darkness. The more talents we develop, the more places and things God can assign us to. He desires to assign us to situations where impossibilities must bow. We become qualified for greater responsibility and authority when we are willing to use all our resources, no matter the cost.

Our assignments, although usually bigger than us, will typically utilize skills, gifts, and talents we already have. These differ from the spiritual gifts, which are always in play. The Holy Spirit is within us, so the spiritual gifts imparted to us are with us no matter where we are or what we are doing. However, our kingdom assignments usually employ natural or physical gifts and talents that we have and are clues to the sector of society God wants us to reach and influence.

For example, let us look at the life of Peter. Peter was a fisherman when Jesus called him to follow Him and advance the kingdom of God (which was the same call given to all the disciples and us believers). However, Peter's given assignment to fulfill that call was fishing for men. This assignment to fish for men employed a skill Peter already had, which was fishing. This was not a spiritual gift; it was a natural one. Yet, it was used for a spiritual purpose. Peter's purpose was to worship God by being an expression of Jesus on the earth. His calling was to expand the kingdom by going into the world and telling people the good news of the kingdom and demonstrating it. He was assigned to a sector of Jewish people, and his natural talent for fishing supported him in fishing for men.

In Apostle Paul's life, we see he shared the same purpose and calling. The sector of society he was assigned to was the Gentiles, first in the marketplaces and then the churches that came out of that. His natural talent for making tents gave him a marketplace to interact with people and demonstrate the kingdom, all while building natural housing—tents. This same skill served him when his assignment changed to building up God's house—the people who make up the Church. He was building both natural houses and spiritual houses.

Many people get hung up on the idea of their purpose when we really should be concerned about where God wants us and what work He wants to assign us to. Our individual purpose is how we express Him. If we just work at what He assigns us to, we will automatically fulfill our purpose. Purpose is not about what we can do with our gifts. It is about those gifts being used in the Master's hands to build His kingdom instead of our own. For example, if I go to Home Depot and purchase different construction tools, such as a hammer, skill saw, tape measure, level, etc., these tools have now been redeemed. I purchased them from the kingdom of Home Depot and transferred them to mine. They are no longer under the jurisdiction of Home Depot; they are under mine. I have rescued them from a useless and empty existence of wasting away on a store shelf, not doing what they were created to do, and not accomplishing anything great.

Now that they have been bought with a price and been redeemed from the kingdom of Home Depot and transferred into my kingdom of Van Schaik Construction, Inc., they now have the potential to be used for their intended purpose. I did not redeem them just because they were bright, shiny, and beautiful. I knew the potential they were created to achieve and what I could do with them to build a more beautiful world and expand the reach and influence of my kingdom. I purchased them because I have a job—an assignment for them to fulfill.

In the project I need them for, they have a specific role only they can fulfill. Each tool has a unique design and function, and I know the potential it carries when in my hand. Apart from me, they can do nothing, but in the hands of a skilled master, they can be used to build something great. I can use them to build my kingdom with their unique and individual functions and talents. As long as they stay in their master's hands, they can accomplish great things. Now that they have been redeemed, they are responsible for being used for their specific functions. All these tools have the same collective purpose: to build. They have been called out of the kingdom of Home Depot to follow me and be used to build my kingdom.

In addition to all having the same collective purpose and calling, these tools also have an individual purpose. How they are uniquely gifted to fulfill and express the collective purpose of building is what their individual purpose is. The saw cuts. The hammer drives nails. The tape measure measures. The level balances and straightens. Even though each of these tools has a unique design and function to fulfill a particular purpose, they have the same collective purpose. Their individual purposes can be used for different assignments. I can use a hammer to drive nails or pull them. I can also use it to demolish something that needs to be torn down. No matter what assignment or job I give a certain tool, it still fulfills its purpose to build.

How I choose to put these tools into action is not their identity. Their assignments are not their identity or even their purpose; that would be limiting. If I said a hammer's purpose is to drive nails, or its identity is a nail driver, that limits it. Building is its purpose. Its assignment within that purpose could change. Its purpose is to build and create, but it can be used in many different assignments and ways to fulfill that purpose. It can be used to drive nails or to pull them. It can be used in demolition. It can be used to tap things into place. None of these things are its identity or its purpose.

Conversely, a hammer cannot be used to paint, nor can any of those tools for building. That would be trying to fulfill an assignment it was never intended to do. Even though painting and decorating can be a part of building, a hammer is not made or designed to fulfill that particular function. These tools (hammer, level, saw, etc.) are not designed to redecorate. They are designed to build the actual structure the paint brushes and rollers can then decorate. Each tool serves a different sector of the building project. Even though they are all working toward the same collective purpose of building the same project, if they try to accomplish an assignment outside the scope of their individual function, the result will be a horrible mess. A hammer expresses the building process differently than a skill saw does, yet each with their unique skills is vitally important to the entire process.

Why are we even talking about this in a book about finances? Because we are expected to take the gifts and talents God gives us and convert them into income. God is a God of investment and profit. God expects everything He makes to be fruitful and multiply. An apple tree cannot be fruitful and multiply if it is busy trying to be a rose bush. The Father invested Jesus, and He expected a return on that investment—us. We are the fruit—the multiplication from the seed of Jesus. If we try to be fruitful and multiply in a function we are not created for, we will not succeed and live a frustrating life.

Our gifts and assignments are clues to our individual purpose, which is our specific role or duty we fulfill within our collective purpose of building the kingdom and how we are to express and reflect God on the earth. God did not give us gifts and assignments so we could entertain ourselves, put on a show, or gain fame. He gave them to us so we might show the world who He is. This is the difference between success for fame and success for platforms. Like a hammer trying to paint, many people are using their God-given gifts for their own personal success and fame rather than kingdom influence. They use their platform to promote and influence people away from the kingdom of God. Success brings platforms, and platforms are for influence. Do we want success for our own fame, or do we want success so we can lead people to Jesus and build His kingdom?

In Genesis, we see Joseph's spiritual gift of interpreting dreams, plus his natural talent for administration, had the destiny attached to save lives and preserve nations, specifically the nation the Messiah would come through (Israel). Joseph's promotion was not about his fame and fortune, although those things were a nice added bonus. His success had the greater purpose of advancing the plan of salvation on the earth. The Israelites were the ones the promised Messiah was to come through; therefore, the Israelites needed to survive the famine headed to Egypt. It would have put the entire plan of salvation at risk if they did not survive. Joseph was prepared and sent to ensure that this young, budding nation survived, and as a result, the pagan nation of Egypt was also spared.

Although Joseph was rewarded for his obedience and faithfulness to God, God's promoting Joseph to that level of success and platform had very little to do with Joseph and was more for the benefit of making sure his very brothers who tried to kill him survived. Meditate on that for a moment—Joseph's success was about blessing and preserving his enemies, the very people who tried to kill him because they were so jealous of his success. We serve a God who desires to rescue our enemies as much as He desires to bless us. Like Joseph, can we be trusted to handle that level of power, influence, and success? Had Joseph used his power to serve himself instead of God by using his power to destroy his enemies, he would have killed his brothers, and there would be no nation of Israel. The entire plan of salvation would have been at risk of delay, causing God to bring it about another way.

Can we be trusted with that same level of self-restraint in positions of power? Can we be trusted to set aside our own agendas and recognize and obey the plan of God? Can we be trusted to use our success for what God wants to use it for and not what we want to use it for? This is why the wilderness of suffering is such a vital part of the preparation process. The wilderness is where we sacrifice our agenda on the altar and trade it for God's agenda.

Our gifts and successes are about advancing the kingdom of God, not the kingdom of self. God promotes character, not talent. As seen in the parable of the talents, it is always our choice whether to use them or not. We can get in the game or not. We can invest our gifts and talents wisely and gain returns or not. I want to emphasize this because when these talents begin to produce income, it is still about kingdom purpose. Our focus must always be on pursuing God so we do not become corrupted by these things. We must only find joy and fulfillment in Him, never finding significance or fulfillment in what assignments He has given us.

Read Psalm 37:4.

Our job is to delight in the Lord, not the stuff, the positions, the purposes, the gifts, the talents, or the assignments. Romans 11:29 (NLT) says, "*For God's gifts and his call can never be withdrawn.*" This means God gives us these gifts whether we answer His call to use them for the glory of His kingdom or not. People can use their God-given gifts and talents outside of a relationship with Him and without kingdom purpose.

Let's say a certain person has a gift for singing and songwriting. They get picked up by a record label and begin releasing albums, performing concerts, and making an incredible amount of money. They are technically fruitful and multiplying and building wealth, success, and a platform with those gifts. However, by leaving a relationship with the God who gave them those talents out of the equation, they not only miss God but also their God-given purpose and call. Even though they are operating in their gifts, they are not fulfilling their purpose. Their gifts are being used to build their own kingdom instead of God's.

It has nothing to do with the type of music, per se, that this person is making (although many lyrics written by today's artists do not reflect a godly lifestyle or values). Even if the lyrics are neutral, if the platform of success and influence these gifts have created is not being used to lead people into knowing God, then the opportunity to show people who God is and lead them into a relationship is wasted. To do this is to be like the rich young ruler Jesus warns us about in Luke 12:16-21, where He describes this person as foolish for storing up worldly wealth but not having a rich relationship with God.

This is why so many people who seem to have it all by the world's standards end up depressed, unfulfilled, and miserable. They are missing the biggest piece of the whole picture. Success, platform, and gifts, apart from a relationship with Jesus and being used for His glory, will still leave us empty and unfulfilled and may even destroy us. Building wealth without the blessing of the Lord comes with sorrow and stress, and it decays with the rest of the world. This type of success can never satisfy, which is why we see so many in this position turn to drugs, alcohol, and, sadly, even suicide.

Keeping a kingdom mindset and purpose in everything we do will keep ambition far from our hearts when we take up our positions as administrative heirs of the estate. Accumulating wealth, the kingdom way has more to do with the condition of our hearts and minds than whatever task or job we do. God's blessing on even the most menial task can bring wealth. God is more concerned with our internal world than our external world. The external is temporal. The internal is eternal. This is so we walk out our assignments not from a place of ambition but from a place of burden.

Sion Alford explains this concept so beautifully in his book *Divine Detours*. To paraphrase how he puts it:

> Ambition seeks position without a preparation process. Ambition wants the prize without the pain, suffering, self-denial, and discipline it takes to achieve great things. This is why so few great athletes make it to the level of competing at the Olympics. Very few are willing to pay the price. Ambition wants to bypass the wilderness of preparation. Eventually, ambition will deny the will of God and seek its own way. People with burdens for what God wants are unstoppable because their motivations are pure, and their actions always radiate the fruit of the Spirit. That is why God leads us through the wilderness of suffering, where our ambitions die, and we learn to be burdened for the things of God. The pit is where God turned the ambitious heart of Joseph the dreamer into the burdened heart of Joseph the redeemer.

King Saul was ambitious for power, fame, and glory. King David was burdened with leading God's people how God wanted them led. Ambitions motivate us from the outside to seek glory. Burdens motivate us from the inside out of love for the one our heart is burdened for. When an administrative heir is ambitious, the other heirs suffer. When the administrative heir is burdened for those under their care, they thrive. The gifts, talents, abilities, resources, assignments, calling, and purposes in our lives are for serving the people we are called to administrate, not for serving ourselves. We must be worthy of being trusted with the true riches of heaven—the people God desires to build into His living temple.

CLASS 5
STUDY GUIDE AND JOURNAL

Invite the Holy Spirit into this time of reflection and ask the Lord to reveal anything and everything He wants to reveal. Ask Him to shine His light into every dark place and renew your mind to His truth.

Key Scripture: *"For he has rescued us from the kingdom of darkness and transferred us into the Kingdom of his dear Son."* Colossians 1:13 NLT

Write Matthew 6:25. What does this scripture tell you your mindset should be when it comes to provision?

If too much of your income is currently being used up on your own needs, what changes could you make to free up some so it can be used to advance God's kingdom?

According to Luke 16:9-13, what did Jesus say money should be used for?

Is there anything you've overcome in life (demonstrated kingdom results)?

How could you begin to share your knowledge with others who might need to overcome the same issue?

According to Matthew 11:5, how did Jesus demonstrate the kingdom, not just talk about it?

According to Matthew 24:45, what did Jesus say a faithful and sensible servant could be trusted with?

Take inventory of your unique talents, giftings, specialties, and abilities. Are there any you are not currently using?

How could you begin using them to serve others or trade with them for income?

Write Luke 12:15-20. According to this passage, why is it foolish to amass earthly wealth that isn't used for kingdom purposes?

According to Proverbs 10:16, what do evil people squander their money on?

As kingdom people, you should use wealth as a means of harvesting people. Why does Jesus say that this is a wise investment in Luke 12:33?

Instead of being heirs who simply are provided for by the estate, how can you gain the authority to become an administrative heir who is given the responsibility of managing the provision of the estate?

For what purpose was mankind created?

According to Mark 16:15, what is every believer called to do?

Luke 16:12 (NKJV) says, *"And if you have not been faithful in what is another man's, who will give you what is your own?"* How can you help your boss or company prosper?

Proverbs 22:1 (KJV) tells us, *"A good name is more desirable than great riches."* Joseph never preached a single sermon. He worked his entire life in secular society serving pagan leaders. By the time Joseph was called to stand before Pharaoh and interpret his dream, Pharaoh told Joseph, "I have heard it said of you…" What kind of reputation are you building that God can use to promote you with later?

Using your unique gifts, talents and abilities as clues, what part of society do you believe you are assigned to serve and advance the kingdom in?

How can you allow your gifts to be fully used in the Master's hands?

How would you use success as a platform to advance the kingdom instead of your own fame and fortune?

If, like Joseph, God asked you to use your resources to provide for and care for your enemies, would you be able to do it?

How can you ensure you have a burdened heart like King David instead of an ambitious heart like King Saul?

For many, knowing that all believers have the same purpose and calling provides great relief and removes a lot of pressure. When people are seeking to know what God created them for and want to live their purpose, what they really want to know is what their kingdom assignments are. What assignments has God already given you that maybe you didn't even realize were kingdom assignments at the time?

Do you think your assignment may change in the future, and if so, where do you feel the Holy Spirit is directing you? (It's okay, if you don't know yet!)

Take a moment to thank God for how He uniquely fashioned you with abilities and bestowed certain gifts upon your life. Thank Him for directing your steps and for helping you to grow in ability to take on greater assignments with greater responsibility. Thank God for His provision. Thank Him for the opportunity to partner with Him and what He wants to do in the earth. Ask Him if there is any area He'd like you to begin to grow in skill or ability.

CLASS 6

WHY DOES OUR BLESSING LOOK LIKE WORK?

"Do you see that faith was working together with his works, and by works faith was made perfect?"

JAMES 2:22 NKJV

By now, we have learned that we do, in fact, have an earthly inheritance in Christ that includes prosperity. We have learned the importance of an obedient heart that puts God first, especially in finances so that we can be trusted to steward more and not become corrupted by wealth. The prodigal son knew he had an inheritance but demanded it before the appointed time and ended up squandering it. Remember, Proverbs 20:21 (NLT) tells us, *"An inheritance obtained too early in life is not a blessing in the end."*

We must be developed into stewards who know how to create and steward wealth with a kingdom-first mindset. We have also learned that how much prosperity we are responsible for managing is proportionate to our ability to handle and eventually manage more. We have learned how to bring the economy of heaven to earth through the three areas of biblical giving. We have learned that when we are faithful with the little and what belongs to another, we will be given our own, and the bigger problems we can solve, the more the marketplace will pay us.

We have learned that we all have the same purpose and call on our lives and that we can have numerous different assignments. We have learned that we are uniquely fashioned with God-given gifts, talents, and abilities that help us in our assignments. We are to engage the world by trading and serving humanity with them. By doing so, we build the kingdom of God by expressing our Creator and earning an income at the same time.

We have learned that worship is not limited to singing songs and that every time we use the skills God has given us can be an act of worship to our Creator. We know using our skills is our reasonable act of service as bondservants of our Creator. Next, we are going to find out what happens when we put our talents to use and how faith and action together bring the manifestation of God's promises into our lives.

But first, I want to address—the fact that we seem to be held in this weird tension between being both a co-heir and child of the King and a bondservant. How is it that we can be both? These two positions seem to contradict one another. To better understand this dichotomy, let's dive a little deeper into the concept of bondservant and why it benefits us that although we are children and heirs, we should take on this heart-posture of bondservant.

In most instances in the New Testament where the term "servant," "bondservant," "slave," or "bondslave" is used, it is the Greek word *doulos*.[66] This word is different than servant. A servant is one who is hired but free to go elsewhere. *Doulos* means "someone who belongs to another," a bondslave without any ownership rights of their own. It means one who gives himself up wholly to another. A bondservant was different from other forms of slaves or servants who, after working off debts or obligations, could be set free. A bondslave was a purchased slave. This type of slave was owned for life, not merely a hired servant who could be fired or quit or hold a temporary position while working off a debt. So why on earth would so many of the New Testament writers, including Paul, who also wrote Galatians, which gives us the revelation of our adoption as sons and daughters, refer to themselves this way? Here are some examples (NKJV):

- James 1:1 - *"James, a bondservant of Jesus Christ"*
- Jude 1:1 - *"Jude, a bondservant of Jesus Christ"*
- Philippians 1:1 - *"Paul and Timothy, bondservants of Jesus Christ"*
- Colossians 4:12 - *"Epaphras, a bondservant of Christ greets you"*
- 2 Peter 1:1 - *"Simon Peter, a bond slave of Jesus Christ*
- Titus 1:1, Galatians 1:10, Romans 1:1 - *"Paul, a bondservant of Jesus Christ"*
- Revelation 22:9 - an angel refers to himself as (*sundoulos)* a fellow servant. Same word - "doulos."

At first, it seems strange that Paul continuously refers to himself and others with this term since he is also the one who gives us the revelation of being co-heirs with Christ in the book of Galatians. Galatians 4:7 says, *"Now you are no longer a slave [doulos] but God's own child. And since you are His child, God has made you his heir."* In this instance, he points out that we are no longer slaves to sin and have been adopted into God's family as His own children and heirs. How can Paul say we are not slaves but rather children and yet continuously refer to himself and others as slaves?

When trying to explain this, many improperly teach that a bondservant was a voluntary servant, like in Exodus 21:6, which lays out the procedure for a debt slave to become a life-long slave. After their service was up, they could go free, but some chose to remain servants because they either loved their master or perhaps they had a wife and children that they loved who would remain with the master. They could choose to stay together and remain a servant of their own free will. This decision was sealed by the piercing of the ear with an awl. They improperly teach, I have even done so myself, that the use of the term bondslave, rather than slave or servant, referred to this voluntary form of slavery described in Exodus 21.

The problem with teaching this is that it does not hold up when we study the original languages or even some archaic or outdated English words. Etymology is the study of the origin of words and the way their meanings have changed throughout history. So, etymologically, bondservant distinguishes a purchased slave owned for life by his master from a servant, who is simply hired help for a season but is essentially free to go elsewhere. A servant can quit their job and abandon their assignment, but a slave or bondslave cannot.

Bondslave arises from the same origin and is a direct synonym for slave. The use of this term as opposed to mere servant is purposeful. Paul (and others) simply use the basic word for slave, which makes any idea of volunteerism wrong. There is no inherent idea of free will choice in this word. It is absolutely the same word used for a slave purchased at a slave market. Paul is being abundantly clear using this word—a person owned by another person, an owned slave.

Exodus 21 does not support this term meaning a volunteer either. In this passage, the Hebrew word for slave, before the ear is pierced, doesn't change to the word servant after his ear is pierced. The same word is used before and after. If there is any difference to point out, it would be between an Israelite debt-slave, which could only be held for seven years, and a bondslave, which is an owned slave, and a much more severe and permanent form of slavery.

Paul deliberately used the word for slave, not debt-slave, and it is even more unlikely that the Greek audience to whom he was speaking would have been familiar with ancient Israelite slavery regulations. There is no question Paul is identifying himself as being "bound for life" to serve God because he was purchased with the blood of the Master Himself. Paul purposefully and willfully uses the word, meaning the most servile state one could have in the Greco-Roman world—slave.

So why would Paul intentionally use this description when he knows we are children of the King and co-heirs with Christ? Part of the answer may be that Jesus used it first. Philippians 2:6-8 shows that although heir to all of heaven, Jesus postured Himself as a bondservant. Though He was God, He did not think of equality with God as something to cling to. Instead, He gave up His divine privileges and took the humble position of a slave *(doulos)* when He was born a human being. When He appeared in human form, He humbled himself in obedience to God and died a criminal's death on the cross. Therefore, God elevated Him to the highest honor and gave Him the name above all other names.

In God's kingdom, the way up is down. Jesus did not cling to His status as heir. Instead, He gave up all to serve God and humanity and, as a result, gained everything back. In the same way, Paul and the other self-professed bondservants knew that being an administrative heir meant serving the estate. He stated in 2 Corinthians 4:5 (NLT), *"You see, we don't go around preaching about ourselves. We preach that Jesus Christ is Lord, and we ourselves are your servants for Jesus' sake."*

Ironically, *doulos* or bondservant is used with the highest dignity in the New Testament, describing believers who willingly live under Christ's authority as His devoted followers. They willingly give God full possession as an act of worship because they recognize the price paid to buy them out of slavery to sin. God paid to purchase us out of our slavery, but instead of buying us to make us His own slaves, He bought us and set us free. Paul and the others are saying, "How can I want to do anything other with my life than give it back to this very God who would do such a thing for me?"

Paul and the others are not saying we are slaves to God in the idea of religious or legalistic works or out of religious or legalistic duty. They are declaring their desire to be bound for life to God who bought them and then willfully set them free. They are declaring the level of commitment they want to make, knowing the value of the cost of the purchase. They know God paid a high price for us not to be enslaved to the world, so it is their highest act of worship, in return, to become a slave to Christ.

Unlike being enslaved to sin and the kingdom of darkness, Christ's yoke is easy, and His burden is light. They did not cling to their status as heirs but laid their inheritance down in complete submission and obedience to the one who gave it. Being a bondservant of Christ is not drudgery; it's an honorable position! *Doulos* is the same word Jesus uses in Mark 9:35 (NLT), *"...Whoever wants to be first [wants to be the greatest] must take last place and be the servant [doulos] of everyone else."*

Jesus taught that the greatest in God's kingdom would have to become the servant of all. Jesus also taught us in Matthew 16:25 that we find our life when we lay it down. These self-professed bondservants knew this secret: they, too, would find their lives by laying them back down.

Read Romans 6:20-23.

This passage says we were free from the obligation to do right but now have become slaves to God. Slaves (bondservants) have assignments to fulfill for their masters. Again, how can we be a child or heir and a bondservant or slave? To help us understand, I will use my own children as an example. All three of our children work in and for two of our companies. They are heirs to our entire estate, yet they know they will never get to administrate the estate unless and until they learn the proper management of it. Why would we have such a requirement? Is it because my husband and I are mean and want to keep their inheritance from them? Of course not! It is because we are not going to set them up to fail. Proverbs 1:32 (KJV) says, *"... The prosperity of fools shall destroy them."*

My children are having the foolishness trained out of them so prosperity will not destroy them. They are learning that to lead means to serve. Power and authority without a servant's heart lead to corruption and tyranny. They have been invited to work with us, not just for us, to learn administration and grow in ability and responsibility. Handing them an estate and companies they have no ability to administrate and manage would cause them and the assets to crash and burn. It would not only affect them but also the lives and families of all our employees.

Being the owner of companies may sound glamorous, but it really means we carry the weight of responsibility for the livelihoods of every employee working for us. Could we just sell the companies upon our death and leave our children the money? Yes, but which is more valuable, a pile of cash to blow through or wealth-producing systems with the knowledge of how to administrate those systems providing an endless supply of cash? Would it be better if we left them a golden egg they could sell to feed themselves one time, or a goose that produces golden eggs to feed them for life? If they are going to inherit a golden goose, they must learn how to properly care for the goose and keep it healthy. They must learn how to administrate and take care of it. They are both heirs and bondservants to those companies.

Again, are my husband and I mean to make our children work for their provision? Certainly not! A vehicle I do not know how to drive does me no good. In the same way, a wealth-producing vehicle my kids have no clue how to drive will do them no good, and they will crash. For these same reasons, we are invited to work both for and with God. This is not about works or striving for God to give us provision. We are not working for God to earn our salvation; we work with God because of our salvation. We are invited to work with God to build His kingdom through assignments, and then we get to share in that inheritance both here and in eternity.

As heirs and bondservants, we have a responsibility to respond with our abilities to our assignment or task. We have an obligation to our Father as heir and to our Master as bondservant to do something with the gifts, talents, and abilities He has given us to build His kingdom. The amazing thing is when we answer the call and put our talents to use for kingdom purposes, it will simultaneously provide for our physical needs.

There will come a day when we will be held accountable for what we did with the talents God gave us. So it's important to ask ourselves, "What talents are we sitting on that can start being used to both build God's kingdom and provide income and provision for ourselves and our families?" It could be the very thing He wants to use to prepare us for our platform of influence. Whatever our platform of influence is, telling people about the kingdom will come from it.

Most people are missing it in the administration of what they have already been given. They get a plan, and they are given gifts and talents to support their assignment, but they do not step out and administrate the plan. It is great that Joseph received a plan of action through his gift or talent of dream interpretation, but what if he stopped there? What if he was so caught up in the awesomeness of his gift, enabling him to do something no one else could do, that he missed the very reason for being given that gift—to ensure the survival of the nation of Israel? What if he became full of himself? He would have missed the entire point. The reason for the opportunity was to give Joseph a plan to act out and administrate.

We will never occupy what we are unwilling to administrate. To administrate means "to oversee, to govern, or to supervise."[67] It means that work is involved. It takes active participation, not just bossing others around. If we do not learn how to submit, we will never know how to manage. Jesus wielded supreme authority because He Himself was under authority in full submission to the Father. He did not use His authority over everything to manipulate people and hijack their free will, and He certainly did not use it for selfish ambition or gain. He was in full submission to the plan, purpose, and will of His Father.

In the same way, if we do not submit our gifts and talents to the plan of God, which requires the working and administration of that plan, we will never understand that the whole purpose is not so we can feel awesome and powerful when those gifts and talents are in operation. Our gifts and talents have souls attached to them and are there to support an assignment God gives us of harvesting and leading people to build God's kingdom.

The fact that we are given an inheritance that includes prosperity in this life is not so we can live like the prodigal son, spending it on our own pleasures. Our inheritance is so we can live in our Father's estate and serve Him with that inheritance. Our inheritance is not for our provision, but rather, our provision is for our inheritance. All these principles we have covered are not about "how do we get more provision" as much as they underscore that the provision is already here, and this is what it is and is not for.

Provision is not the end game, as when we figure out how to receive abundant provision, we can just rest and enjoy life. That is not what the provision is for. The end game is about what to do once we have it. That is why this entire discussion has been about principles that train our hearts, not our behaviors. Provision is the means that support our assignments as heirs on the earth. Yes, we are allowed to eat and enjoy, but not at the expense of neglecting our assignments.

As a matter of fact, receiving provision does not signify our status as heirs; receiving provision is supposed to be a foregone conclusion. What is significant is the way we now receive provision. Because Christ restored us, we get to work from provision, not for provision. The way God provided for the Israelites in the desert is a picture of this. In taking the Israelites into the wilderness to prepare for the Promised Land, God changed how they received their provision.

In Egypt, they had to hunt, work, and exchange hard labor for it through painful toil and sweat. In the desert, they simply had to get up and gather it. It is much easier to gather what is already there than to labor and sweat, seeking to find provision. Of course, the manna did not just show up in their tents or on their tables every morning; they still had to participate by collecting what they needed for the day. They did not get to just sit around and do nothing.

This concept gives us a picture of something we will dive into momentarily: working from provision, not for it. When they got up to gather, the provision was already waiting for them. They did not have to hunt for or find it. This is working with God rather than for God. 2 Thessalonians 3:10 tells us simply that if we do not work, we do not eat. This does not include those who are unable to care for themselves. It is our duty to care for them. However, lazy, able-bodied people who refuse to look after their own needs, always expecting to be cared for by others, are vastly different.

God's Word advocates a strong work ethic and does not promote the use of welfare systems for able-bodied people. Welfare is for widows, orphans, and lepers—those who have no ability to provide for themselves. If we are not experiencing God's blessing of abundant provision, we may be sitting on our talents instead of converting them into income. We must convert our talents into a system of trading and management and be diligent and hard-working. Proverbs 10:4 (NLT) says, *"Lazy people are soon poor; hard workers get rich."*

In other words, diligence as a lifestyle brings prosperity. In the Bible, laziness is the same as wickedness. To be prosperous, not just rich, we must work as unto the Lord. Prosperity takes physical work. A condition of prosperity is that we are not allowed to be lazy. This does not mean we should be workaholics, either. It simply means whatever job or assignment God provides should be done to the best of our ability, even if our work is maintaining a household and raising children.

Deuteronomy 8:18 (NKJV) says, *"And you shall remember the Lord your God, for it is He who gives you the power to get wealth, that He may establish His covenant which He swore to your fathers, as it is this day."* Here is what most people do not understand—God does not give us wealth; He gives us the power to get wealth. God did not give the Israelites manna. He gave them the opportunity to get up and collect manna. God will give us gifts, talents, abilities, ideas, and opportunities, but we must be the ones who convert those things into wealth. Prosperity is not a byproduct of nothing. To prosper means to do well. For something to prosper, it must be doing something.

Let's say God put a dream and desire in me to become a bodybuilder and generate wealth through bodybuilding. Just because God gave me this dream doesn't mean I would magically wake up one day with a bodybuilder's physique and wealth accumulated in my bank accounts. It would mean God would be giving me the choice to work with Him to achieve this. I would have to act based on my faith. I would have to pick up weights and train my muscles, not just once, but many times over many years. God would then put His power on that action and effort, causing them to take me further than I could ever get on my own. Faith without work or action is dead. That's why Hebrews 11 says that by faith, those listed there took certain actions and then received their promises. Faith is not passive; it is active.

We didn't just wake up one morning wealthy business owners. It began with us exchanging our desires (for God to bless my husband's job and give us a good paycheck) for God's desire for us to own our own business. That's the difference. God led us to start a business by first giving us the idea. We then put the idea through the fire by taking it to God in prayer to see if it was coming from Him. Based on our faith in what God was saying, the idea became a desire. We previously had no interest in owning a business, but because God deposited the idea within us, our desire for it grew.

We then began to take faith-based action to build the business, believing that God would bring the blessing, and He did. After a period of development, it began to produce wealth. This is another detail people often miss. They expect blessings to come right away. Even plants have a period of development before they produce their fruit. The period of development tests to see what you can handle. Many people give up when they don't get the instant gratification of a blessing and forfeit their promise.

Like the analogy of the bodybuilder, there is a development process. How hard they are willing to work, how much effort they put in, and how disciplined they are determines how much they develop and, therefore, what success they will see. Just like faith without work is dead, work without faith is futile. It's only when the two come together that God has something He can bless and put His power on. Go to God and get His plan. Then, choose to desire and act on that plan.

Motivation and desire without action are useless. However, motivation and desire partnered with action is proof of faith. What does this mean? Well, if I have the motivation or desire to be physically fit but don't act and work out, it's useless. However, I also wouldn't put forth the effort of hours in the gym if I didn't have faith that it would create a physically fit body. This action is proof of my faith. Faith in the body is useless without work and effort. The work and effort wouldn't get started without faith. This is how faith and action work together to produce the promises.

If we desire a healthy body and have faith that God will help us, does God bless our body or our efforts? Do we magically wake up one day with a blessed, fit body, or does God bless our faith-based efforts when we get up and exercise? Again, don't get confused by a works-based theology. We don't work for our blessing; our blessing is for our work. The blessing is already there. Our effort is a physical expression of our faith in God's help.

Abraham and Sarah had faith for a baby, but Isaac didn't just show up. They still had to have sex. They did so in faith that God would fulfill His promise and bless their efforts. In fact, they only acted because of faith in God's promise. Effort and faith work together to partner with God. This is not just us doing whatever we want and expecting God to bless our efforts. This begins with allowing God to initiate what our desires should be and what our efforts need to be. Our effort is a response of obedience in faith that

God will do what He said. We don't get to flip-flop and choose any old effort and expect God to bless it. It begins with us laying aside our own ideas, plans, and agendas, allowing God to give us ideas, and choosing to desire God's plans above our own.

For us to prosper, we must be doing something. Our hands must be "to the plow." We must give God something to bless. In the Promised Land, they did not sit in their huts while prosperity came to them; they had to work their fields. They had to grow something, and God's blessing was on whatever was grown. If we want provision to come to us, that's manna. Manna is given in the wilderness, and we will only be given just enough. They were never allowed to collect more manna than needed for just that day.

Manna was about learning obedience and trust and that God is the source of all our provision, no matter where it comes from or how it comes to us. They had to learn to obey what God said to do with their provision—collecting only the amount He said—and it was about learning to trust Him as their source of provision. There is no abundance from God until obedience and trust are our priorities.

Once we trust God alone as our source and we are obedient to do what He says with it consistently, if we want abundant provision, we receive it by God putting His power to get wealth on our efforts as we work as unto the Lord and partner with Him. The inheritance we are given is so we will have the provision to fulfill our assignments while building His kingdom. This means we are going to have work to do.

Ephesians 6:6-7 (NLT) says, *"...As slaves of Christ, do the will of God with all your heart. Work with enthusiasm, as though you were working for the Lord rather than for people."* This implies that, although we will "secularly" be working for other people, we should treat all work we do with the same enthusiasm as if we were working for the Lord. There is no sacred or secular divide. It does not matter if we work in and through the church or in the marketplace; it is unto the Lord.

So, because we are both heir and bondservant, we are invited to work with God, not just for Him. Because of Christ, we are restored to our original position, for which God intended and created man. Adam, while in the garden, had all things already provided for him, but he still had work to do. In the garden, Adam had dominion over all things. He worked from provision, not for provision. He had work to do, but it was not until after the fall that he came under the curse of working for provision.

After that, Adam's time was consumed with first working to support his needs rather than the work of simply ruling over creation. If he had always worked for provision, this would not have been included in the curse of which Adam was told, *"By the sweat of your brow will you have food to eat..."*[68] In God's original creation, man worked simply because there was work to be done, not because he needed provision. Man worked because there was stuff to do, building and cultivating the kingdom his Father made, not because he needed provision. Everything was already provided.

This is the status to which Christ restored us. In the garden, man simply gathered provisions off the plentiful, fruitful trees of the garden. Out of the garden, he had to labor by planting and cultivating his own crops in the ground that was now full of thorns and thistles. In one scenario, we simply receive as we rest in God's blessing, working on the assignments given to us. In the other, we strive and toil for that same provision.

We see a picture of this with the Israelites in the desert. They did not have to work for provision in the way they did in Egypt; they simply gathered their provision every day. This was God giving us a type and shadow of the status Christ would return us to. Manna did not just fall in their laps. They still had to pick up their provision. It was God's way of training them to see Him as their provider. During their time in the wilderness, it was preparation, training, and learning how to trust before God could send them to slay giants. Their daily portion of manna was "just enough" and trained them to trust and obey.

When contrasted with Adam and Eve in the garden, they started from a relationship of trust and obedience and, therefore, gathered from the abundance around them. The Israelites got a taste of this system of provision but were given limitations on the amount they could gather because they needed to have their minds renewed to see God as their source and learn to live a new way. God had to take them through this season so they could detach from their old way of life, which was all they had ever known up to that point.

Just because God used their food provision as a means of training them this way does not mean they went into the wilderness poor. During the Israelite exodus, in Exodus 12:35-36, we see the Israelites plundered the Egyptians. They were given articles of silver, gold, and clothing. They left with all the Egyptians' wealth. The weight of silver and gold, in estimates of today's U.S. dollars, would be valued at $37,376,486.88 for the gold and $1,751,465.33 for the silver. It is estimated that about 2.4 million people left Egypt. If this amount were divided equally amongst the people, it would equate to over $900,000 per person. They were pretty much instant millionaires. Not only were they suddenly free from bondage, they were also simultaneously wealthier than they had ever been!

However, as with all of us, the wealth they plundered had a purpose attached to it—to build the Tabernacle of God—so this wealth was used to test their hearts. In Exodus 25:2 (NLT), the Lord told Moses, "*Tell the people of Israel to bring me their sacred offerings. Accept the contributions from all whose hearts are moved to offer them.*" (Although tithing existed as a principle as we established previously, the law had not yet been given to Moses at this point.)

Only a few chapters later, after Moses's mountaintop experience of receiving the Ten Commandments, he discovers some of his people made a golden calf for themselves. The only gold available for that would have been from those who held back from giving to the Lord for the building of the Tabernacle. This gold was already an idol in their hearts before it was ever a calf. As a result, three thousand people died that day for their idolatry. Idolatry to money can have profoundly serious implications. We never have to worry about loving provision more than we love the provider when we willingly give that provision right back to Him.

Just as the Israelites had to choose to leave Egypt behind along with its system of doing things and follow God to learn a new paradigm, we are invited to do the same in our finances. We are to rest in the knowledge that our Father will provide all our needs and give us the opportunity to learn, grow, and steward more than just what we need.

WE MUST STOP FOCUSING ON OUR OWN PROVISION

Read Matthew 6:25-33.

What is Jesus saying? He wants us to stop focusing on our provision. We must stop looking at our jobs, businesses, or other sources of income as our providers. God is our provider, and He can provide through those sources or any other source He may choose. We allow ourselves to get hung up on the how instead of resting in the knowledge that He will provide everything we need, not everything we want. Those thoughts dominate the minds of unbelievers; they are not supposed to dominate the thoughts of the children of the house.

My children do not come into the kitchen and ask me for eggs for breakfast and then sit, wonder, and stress if I'm going to provide them breakfast today. They do not try to figure out how I am going to get the eggs to them. They are not concerned with where breakfast comes from; they just know that when they show up at the table to eat, there will be food on it. That is what Jesus communicated about how we should be in Matthew 6. My children rest in their status as children, and they let me handle the status as parent and provider. They are children of the house! What is mine is theirs. They do not have to ask or beg for my provision; they know that if I have it, then they have it.

The only way or reason they would worry is if they were not sure I had the provision. Is our heavenly Father lacking provision? Then why are we even worried whether He will share it with us? My kids know that if I have it, they have access to it based solely on their status as my heirs. Certain things they know they have access to automatically, such as milk, eggs, and electricity. They ask permission for other things above and beyond basic provision, just in case I have it set aside for a special purpose (e.g., if I had a special pie in the fridge). They would probably ask to make sure the treat was not intended for company or a special event before taking a bite. Not because they are lowly or unworthy but rather out of respect for me.

In the same way, if I give them an assignment to clean the bathroom, they do not stress and worry about where the provision of cleaning supplies will come from. They know that if I give them an assignment, I carry the responsibility to provide them with what they need to fulfill it. This type of trust is what it means to enter the kingdom as a little child. Somewhere along the way, we have forgotten how to be children.

On the flip side, resting in the trust of my provision also does not mean that if I provide them with chicken, they get to demand beef. I have supplied their sustenance, and they can take it or leave it. A grateful heart would not dare demand something else be given. In the same way, as a good, loving parent who desires to give good and perfect gifts, if I know my children absolutely hate the taste of something, I do not antagonize them by purposely forcing it on them out of a power trip. That would not be love. If it was all I had, that is one thing. The same is true with our family's perspective on vegetables. It is important that they get the nutrients, not the exact vegetable they are or are not eating.

I have taught my kids that eating a diet abundant in vegetables is important for their health and for their bodies to work properly. To associate positive feelings with health and garner their cooperation, we explored different options and varieties and tried those vegetables prepared in different ways. I could force my will on them and make them do what I know is good for them, or I could find ways where not only do they eat what is good for them but they desire to, as well. Our heavenly Father is the same way. He gives every good and perfect gift. If we ask for a fish, He does not give us a snake and expect us to tolerate it.

There is a fine line between a secure child and an entitled child. As a parent, I will not back down from living truth; I'm not going to allow them to eat candy for dinner just because that is what they like. But I will work with them to find a way they can live the truth of the importance of healthy eating rather than forcing my will on them. That would breed rebellion. Instead, love says, "Here is a principle you should live by. Let us find a way for you to live it in a way that's sustainable for you." When they see you are coming from a place of love, not control, and from a place of guiding them to do things that are good for them, while acknowledging their own free will, cooperation results.

So why are we so worried that when we ask God for provision, we must hold our breath wondering if He is going to come through, or when He does come through, is it going to be something we do not really like or want? My children have a need to consume healthy food. If I can meet that need with something they like and enjoy (e.g., broccoli), I'm not going to try and meet it with something I know they hate (e.g., Brussels sprouts). Why force the Brussels sprouts if I can just as easily provide broccoli?

Just because my children are the heirs of my house and all their needs are provided, does not mean they get to do nothing but sit around on the couch and play video games all day. They have work and chores that contribute to managing and stewarding the house. There are no free rides; everyone contributes. But therein lies the difference: they aren't working for their provision; their provision is a foregone conclusion. They work simply because there is work to do to manage the estate. Their work and their provision have nothing to do with each other. They are not provided for based on what they do, they are provided for based on who they are—my children. They work from having their needs met, not for getting their needs met. They work with the parents of the house to contribute. They approach work from a completely different mindset. This is how we need to recalibrate our minds on the topic of work in the kingdom.

WORKING WITH GOD

Provision is pro (for) vision. Provision is for vision. Without provision, there is no vision, only survival. God has a vision for our lives that includes provision to see it through. God has a plan to prosper us. We should ask Him for His plan instead of asking Him to prosper ours. We need to ask God for the plan and then work it. That is working from provision, not for it.

Just like Joseph, upon interpreting the dream for Pharaoh, Joseph received the plan from the Lord, then he worked that plan. He acted it out; he did not sit on it. Joseph had to be willing to see past who he had been up until then and who he still was in that moment—a prisoner and a slave. He had to see beyond his past and present and see into who God was assigning him to be. In the same way, we need to see past who we think we are and decide, like Joseph, that it does not matter. All that matters is that we work the plan God gives us, and by doing so, we will become who God says we are.

God's provision always comes with His plan. His provision does not only include material things, either. It also includes the grace to be who we need to be to carry out the mission. Joseph did not become an administrator and then work the plan; he became an administrator by working the plan. He was willing to learn and work. We need to be the same way. To do this, let's look at more scripture regarding what it looks like to work with God. We are going to look at a parable where Jesus explains not only His role versus our role in things, but He gives us insight into the heart of the Father.

Read Matthew 25:14-25.

This servant had a wrong view of his master. The first two servants recognized their master as their source and were grateful, as evidenced by their stating, "You gave me..." They were grateful they were given something they could work and trade with. The last servant saw his master as someone "harsh" who wanted to take from his servant's hard work. This servant did not value what he had been given and viewed his master as unfair. The unprofitable, one-talent servant was in the greatest danger because his attitude was "I don't have much, what can my master expect of me?" This attitude reveals fear, apathy, laziness, and lack of faith. This servant gets cast into outer darkness. That should be very sobering.

No matter how much we do or don't have, we can still do something with what's in our hands. Everyone can do something. Notice every servant received something from the master. How much they were initially given was based on their proven abilities, not God preferring one over another. However, two of the servants took what they were given and got to work with it. As a result, they grew and developed in their ability to handle more.

Organized religion dominated by a religious spirit teaches that God is mean and unfair and wants to take from us, yet fails to recognize all that has been given to us. This last servant felt that since he was the servant planting and harvesting, the money should be his. He couldn't see how if it were not for what God had created, he would not have anything to plant or harvest from. The very ground we work with is created by God. We would not even have a life to live if not for God. This servant could not see how his planting and harvesting was actually a partnership between himself and God.

God provides all the resources and our physical abilities while we provide the effort. How many of us have this attitude about our incomes from our jobs? Many believe, "I am the one who worked for the money; why should I have to give God any of it?" This attitude only sees our human effort and fails to recognize or give God any credit for His part in it—everything He provided for us to be able to do that job. The servant felt that since investing for his master would cost him time and effort, and he did not get to keep the dividends, he did not want to participate. By the servant's remark of *"harvesting where you have not sown,"* in effect what the servant was saying was, "You're going to take my stuff. I don't want to participate in this assignment, but I'll hold onto it for you." Never mind that the land he buried it in belonged to the master.

Why did this servant hoard and hide the money instead of putting it to use? Fear of loss. His wrong view of the master made him afraid of loss. What will a poverty spirit make us afraid of? Losing what we have. A poverty spirit will also make a person fear there will not be more to replace what was used or given away. This wicked and lazy servant chose to believe and serve poverty rather than have faith in God. Religion, void of a true relationship with God, teaches us that God wants to take everything from us and that following God will cost us everything. Yes, following Jesus does cost us our lives, but not in a drudgery or bondage kind of way. To think that is to not know or understand our God, who is love.

Read Matthew 25:26.

We all know how the rest of the story goes, but right now, I want to focus on the question, *"Why didn't you deposit my money in the bank? At least I could have made some interest on it."* What does a banker do? They take someone else's money and give it an assignment. A banker will take someone else's money and put it to work to produce a profit. This verse shows us that God is a God of profit who fully expects a return, not loss. He expects a profit on what is invested.

What is the call every believer has on their life? To build His kingdom by harvesting people. God cares about people. Our assignments are all about harvesting people for the kingdom. So what is He saying when chastising this *"wicked and lazy"* servant? He is saying to this servant and to all of us that if we cannot get involved or participate in a project or assignment to harvest people, the least we can do is fund it and let that talent go to work through someone else's hands.

Do we give a lot of money to fund kingdom assignments? Great! God says that is the least we can do. If we do not want to trade with what we have been given to advance the kingdom, then, *at the very least*, we can bankroll someone who is. Giving does not make us the greatest. It makes us the least! Giving is entry-level participation in the kingdom; it is nothing we should be prideful about. If someone wants to put his or her talents to use to harvest people and build them up in the kingdom, the very least we can do is fund that assignment if we do not want to participate in it or if we are actively working on a different assignment.

When we compare the good and faithful servants to the one Jesus refers to as wicked and lazy, we see several key things. First, their different mindsets caused them to behave differently and take different actions. How we think about things determines what we do. What they believed about the character of their master determined their attitudes and level of participation in building their master's kingdom. The wicked and lazy servant did not want to use his effort to build his master's kingdom because he was focused on what he might lose. Playing it safe caused this servant to build nothing.

Second, being referred to as good and faithful or wicked and lazy had nothing to do with church attendance, how much worship music they played or sang, or how much Bible reading they did. It was based on whether they desired and took action to increase the resources they had been given for their master's sake and profit. The good and faithful servants saw their profit and their master's profit as one and the same. They wanted to do good for their master, but they were also faithful to act on that desire. The good and faithful servants wanted to take what they were given and make it more valuable so they could bring back to their master a larger return than they were given. This is not just money!

What are we doing to increase the value of all the resources we have been given? Some often overlooked resources are our houses, cars, talents, or even a dash of time. Do we prioritize one resource (money) to increase our other resources? Do we take money and invest it into our homes, upgrading them to increase their value? Do we take money and invest it into our vehicles with proper and good maintenance, causing them to last longer and hold more of their value? Do we take money and invest it into our time by taking classes to increase our knowledge and skills so our time is more valuable and we can be paid more for it?

The time of a brain surgeon holds more value and can be charged more than the time of an entry-level clerk. Each one has made vastly different investments into their knowledge and skill sets, so one earns hundreds to thousands of dollars per hour for their time, while the other earns around ten dollars. One is not necessarily more honorable than the other. Simply, a ten-talent servant requires ten-talent ability and work ethic. Being a five-talent servant is going to require five-talent ability and work ethic. It does not matter what level of ability we start at; what matters is what we are doing to increase the value of our talents. The servant, called wicked and lazy, did nothing to grow or increase. At the very least, he could have asked one of the other servants to help him or invest for him but instead chose to do nothing!

Read Luke 19:15-17.

Worldly wealth is the test of how we will handle true riches. What are we doing to make sure we pass the test? People put more effort into helping themselves pass the SAT®, which has no eternal significance, than learning what they need to know about handling worldly wealth. We all get a start and end date. What are we doing with the time in between? What are we doing with the dash of time entrusted to us? Are we increasing our Master's kingdom using all the resources He has placed in us and around us?

We must find and develop our gifts, then deploy them to build the kingdom. This isn't just funding ministries; it is also developing businesses that do things the kingdom way. It is working for our employer with a kingdom work ethic and bringing kingdom solutions to needs in our workplace. It is using our homes and vehicles to help, host, and to grow in value. We must look at every single area of our lives and every single possession we own as having kingdom potential to be fruitful and multiply. This next passage shows us a picture of working *with* God instead of *for* God.

Read Luke 10:30-37.

Most of us read this passage and think we are the Samaritan, and this is how God wants us to treat people. While part of that may be true, I believe we have been interpreting this parable all wrong. We are not the Good Samaritan; God is. This story starts off with a man who gets beaten up, robbed, and left for dead—a picture of what Satan has done to mankind since the fall of Adam. The beaten man left Jerusalem (the city of God) and descended to Jericho. Jerusalem is about 2700 feet above sea level, whereas Jericho is about 800 feet below sea level. Jericho is also one of the oldest known cities. Perhaps this represents the fall of mankind, descending from his position in paradise. The man was stripped of his clothes, which signifies a loss of status.

A priest came along and did nothing. Religion, as an institution, and religious people cannot do anything to fix man's broken condition. The same thing happened when a temple assistant walked by. Maybe this symbolizes the average churchgoer who falsely believes ministry should be handled by "official ministers" like pastors.

Lastly, a Samaritan came along. Samaritans were despised by the Jews because they were considered half-breeds between the Jews left behind while most of their brethren were led away to Assyria during the Assyrian captivity and the Assyrian occupying force left behind in Israel. These two groups intermarried and created the half-breed of Israelites, even creating a half-breed theology adopting some of Judaism and some of the idolatry of the Assyrians.

God compares Himself to the Samaritan because God is despised by most at first. Many lost people are at enmity with God. They keep Him at a distance and don't want to associate with Him or have anything to do with His ways, His Word, or His Church. This is how it was between the Jews and the Samaritans in that day. However, even though this Samaritan was despised by this beaten man from Jerusalem when the Samaritan saw the man, he felt compassion for him and came to his aid.

Through this parable, Jesus is teaching us the Father's heart concerning people that although we despise Him, He comes for us. Jesus shows us what God would do if He were there. He came after the wounded man and bandaged him, applying oil and wine. The oil is symbolic of the Holy Spirit; He applies life. The wine is the antiseptic—the blood of Christ—which cleanses us of unrighteousness and sin. God came to us; we did not come to Him. He applied life and healing to us and cleaned us up. Now, because of God in us, we go to others and do the same thing.

Next, the Samaritan puts the man on his own donkey. God will take us where we need to go and provide the means to get there, even though we may be unconscious or unaware He is doing this. The Samaritan then brought the wounded man to an inn. This is where we come in. The inn is the church. The church is where God brings people to heal who have been beaten up by the world. He even personally tends to them there to complete the healing, so the applied oil and wine have time to do their work while the wounded person recovers. The healing is not instantaneous. Even though the oil and the wine were applied, the beaten man still needed to be somewhere safe where he could heal and recover from his wounds. The innkeeper (that's us) is the one who gets to partner with God to look after the wounded people who are healing.

A religious spirit will try to say, "You have this nice inn; you have the extra room, and you owe it to God to take care of this man, so you should take care of him. You ought to because of how blessed you are." Religion says we should feel guilty because we have been so blessed, and we have a duty to sacrifice what has been given to us to do God's work. Religion tells us we must work for God out of obligation; however, the Samaritan never demands the innkeeper's help! Instead, he invites him into partnership with an offer too good to refuse.

The Samaritan says to the innkeeper, "Hey, if you'll partner with me, if you'll work with me to complete this man's healing and restoration, whatever you spend to do so, whatever it costs, I will pay you back in full." That shows God's heart in the matter. He is just looking for people to partner with Him by using the resources they have, knowing they will be reimbursed for their sacrifice. The innkeeper had the resources, but he was never demanded or commanded to help out of duty or obligation. Instead, the innkeeper was told that if he partnered up, even though it would cost the innkeeper up front, the Samaritan would foot the bill by reimbursing him whatever it cost!

What did the innkeeper hear? Profit! If he partnered with this Samaritan to help the wounded man, there would be profit in it for him. Why profit? Because the Samaritan said, *"Whatever it costs, I will repay you."* To understand this and why it is significant, we need to understand business and how a business owner thinks. This inn was his business—how he made his income and fed his family. Businesses do not operate for free; they have costs whether customers come or not. From a business sense, not only would the innkeeper have the outright expenses of this guy's care, but he would also have the business losses of not being able to sell that room while using that room for the wounded guy's care.

Every day this wounded man takes up a room is a day that room cannot be sold. In addition to the cost of feeding, clothing, and medical expenses, it costs this innkeeper profit he would have made. That lost profit is part of "whatever it costs" to see after this man's care. So let us say the innkeeper's expenses are $20 per day for food, clothes, and medical supplies. Next, just to make that room available for sale, his mortgage on the inn, utilities, and cleaning staff comes to another $20 per day. Let us then say the innkeeper charges $50 per day to rent that room, which means he has a profit of $30 per day for that room. So caring for the man costs the innkeeper $50 per day ($20 hard cost plus the $30 lost profit), plus the additional $20 in expenses of feeding and caring for his injuries with medicine and bandages, etc. That adds up quickly! So what is the Samaritan saying? This is not just reimbursement; it is whatever it costs. That "whatever," as we now see, includes the innkeeper's profit.

God is not a harsh master or dictator who blesses us so that He can make us do things for Him out of religious obligation. To believe this would be a twisted and perverted view of who He is. We must fix that religious mindset of God's character. He says, "Partner with me, and I will reimburse you whatever it costs, in full." God is not concerned about the cost. He has an unlimited account. He tells the innkeeper that because he knows the innkeeper does not have an unlimited account, it might be scary for him to lay out those expenses. The Samaritan says there is an unlimited amount of provision to care for people if the innkeeper is willing to partner with him.

What if the innkeeper spent money on upgrades to make the wounded man more comfortable? Do you think the Samaritan would get upset about that? No! (Only if spending that money on upgrades interfered with the ability to care for the man in the way he needed or caused him to not have the money to now care for the man properly.) Since we are the innkeepers, the Church is the inn, and the Samaritan promises to cover the costs, we need to quit being so concerned with what churches are spending unless they neglect their assignment to care for the people. We can do both. In fact, in any religion, it is a sign of honor to that god to make a lavish temple to worship them.

This is why Solomon made every other temple pale in comparison to the temple built for the one true God. No expense was spared, and it was as lavish as could be made by human hands. This was a sign of honor and showed others the splendor of God. The world knew there was something different and magnificent about the God of Israel because of the exquisite cost and attention to detail of that temple. Many of today's Christians would look at Solomon's temple and say, "Look at all this waste! Instead of covering everything in gold, we could have used that gold to feed the poor!" Okay, Judas! This only exposes a poverty mindset these people held that assumes there is not enough to do both. The innkeeper spoke of no such limitations.

What was the innkeeper's response? "Unlimited funds if I take care of this guy? I must spend a little up front, but ultimately, I lose nothing and get to make all my profit, too. Hey, you got any more guys like this?" This is what it looks like to work with God! This is what it looks like to gather provision rather than hunt. We do not have to hunt for the people to fill the rooms. God will bring them if we just agree to use all our resources to care for them knowing He is good for fulfilling His promises and paying us back in full. It is okay to expect profit when partnering with God. In 1 Timothy 5:18 (NKJV), we see, "*... The laborer is worthy of his wages.*" God does not expect people to work for free, and He certainly does not want partners out of religious obligation or duty. That would make God a user.

In other sectors of society, we do not expect people to work for free because it may be for a morally worthy cause. We do not use people like that because we know it is wrong and it would be exploiting people. So why do we accept this in the Church, letting religion tell us this is how things are supposed to be and that it is an acceptable view of God? Why do we let religion and religious people, who obviously do not understand the heart of the Father, tell us it is our moral obligation to give and take care of people with no expectation of return? That is wrong, and it is not biblical. The only catch, if there is one, is that the innkeeper does not get the unlimited checkbook if he is not fulfilling the assignment of caring for the people.

Also, this does not mean people cannot volunteer to help an organization for free. However, someone cannot devote all their time to that because they would not be able to provide for their own needs. The point is, in an actual profession where someone is working to provide for their families, people are paid for the work they do. Even non-profit organizations have people in paid positions for proper administration and management. Although volunteering can be good, no one is expected to spend their life volunteering to the point where they cannot work to see after their own needs.

We see to the needs, obligations, and bills of our own house first, and then we are free to volunteer if we want to. Volunteering, by its very nature, means someone wants to give their time, effort, and skills of their own free will. They are never coerced or forced. It would be unrighteous to expect people to do so. The Lord does not expect people to work for free, nor should we, in the Church or otherwise.

Read Mark 6:35-44.

This is one last area for us to look at when it comes to working with God. Unlike the innkeeper, who already had some provision and a good business to start with, this passage shows us what it looks like to partner with God when we have nothing. The miracle of multiplication was not only that there was enough for everyone to be fed as much as they wanted. As great as that was, the miracle did not stop there. The real abundance was the leftover fragments that seemed so insignificant they were almost overlooked.

The leftovers did not look like much until they were purposefully collected. Even the disciples almost overlooked their importance until Jesus said to go back and gather them. Only then did they discover how much was truly there. Where might we have fragments of abundance around us that we mistakenly perceive as insignificant?

When I read this passage, the biggest question I have is where did the baskets come from? They were in a remote place, having traveled many days. I doubt they came from the people because no one there was supplied with any kind of provisions on them. It appears they were all traveling light. They were not even prepared with food and likely did not have any baskets on hand they were walking around with to collect the leftovers.

When we obey God and care for people, the provision to fulfill that assignment shows up! Whatever is necessary to carry out the task shows up, in this case, baskets, in addition to the abundant provision to care for the people, which was the actual food they needed. So where did the baskets come from? Who cares! All that matters is that they did. We simply obey by taking care of people and collecting our provision, and the baskets to contain it will show up!

Proverbs 14:23 reminds us that work brings profit, but mere talk leads to poverty. It is not enough to just learn these principles and talk about them. The profit is in putting them to work. Proverbs 12:14 (NLT) says, *"Wise words bring many benefits, and hard work brings rewards."* There will be some benefit in the wisdom, but the reward is in the work. Lastly, Ecclesiastes 3:13 tells us people should eat and drink and enjoy the fruits of their labor, for these are gifts from God. God is not a harsh dictator. Jeremiah 29:11 (NLT) says, "*'For I know the plans I have for you,' says the Lord. 'They are plans for good and not for disaster, to give you a future and a hope.'*"

Did you catch that? God has plans (plural), as in more than one plan to prosper us. We just need to ask Him what they are. The problem is too many of us create our own plan and ask God to prosper it. We need to ask Him how we can trade the talents and resources He has given us to both build His kingdom and our incomes. They go together, just as we are meant to work together with each other and with God.

CLASS 6
STUDY GUIDE AND JOURNAL

Invite the Holy Spirit into this time of reflection and ask the Lord to reveal anything and everything He wants to reveal. Ask Him to shine His light into every dark place and renew your mind to His truth.

Key Scripture: "*Do you see that faith was working together with his works, and by works faith was made perfect?*" James 2:22 NKJV

Why is viewing yourself as only a bondslave or only a child an incomplete picture? Why is a balance found in both?

According to Proverbs 20:21, why is an inheritance obtained too early in life not a blessing in the end?

In Mark 9:35, Jesus taught that whoever desires to become greatest must take last place and become a servant of everyone else. How can you use your money to serve others and not only yourself?

Proverbs 1:32 says that the prosperity of fools shall destroy them. What foolishness do you believe the Lord is seeking to train out of you?

What talents do you have that you can begin to put to kingdom use by using them to serve other people?

What skills could you potentially make a business out of?

(Please keep in mind that "service to people" doesn't necessarily equal "doing it for free." Just because one receives money in exchange for serving, doesn't mean it's not still service or kingdom service. This is the very essence of business. Businesses still serve people, even though they receive money in exchange for their service. Businesses that do not serve people well do not stay in business long. For some reason, Christians have adopted the mistaken belief that serving people means it must be done for free. Kingdom service, and therefore kingdom business, means you serve people from kingdom ethics, principles, and law—loving your neighbor as yourself, treating them the way you would want to be treated.)

How can you change your mindset to work from provision, not for provision, and from success, not for success?

According to Deuteronomy 8:18, God does not give us wealth, He gives us *"the power to get wealth."* What is significant about that difference?

If someone has a dream to become a world-class bodybuilder, how would faith and action have to work together to see that desire become a reality?

When it comes to the desires of your heart, how do faith and action need to come together to make them a reality?

To prosper, you must give God something He can bless— a "field" growing some kind of crop, e.g., a business, investments, etc. How much you then prosper is up to you. Do you want to put in the work to grow two tomato plants or a thousand? Does your field have the capacity to grow a thousand plants, or do you need to invest in a bigger field? How can you begin to convert your talents into a field God can bless, or if you already have the field, how can you invest in increasing its capacity?

According to the parable of the talents in Matthew 25, whether you are given one, five, or ten talents to start with is based on your ability. How can you increase your ability to grow what you have already been given?

Why is funding other kingdom assignments the least you can do, not the greatest?

From the perspective of the innkeeper, while God is the Good Samaritan, how can you begin to partner with God to take care of people?

According to this same parable, why should you not be concerned about what it costs to take care of people?

When Jesus multiplied the five loaves of bread and two fish, as found in Mark 6:35-44, not only were people fed to fullness, but there was also an abundance of leftovers. Not only did God provide the abundance, but He also provided the tools and ability (baskets) to collect them. What fragments of abundance might be hiding in plain sight all around you?

CLASS 7

TEN PRACTICAL STEPS TO KEEP MORE OF OUR MONEY AND PREPARE OUR FIELDS FOR ABUNDANCE

We learned from the miracle of Jesus multiplying the fish and bread that the true abundance was not that everyone's need was met; it is what is left over after needs are met. From the account of this miracle, we can see that the abundance was in the pieces left over after everyone was fed and satisfied! Those fragments seemed so small and insignificant like they would not amount to much until they were purposely sought after and gathered.

Oftentimes, we are surrounded by abundance that we are blind to, which is why we are going to look at some of the areas where there are commonly uncollected fragments of our wealth. We will discuss areas that consume more of our wealth than we are aware of and how to restructure them so we keep more of our wealth by giving those same dollars an assignment. Many of us do not need more provision; we must better allocate what we already have.

We have also learned that there are two different systems of economy competing for our faith. We have the physical system that has been cursed, where provision is gained through painful, hard labor and sweat or by selling ourselves into the slavery of debt just to meet basic needs. Then there is the spiritual system in which we tap into the unseen realm of the kingdom of God and simply receive provision the way humanity was designed to all along. However, receiving provision does not mean we sit on our couch while angels simply deliver money to us. There is still work to be done, but we approach work from an eternal kingdom mindset of working from provision, not for provision.

Once we move from the wilderness to the Promised Land mindset, how we receive provision changes. We receive our own plot of land to administrate. As we cultivate and work that land, God's blessing on the work of our hands leads to abundant harvests where needs are met, and there is abundance to store up and share. This overflow then gets funneled back into the kingdom through seedtime and harvest. We bring heaven's economy to earth by using finances for kingdom purposes—tithes of honor, sowing into and supporting kingdom assignments, and giving to the poor. Because God gives seed to the sower, these activities result in more seeds flowing into our lives, which keeps the whole cycle going and growing.

As we look at some practical ways to administrate our financial fields, some may experience a feeling of relief. This is because we are conditioned to "do" instead of "be." We are conditioned to look for a quick-fix checklist like: "Five Steps to _____," or "Three Keys to ________." We open article after article, promising a quick and simple "To-Do List" to get the things we want, not realizing that we have the equation backward. If we can change how we think, we will automatically change what we do.

Our actions are birthed out of what we believe, so if we do not start by tearing down and rebuilding the foundation of what we believe, nothing else will matter. This is why we have spent so much time covering beliefs and principles about money and provision first. If we do not start by restructuring our beliefs, we will not have the stamina or ability to see a to-do list through. We cannot prepare for abundance if we first do not even believe God wants us to have it.

If we receive abundance before our hearts are postured correctly or before we know how to manage it, it will own us instead of us owning it. If we cannot handle worldly wealth well, we won't be trusted with true riches. It is only after beginning the journey of going through these processes first that we can begin to take practical steps. Then, we can begin to put our faith into action and see things come to life.

Hopefully, those who have not before have now begun honoring the Lord with their finances and putting Him first through tithing, thereby enacting a covenant of financial protection. We don't tithe for money or to be blessed. We tithe to honor the Lord with what we are already blessed with.

It is also my hope that we have begun to seek the kingdom for our needs, resting in the assurance that our God will provide every legitimate need simply because He is a good Father who takes care of us, not simply because we sow. Once we've mastered this basic trust, we can then begin to grow our finances by sowing a seed and expecting the Lord to do exceedingly, abundantly above what we could ask, think, or imagine instead of turning to debt when we need or want something that goes above and beyond provision that meets our basic needs.[69]

As we focus on simply abiding in Him and doing everything from our connection to Him, we will be able to act in His strength instead of relying on our own limited willpower. As we abide in Him and meditate on His Word, these principles will become habits in our lives. Then we can take things a step further by learning financial management and the proper administration of our finances. We can work on the practical steps to keep more of the wealth we already have. Even small leaks sink ships, so we need to plug up the leaks we currently have that are siphoning off our wealth before we even begin to worry about taking on more.

These practical money management steps may be elementary for some, and some may be doing several of these things already. If so, great! This is in no way intended to dumb anyone down or assume anyone does not know these basic things. I also cannot assume everyone already knows and is doing these things, so if some of these steps seem elementary, try not to dismiss them. It can be good to go back to basics as there may be even more of our wealth hiding. Just like in the miracle of the fish, the abundance was in the fragments! We need to take stock of our finances and see what fragments of our wealth if revisited and gathered, could lead to abundance. We will look at the most common ways our fragments get consumed instead of collected and kept.

Quickly, before we get into these likely familiar steps, we need to be incredibly careful about trying to change ourselves from the outside in via behavior modification instead of from the inside out via belief modification and living by the Spirit of God directing us. Behavior modification programs have their place and can be great for developing discipline, self-control, and learning the administration of finances. However, true freedom is seldom achieved through using willpower to follow the rules.

True freedom is not needing willpower to do something we should or want to be doing. Using willpower to simply rein in spending is like forever being on a financial deprivation diet. It is legalism, trying to live by following a bunch of rules. Just like the law, even if the intent is good, most people cannot follow it long-term. As in the health arena, a person trying to achieve freedom simply through a deprivation diet can only deprive themselves for so long before they break down. If they work on their beliefs surrounding health, food, etc., before attempting to change how they eat, the changes are easier to make and are more permanent.

This is not to say that rules are not good and that we should not follow them. However, rules by themselves will never produce true freedom. Freedom can only be found in the kingdom of God, accessed through Jesus Christ alone, and abiding in Him in our decision-making. So it is not that rules do not have their place; it is that living a life of rule-based deprivation is not our inheritance. God's plan for us was not to deprive ourselves for so long that we amass enough money and material things "to one day be financially free." On the other side, this does not mean to use debt to indulge our desires, either. Jesus said to repent.

Repent means to change our minds. When we change our minds first, our behavior will follow and will change on its own.

The kingdom is based on principles, which are not necessarily rules. Principles are dynamic, not static. For example, as a principle, we should avoid debt. Legalism says, "Never use debt!" Oftentimes, a rule or law is a man-made version of a principle. As a principle, one should want to avoid debt, but there is a time and way to use debt to our advantage instead of it taking advantage of us.

We must be careful about taking the principles of God and turning them into legalistic rules, which is why these behaviors are the very last part of these teachings. These steps are not necessarily new information. I myself have adapted this list from various books, seminars, and financial planners I have gleaned from.

STEP 1– STOP USING DEBT AS A SOURCE OF INCOME.

Until we are financially stable and free, debt must be viewed as a mortal enemy of our financial freedom and well-being, not as a source of meeting our needs. This is why we are going to spend a lot of time focusing on this step. We cannot live in slavery and freedom at the same time, and we can never live in freedom if we have sold out our financial futures by using debt. For most, we are already in debt perhaps with a mortgage, car payments, and possibly even some consumer debt on credit cards, student loans, finance loans, and second mortgages.

The first practical step to shrinking that mountain is to purpose in our hearts to not add to making the mountain any bigger with further debt unless expressly instructed to do so by the Lord. Once we are debt-free and have mastered the skills of financial management and our credit scores have improved, we can begin using debt and the hidden loopholes in their contracts against these lenders instead of debt using us.

For example, when we purchased my last vehicle, we went to the dealership prepared to pay cash. Their finance company really wanted our business, so after some negotiations, they agreed to loan us the money for the car at a mere 1% interest. We knew we could take that same lump of cash and invest it, receiving at least 7% to 10% in return. After accounting for the 1% interest paid by financing, we could still earn 6-9% on our money, so in this instance, using debt was the smarter choice if we invested that money and not spend it on lifestyle stuff.

We invested the money by using it to purchase, remodel, and flip a house, actually still making about 10% on that money after all was said and done. However, keep in mind: we are debt-free already. We do use loans and things from time to time, but the difference is that we have the money set aside to pay them off at any given time, or we are diligent to pay them off very quickly by throwing every extra dollar at them.

To me, "debt-free" does not necessarily mean we never leverage debt. It means we can pay it off anytime we choose. While we were still in debt, with no hope of getting out, this would not have been a wise strategy, especially since the interest rate would have been incredibly different. Therein lies the difference. Debt can and should be used to acquire and grow assets, so we do not tie up our own cash flow. Debt should not be used for consumer purchases like clothing, vacations, household goods, or anything else that cannot be turned around and sold for more money than it was just purchased for.

Using debt for consumer purchases is about the most financially destructive thing one can do because it means paying astronomically more for the same stuff when the interest on that debt is factored in. Why would anyone go into a store and pay 20-30% above asking price? Yet, that is exactly what they are doing when putting purchases on credit.

For a season, until we are no longer enslaved in debt any longer, it is imperative to make a firm decision not to go into any further debt. This must be an unshakable stance that we and our spouses if we have one, are in a strong, no-compromise agreement. Have a card-cutting party where any open credit cards (not debit cards) are cut up, so there is no temptation to use them. We must resolve to be ready to experience God's provision and quit doing things our own way and in our own strength.

This begins with truly facing every area where we are already in debt and where our money is currently going. Write it down. Remember: we cannot conquer what we will not confront. We must get a clear picture of the true size and scope of the mountain of debt we have built through our overspending. We will not face it with fear but with faith that as we learn to live by His kingdom, He will show us that He will do exceedingly, abundantly, above what we could ask or think. He will provide for us in creative ways and will show us unique strategies to pay debt off.

We serve the God who gives us authority to move mountains and cast them into the sea, and debt mountains are no different. But it all begins with a no-compromise decision to get out of the world's system of slavery to debt. We can live in Egypt as a slave, or we can leave Egypt behind, break free from slavery, and journey to the Promised Land, but we cannot do both. We must choose whose kingdom we will live in and then obey that king. We cannot serve two masters; we must choose one. We must choose between obeying Jesus as King of our money or Egyptian debt masters. When we willingly put ourselves in debt, we are making the willful choice to submit ourselves to obey an Egyptian debt master.

STEP 2—SEE EXACTLY WHERE OUR MONEY IS GOING NOW.

The next thing we must do is go through all our financial statements and see exactly where our money is going every month and make a list of it. This is going to be the first of three different lists we are going to create. Most people try to set a budget based on what they think they should be spending, instead of starting from what they actually are spending. We must go through three months of bank statements, credit statements, and cash receipts and add up what was spent. It is helpful to "chunk" it into different categories (e.g., household for expenses of home maintenance, groceries, debt payments, clothing and shoes, utilities, and insurance; vehicle for repairs, gasoline, etc.; mortgage, entertainment, and frivolities).

We have a certain amount of dollars coming in and must be aware of what they are spent on. Some people would call this making a budget, but as I said, it makes no sense to sit down and make a budget based on what we think we should spend, it should be done by figuring out what is already being spent. For this reason, I do not like to use the term budget. I think budgets are like diets; they feel like deprivation; therefore, only those with the strongest of wills will stick to them. We can call it our "Financial Battle Plan," "Spending Plan," or whatever makes us feel empowered about regaining the position of overseeing our money rather than our money overseeing us.

It is time to quit playing defense and start playing offense. The only way to do that is to find exactly where and how much money is being spent and face it head-on. Most people are amazed at how quickly seemingly insignificant purchases (fragments) add up. However, as I said earlier, even small leaks sink ships. This is part of beginning the journey into the wilderness, where anything unnecessary for survival gets left behind because the weight will only hinder us on the journey and make the trip slower and much more difficult.

Walking twenty miles with a five-pound backpack will go much faster than trying to carry a five-hundred-pound backpack. The same applies to our journey out of debt and into financial freedom. Continuing to spend money on even these trivial things will make this journey much longer than if we made that sacrifice for a season, threw that same money at our debt, and reduced that mountain much quicker. Some common trivial things that add up are things like streaming subscriptions, grabbing things from a drive-through instead of making those things at home, gas station purchases, getting our nails done, cable TV, entertainment tickets, etc. People who live paycheck to paycheck waste a significant amount of money on things like these instead of taking those same dollars and investing them.

Once we have the list of exactly where our money is going, we will look through it and let the Holy Spirit tell us what must be sacrificed on the altar of our will. For my family, that looked like cutting the phone, internet, and cable for a season. We cut little luxuries, like fabric softener. We shopped at The Salvation Army for our clothes instead of the malls. It looked like my husband and I sharing a vehicle and carpooling for nearly two years to avoid taking on the debt of another car payment. This meant I was dropped off at work a lot earlier than I needed to be and picked up long after I was already off.

Any inconvenience was far worth not having the stress of trying to pay debt with a ridiculously high interest rate. Whatever was not a necessity was cut so we could get a handle on living below our means instead of above them. For some people, the choices may not be this drastic. For us, they were. But the sacrifice was more than worth the peace of mind we gained in return from no longer being spread too thin financially.

During this journey, my husband and I had to look our kids in the face three years in a row and say, "There are no Christmas presents this year. It is either presents you do not need or electricity you do need. So, sorry, kids, electricity it is. It is not good stewardship to skip paying our bills just to buy you lifestyle stuff."

God honored those sacrifices because the very next year, we were able to pay cash and buy our son a car for Christmas. Many people saw that blessing but did not see the wilderness of sacrifice we walked through the three years previously. It is not that we can do what others cannot, it is that we did what others will not.

STEP 3—DEVELOP TWO DIFFERENT CASH RESERVES.

The third strategy we can use to get out of debt is to create a cash reserve for those unexpected things that come up, which typically would send us running to a credit card or another type of loan to pay for them. Ideally, a reserve of at least $3,000 is preferable to start, with the ultimate goal being to have six months of living expenses set aside. (Six months' living expenses should be the goal only after beginning to pay off debt. We should start by setting aside a few thousand dollars, so an unexpected emergency does not throw us off track and make us go running back to debt.) Most people cannot even fathom this, which is why getting our spending under control and developing self-discipline comes first. Then we will begin funding this reserve by searching for hidden money. (This is not reducing payments; that will come later.)

I find it astounding that most financial programs stop with the creation of an emergency fund. As great as it is to have, it does not lead to freedom; it only has the potential to keep us from running back into slavery. However, there is a second type of fund we want to begin to build. The second type of cash reserve we want to begin to build is a wealth account. This is money we accumulate for the sole purpose of investing. It is great to have debt paid off, but without income we do not have to physically work for—passive income—it will be almost impossible to obtain true financial freedom.

Passive income is generated by investing in something, some sort of asset, which produces its own income. An example of this type of income would be income from a rental property. We accumulate funds in a wealth account we use to purchase a home as an investment that we rent out. We then rent that house out for more than what we owe on it. Let us say a mortgage on that property is $1000 per month. We then rent the house for $1400 per month, giving us a positive cashflow difference of $400 per month. That rental income is passive income. It is money earned that we do not have to physically work for.

Other types of passive income can be business income from building a business that generates ongoing cash once built, interest income from other types of investments, or dividend income from stock purchases and such. Unless and until one has passive income beyond their expenses, they will always be stuck trading time for money. There is no true financial freedom in that way of life because if we stop working, our stream of income dries up.

Most people do not know or realize that money itself can be put to work and can earn more money! If we do not get our money working for us, we will always have to trade our time by working for someone else to make more money. Every dollar we have has the potential to be an employee for us, working on our behalf to reproduce itself. What a waste to turn those potential employees into coffee or some other useless thing.

We must put money away in a wealth account for investing or we will always remain dependent on working income from a job. One of the biggest differences between the wealthy and the struggling is that those who are struggling typically waste much money on things with absolutely no significance, while wealthy people spend their money purchasing assets. Wealthy people build their net worth, not just their income. Net worth is the cash value of everything we own minus any debt against it. Wealthy people refer to themselves in terms of their net worth, while most others refer to themselves by the value of their paycheck income. We can have extremely high incomes and still have no financial freedom because of how we use that money.

Are we purchasing assets that will generate passive income or profit upon resale? Or are we wasting that income on stupid lifestyle stuff like electronics, boats, and flashy cars because we think that makes us look wealthy? Why do we waste so much money buying our child another video game or toy that has no real significance in their life and then use those decisions as an excuse to not build an emergency fund or wealth account? It is ridiculous, and it is why so many people keep struggling. Our children would rather have our time anyway. Why be more afraid of disappointing our children than leaving them a legacy of poverty and struggle?

We can give our children temporary and fleeting pleasure for a moment, or we can leave them a legacy of sound financial management and an inheritance. Which has greater significance and impact on their life? Do my children care now about all the things we did not buy them previously? Did going without Christmas presents for three measly years destroy them? What do they appreciate more now? Having had video games that would already be outdated or destroyed? Or do they much rather prefer that those sacrifices enabled us to not only teach them sound financial management but also help them go further in life with education, assets, and an inheritance? We must stop being afraid to disappoint our children.

I see people make excuses all the time about why they cannot get ahead in their finances, why they cannot build an emergency fund, why they cannot start a wealth account, and yet, I watch them over and over purchase things that have absolutely no significance, like Disney tickets, name brand clothes and shoes, electronics, and more. If they would just make a sacrifice for a season, they could turn things around. It all goes back to Step 2, taking an honest look at where money is being spent now, rising to be the boss, and deciding that those funds will begin to go into cash reserve accounts instead.

It will not just happen. We must take charge of our finances by creating a plan and then following through on that plan. Part of Joseph's administrating of Egypt's resources was being the boss and limiting how much grain the people could have to ensure the provision lasted through the famine. Joseph did not allow the people to have as much grain as they wanted whenever they wanted. He had to tell people "No!" for the greater good of the future. We must have that same mindset with our children and ourselves and quit indulging every whim and desire at the expense of our financial future.

Many people living paycheck to paycheck mistakenly think they have no money fragments to put in the baskets of these two different accounts. This is why doing the work to sit down and face where every single dollar is being spent now is vital. It is easy to forget just how many times we have eaten out, stopped at a gas station for a little snack, or how many times we have hit the Starbucks™ drive-through. All these things are financial leeches that consume our wealth.

When we sit down and calculate where every dollar has gone for the last three months, it is amazing how often we find hundreds of dollars spent on these insignificant things that could have instead gone to fund these different accounts and have been sown into our future instead of being consumed. If we lack the discipline to take control of this, we lack the discipline to be trusted with more. To grow in this discipline is to grow in the ability to handle and be trusted with more. If you gave your child $100, and they could not tell you where that money disappeared to, would you just keep giving them more?

STEP 4—HUNT FOR "HIDDEN" TREASURE.

Once we go through the process of adding up where all our money is currently being spent, our eyes get opened to the truth that we all have hidden money around us; we just could not see it before. Everything we see around us was money at one time. The televisions in every room, the golf clubs sitting in the garage, the excess clothes we do not even wear, the jewelry given to us—all these things were at one time money in our hands. We then traded that money for these things.

We need to look around for anything we can sell for quick cash and tuck that money away. Look around. All that clutter used to be money. Your emergency fund and wealth account are all around you and have been traded for insignificant things. Reclaiming this financial territory means we will find anything we do not need or that is not used so we can sell it for quick cash. This is what we will use to begin to fund our cash reserve or emergency fund. It is especially important to set up a bank account at a different bank than our main one for this cash reserve. We do not want easy access between this account and our checking accounts because when things get tight, it is easy to tap into this money.

We begin by creating a list of these sellable items and the amount we feel certain we can get for them, not what we hope to get for them. When we ask the Holy Spirit, He will show us things we would not have even thought of as we walk through our houses, basements, garages, attics, sheds, or whatever looking for things that can be sold. There are many avenues for selling items, such as apps, websites, and social media groups, where items can be listed at no cost. Even having a garage sale could get many things sold. The method does not matter, just turn that stuff back into cash. There should be no sacred cows. Whatever it is, if they still make it, we can own one again someday.

Financial freedom is our most important goal. Look around. Remember, in this upside-down kingdom, we give up, and then we get. We sow, then we reap. There is no getting without first giving up something. However, when we are making these sacrifices to honor God in our finances and to eventually increase our capacity to handle more in His kingdom, Jesus promises, *"And everyone who has given up houses or brothers or sisters or father or mother or children or property, for my sake, will receive a hundred times as much in return and will inherit eternal life."*[70]Whatever we give up for the sake of following how Jesus said to live will bring a hundred-fold return! Sacrifice in this season to reap in the next. It will be worth it. No item is worth our peace of mind.

In addition to this start-up fund, we will begin making a "bill payment" into this account every month. It is to be treated like any other bill that must be paid. Wealthy people make it a priority to take part of what they have right now and invest it into their future by paying themselves as a bill first before any other bill gets paid. Poor people pay all their lifestyle stuff first and then maybe set money aside if there is anything left over, yet sadly, there very seldom is.

If we continue to overindulge by consuming all our resources and not setting anything aside, we are being gluttonous, unwise, and foolish. If a farmer eats all his seed, he has no future harvest. If we cannot afford to put money into an emergency fund and wealth account, then we cannot afford that latte. One last area we can look to see if we have any hidden treasure in fragments lying around is lost or unseen money. Unclaimed property sites can show us if we have unclaimed money somewhere.

STEP 5—MAKE A LIST OF EVERYTHING WE OWE AND STRATEGIZE TO PAY THINGS DOWN QUICKER.

This goes along with Step 2, but instead of listing all expenses, which do not necessarily have debt attached to them (like our electric bill), we are going to itemize out what is specifically debt. On a third piece of paper (first was everything we spend, second was items we can sell for quick cash), we are going to write down a complete and exhaustive list of who we owe, how much we owe them, what the interest rate is, and what the monthly payment is, even medical bills and personal debts we may owe to friends and family members.

I do not care if it's the $20 we borrowed from our sister two years ago and forgot to pay her back. If the Holy Spirit brings it to your mind, write it down. Every debt payment: mortgages, vehicles, credit cards, bank loans, student loans, back taxes, personal loans, etc. Deciding when and where to spend money is not administrating and managing finances. Taking charge and seeing where our money is going and what things are truly costing us is properly managing our money. We must face the mountain before we can ever conquer it and cast it into the sea. Before we can command a mountain to move, we must fully identify the mountain.

Take charge and administrate your finances by writing it all down: the debts, the payments, the interest rates, and the length of time to pay it off, if applicable. This is where we can have no sacred cows. This is where the Lord may lead us to put some things on the altar. That motorcycle, the ATV, the second car payment, or whatever it may be. If we can live and work without it, sell that item and pay off the debt. Proverbs 10:22 (NKJV) says, *"The blessing of the Lord makes one rich, and He adds no sorrow with it."*

It is not worth our financial health, mental health, or freedom to own these things while they are attached to debt and slavery. They are not irreplaceable. We can own them again one day when we do not need to sell ourselves into slavery to obtain them. We do not want to be like the rich young ruler who lamented over selling his possessions when Jesus told him to. We should never be so attached to a possession that we are afraid to lose it. Stuff is just stuff. Stuff comes and goes. Stuff should support the things we do in life; our life should not be consumed by having to work to support our stuff. Once we have an exhaustive list, we can plug these numbers into amortization schedules.

An amortization schedule makes us face, in black and white, what debt is really costing us. Many people are so worried about investing—how to invest, where to invest, what to invest, etc.—but what they do not realize is that by investing in paying off debt, the money saved on interest adds up to way more than most returns on standard investments. A dollar saved on interest is a dollar earned!

STEP 6—REDUCE OUR TAX BILL.

Taxes are a huge deal, and most of us are greatly overpaying them. *Money Magazine* did a study where they took a single client's more than ten years' worth of tax returns and gave them to over fifty different accountants.[71] They then had these accountants analyze these tax returns for this client to see if they would come up with the same or different answer as to the amount of taxes this person owed for each of these ten years. The results of the study were shocking! Not one of the fifty accountants came up with the same answer as another regarding the amount of taxes this client owed.

What was even more shocking was the range of answers! The tax bills ranged anywhere from $6,800 in taxes owed to $73,000 in a single year! The study discovered that most returns are riddled with errors, costing the average person at least 25% more in taxes than they should have paid! This is an area we should want to get a second opinion, and let the Holy Spirit lead us to the right accountant. I understand we are "to give Caesar what is Caesar's," but the greater question here is, "Who gets to decide what or how much is Caesar's?" The accountant does! I want an accountant who knows all the legal deductions and codes and comes up with the correct answer while saving me the most money!

Overpaid property taxes are another area where we lose money. Many times, if a mortgage is refinanced, that year's property taxes are added to the transaction, often not considering whether those taxes have already been paid. Here is the sneaky thing, too: most states don't automatically refund the overpaid tax money; they make a person come to claim it! The state hangs on to that money unless and until the homeowner ever thinks to come to claim it. Many states are sitting on millions of dollars of overpaid property taxes.

Another area where we can save on taxes is deducting our mileage to and from church when we serve. (Not when we merely attend.) For those of us who may have "at-home" businesses, if it is not set up like an actual business by creating an entity, we will be taxed as an individual instead of a corporation, which would cost us thousands of dollars that we could be saving on our tax bill. Part of being a good steward is not overpaying for things that could cost us less, and taxes are no exception. This is an area where being cheap and trying to do things ourselves just to save the few dollars paid to a qualified accountant can really backfire. We don't want to waste the Master's money simply due to lack of effort!

STEP 7—SHOP INSURANCE RATES.

A good place we can start to free up some extra money is to cancel life insurance and disability insurance that is attached to loans. (This is insurance that will pay off loans in the event of death.) Often, this is a waste, and the rates are ridiculous. When it comes to other types of insurance (e.g., vehicle, homeowner's, etc.), most states will give a list of all insurance providers and what their rates are. We should continuously be evaluating and re-evaluating these rates.

Another way to save on insurance bills is to pay for the entire year or six months upfront in a single payment rather than spread these payments over the insurance period. In many cases, the savings can add up to several hundred dollars. Strategizing with a good financial planner will help ensure that we have enough insurance for important things without wasting money being over-insured on insignificant things.

It is one thing to continually shop around for fair market rates on things like insurance; it is a completely other thing to ask or expect discounts from every business we go into. Stop asking people for discounts and calling that good stewardship. That is not good stewardship; that is called being stingy, and business owners dread doing business with those people. Every business has hard costs they must pay to make a product or service available, and for doing so, they have a right to expect profit for the risk they incur to bring that product or service and make it available to people. It is extremely disrespectful to ask them to accept less money and work at a discount.

How would we like it if someone came into our place of work and asked our boss to pay us less to do the same job? We would be extremely insulted. Yet, that is exactly what we do when we request discounts from people we do business with. I see Christians do this garbage all the time, especially when doing business with other Christians. They feel entitled to receive products or services at a discount and then have the audacity to act like that is what makes them a good steward. If they are not turning around and investing that savings, then simply saving a few bucks does not make a person a good steward, it makes them cheap.

Christians generally have a reputation in the marketplace and at places like restaurants for being cheap. Christians are the worst tippers at restaurants, and they are usually the pickiest and most demanding because if they can find fault, they have an "in" to ask for a discount! What kind of message are we sending? Sunday afternoon lunch is the most dreaded shift in the entire restaurant industry because of the after-church crowd. When did Christians adopt the idea that being cheap and getting discounts makes them good stewards? (Never mind the fact most of them are in debt up to their eyeballs.)

We represent the kingdom of unlimited resources. Our dad is the King of kings and Lord of lords. The gold and silver are His. We are the ones promised the abundant life. Why should we be concerned about price? If it is too expensive, do not buy it! People should walk away from financial transactions with kingdom people feeling astounded and blessed. It should be a joy to do business with us! In no way am I advocating for overpaying for things, either. That is not what I am saying here. That would not be wise, either. I am simply saying that in business transactions, both people should win.

We are ambassadors of the kingdom of God, so how we do things sends a message. We are seeking to entice people into the kingdom. Why would they want any part of it when we preach abundance yet practice stinginess? Remember what Jesus said money was to be used for in Luke 16:9? We are to use it to benefit others and make friends, not for our own benefit.

Now, I am also not saying not to use coupons and such. Many businesses use them as tools to draw in customers, and it is great to take advantage of the opportunities. The difference is that in these cases, the discount is their choice; it is not being forced on them by someone who simply feels entitled to pay less.

STEP 8—CHECK UTILITY BILLS FOR ERRORS.

Most bills, usually phone bills and cable bills, are full of errors. We should make sure we know what we agreed to pay and read those statements to make sure everything lines up with that agreement. Many of these utility service providers are sneaky about building rate increases in their plans over time. Many times, by simply calling them and threatening to cancel service and go to a competitor, they will reduce these rates back down.

I'm not going to spend much time here, but we must actively administrate and not just blindly pay for every little thing without question. We cannot afford to assume that these companies have their stuff straight. It is shocking how often this is not the case. I find errors in statements all the time. Yes, it is annoying to have to make the phone calls to get it corrected, but that is what management is. It is not simply paying the bill without question. What is the alternative? Should we just let them keep those overages when that money can be thrown into our wealth accounts? If we are not actively staying on top of these things, why should we be trusted to handle more?

STEP 9—SELL OUR LIFE INSURANCE.

There are companies that will buy our life insurance, take over the payments, etc. It is an investment for them. We get a lump sum now, and they get ownership of that policy and become the beneficiary. We can then buy a cheaper term policy (for now). Later, once things are back in balance in our finances, there is a way to use life insurance to keep our wealth off the radar with whole life policies to stash cash into that we can then turn and draw from later. In this strategy, we wouldn't be using the insurance for the death benefit, but as a way we can stash money that earns pretty good interest, which we can withdraw the money later without penalty or fees. Again, it's wise to have a financial planner help create the right investment plan.

As for buying other people's insurance policies, it is a pretty solid investment, but for now, anything but term insurance is going to be too costly. The difference in the cost of these policies can be reallocated towards paying off debt. Once out of debt, a whole life policy that accrues value might be the better choice, or even a minimal policy to cover funeral expenses. Think about it: Why do we have life insurance to begin with? Is it not to pay for the funeral and pay off our debts in the event of our death to not leave our families stranded? Once we're debt-free, this burden goes away. Then, we can choose to have a higher dollar policy, or not, to leave behind for our family or whomever, or just a small policy to cover funeral expenses. This is one of those things we can strategize with a financial planner on later, but for the sake of this conversation, we are looking to gather up all the fragments that are being wasted so we can throw them at our debt.

STEP 10—CREATE A CASH MACHINE.

Another idea is to assess what talents we might be sitting on that can be converted into cash. Most of us have skills other people are willing to pay for, we just have not opened our eyes to them yet. We all have things we do well or better than others, but very seldom do we think of taking those skill sets and turning them into quick cash where we can either begin to fund our wealth account or end up developing it into a business that can one day replace our job. What are we really good at? Do we bake cookies better than anyone else? We can bake for special events. Can we sew? People need special costumes or garments fixed. Can we teach? Many children need extra tutoring. Are we great at organizing and decluttering? Many people are not and need help with this. It is amazing what people will pay for!

There are literally hundreds of money-making opportunities hidden in plain sight all around us. We only need to pause, pray, and ask the Holy Spirit to open our eyes to them. All these things represent potential talents we can begin to trade with and convert into quick cash. All of us are sitting in untapped potential.

In the beginning, we will not worry about how to turn these things into an actual business. We will just make the decision to begin and find one person we can help with those skills. One will lead to two, then three, then so on. Then we bank that cash. We know God won't drop golden eggs in our lap in the form of cash. The skills He has given us are like a golden goose that can produce endless golden eggs. It is up to us to get producing. We are partners with God, which means we have a part to play, too.

Once we get our goose-producing eggs, we can worry about what to do with them. Master converting skills into cash, then we can decide if we want to create a full-time business around it. Most people never do anything because they want the entire plan and all the steps before doing anything. This is backward. If we plan to take a trip, there are thousands of possible paths to take. Trying to plan out a path before first deciding on a destination is crazy. However, once we make the decision to go to a specific destination, the path to get there appears before us.

The same is true here. First, we decide to convert our talent into cash, and then the path to get there will show up. We do not need to see the whole path at once. When driving from Florida to California, I do not see the entire path at once. I can get there, even at night, by just seeing the next 200 feet. Then the next. Then the next. By focusing on the part exactly in front of me, I can end up at my destination, even if I end up having to take detours around roadblocks along the way. Unsuccessful people let excuses stop them. Successful people act despite all the excuses not to.

Money management is simple. Take talents and skills we already have, trade with them to bring in as much money as possible, continue to grow in those skills, increase in value, and diligently watch the money that goes out. We must monitor and reduce how much is going out and discipline ourselves not to spend it in harmful ways. That's it, in a nutshell. Increase what is coming in and decrease what is going out, which will help us keep more of what comes in.

When we become faithful with these little steps, we can grow in knowing different ways to invest what we have, thus putting money to work for us instead of having to work for it. But these disciplines must be mastered first. When we correct our improper mindsets, learn and live by God's principles, and take these necessary actions in the natural we will be astounded how God will multiply our seed to work for us and accelerate our plans.

God does not multiply chaos or lack of diligence. To do so would be to contradict His Word. If we want to grow in the number of talents we are given, we must be diligent to grow in our ability. We must be doers of His Word, not hearers only. The goal is to have a prosperous soul, not just a bunch of cash. By following the principles laid out in this book, it is my sincere prayer that we all *"would prosper and be in good health, even as our souls prosper."*[72]

REFLECTION QUESTIONS

How has your view of God changed because of these classes?

How has your view of yourself changed because of these classes?

Which principle discussed has had the greatest impact on you?

How can you begin to share these truths of the kingdom with others?

Life is lived from the inside out, not the outside in. This is why this book has focused on the internal life. Once you get that oriented to the kingdom, it will begin to manifest in your outward life. What has been the biggest change to your inner life?

ABOUT THE AUTHOR

Melissa Van Schaik is living proof that it doesn't matter how lowly one starts out in life; with God, all things are possible. Struggling financially from childhood into adulthood gave her a relentless desire to figure out what was causing her to stay in a cycle of poverty and loss. Having little to no financial education drove her to read as many books and attend as many business and financial seminars as she could. As helpful as these things were, nothing ever seemed to change.

In her frustration, she cried out to the Lord for answers. He led her to put the books, seminars, and classes aside and turn to the Word of God as the study manual for finances. As she dedicated herself to learning what God's Word said about money, she allowed the Word to challenge her, correct her, and change her beliefs entirely.

As she studied, she discovered principles that when put into practice through faith, unlock kingdom provision. As she applied these principles to both her personal and business finances, the windows of heaven opened and dramatically changed her life forever.

Noticing the dramatic changes in her life, people began to ask her to teach them what she had learned. As she stepped out in faith to do so, the Holy Spirit continued to expand the revelation she received, giving her the outline and messages that became her online Kingdom Finance class. Seeing students from all over the world learn and experience financial freedom as she did has fueled her passion to continue to share these principles with anyone who will listen and help people put them into practice.

Although Melissa never aspired to be an author, getting this information into the hands of as many people as possible is what has led her to compile these principles into a book. Having a heart of extreme generosity, she hopes to one day be able to give away houses, cars, and pay off church mortgages so God's house doesn't sit in debt. Melissa currently resides in Florida, with her husband, their three children, and three grandchildren.

MelissaVanSchaik.com

ENDNOTES

1) Shalom." *Strong's Exhaustive Concordance: Hebrew 7965. מוֹלָשׁ (Shalom) -- Completeness, Soundness, Welfare, Peace*, biblehub.com/strongs/hebrew/7965.htm.

2) Matthew 6:10

3) https://www.merriam-webster.com/dictionary/sophisticated

4) Zechariah 4:6

5) John 8:32 NLT

6) See Genesis 3, Matthew 4, and Luke 4

7) John 1:1

8) John 14:26

9) Genesis 3:5

10) Proverbs 3:10 NLT

11) Genesis 37-43

12) Qalal." *Strong's Exhaustive Concordance: Hebrew 7043. לָלָק (QALAL) -- to Be Slight, Swift or Trifling*, biblehub.com/strongs/hebrew/7043.htm.

13) "Psuche." *Strong's Exhaustive Concordance: Greek 5590. Ψυχή (Psuché) -- Breath, the Soul*, biblehub.com/strongs/greek/5590.htm.

14) Psalm 1:2

15) Charlton, Laird. "Prospering." *Webster's New World Thesaurus*, Simon & Schuster, 2003.

16) Matthew 6:8 NKJV

17) Isaiah 28:10

18) Romans 12:2

19) 2 Samuel 21:2

20) John 12:31, John 16:11

21) Galatians 3:13

22) Deuteronomy 28

23) Ephesians 2:19

24) *Strong's Greek: 1659. Ἐλευθερόω (Eleutheroó) -- to Make Free, Fig. to Exempt (from Liability)*, biblehub.com/greek/1659.htm.

25) *Strong's Greek: 1658. Ἐλεύθερος (Eleutheros) -- Free, i.e. Not a Slave or Not under Restraint*, biblehub.com/greek/1658.htm.

26) James 1:22

27) *Strong's Hebrew: 4643. מַעֲשֵׂר (Maaser or Maasar or Maasrah) -- Tenth Part, Tithe*, biblehub.com/hebrew/4643.htm.

28) *Strong's Hebrew: 4442. מַלְכִּי־צֶדֶק (Malki-Tsedeq) -- "My King Is Right," an Early King of Salem*, biblehub.com/hebrew/4442.htm.

29) *Strong's Hebrew: 4428. מֶלֶךְ (Melek) -- King*, biblehub.com/hebrew/4428.htm.

30) *Strong's Hebrew: 6664. צֶדֶק (Tsedeq) -- Rightness, Righteousness*, biblehub.com/hebrew/6664.htm.

31) *Strong's Hebrew: 8004. שָׁלֵם (Shalem) -- "Peaceful," an Early Name of Jer.*, biblehub.com/hebrew/8004.htm.

32) *Strong's Hebrew: 1700. דִּבְרָה (Dibrah) -- a Cause, Reason, Manner*, biblehub.com/hebrew/1700.htm.

33) Romans 4:11

34) Hebrews 7:4-10

35) Hebrews 7:7-10

36) Psalm 110, Hebrews 7:11

37) Hebrews 7:8, 15-16

38) Hebrews 7:26-27

39) Hebrews 7:27

40) Hebrews 8:5

41) See Malachi 3

42) Exodus 20

43) Genesis 3:19 NIV

44) Matthew 6:33 NLT

45) 1 Timothy 6:10

46) Matthew 11:11

47) Matthew 6:33

48) Isaiah 53:5 NKJV

49) Psalm 103:3 NLT

50) Based on Matthew 4:23 and 9:35

51) 1 Corinthians 11:18

52) 1 Corinthians 11:22

53) 1 Corinthians 11:27

54) Colossians 2:13-15

55) Hebrews 9:12

56) Luke 8:11

57) Luke 6:38

58) "Commerce Definition & Meaning." *Dictionary.Com*, Dictionary.com, www.dictionary.com/browse/commerce.

59) James 2:26

60) Matthew 6:25, Luke 12:22

61) Luke 16:9

62) Matthew 11:4-5 NLT

63) Johnson, Bill. *Facebook*, www.facebook.com/BillJohnsonMinistries/posts/the-holy-spirit-is-in-me-for-my-sake-but-upon-me-for-yours/10151211324438387/.

64) Genesis 41:15

65) Mark 16:20 NLT

66) *Strong's Greek: 1401. Δοῦλος (Doulos) -- A Slave*, biblehub.com/greek/1401.htm.

67) https://www.thesaurus.com/browse/administrate

68) Genesis 3:19 NLT

69) Ephesians 3:20-21

70) Matthew 19:29 NLT

71) Anrig, Greg. "Even Seasoned Pros Are Confused This Year Money Asked 50 Tax Preparers to Figure One Family's Taxes—and Got 50 Different Answers." *CNNMoney*, Cable News Network, 1 Mar. 1988, money.cnn.com/magazines/moneymag/moneymag_archive/1988/03/01/84339/index.htm.

72) 3 John 1:2

Made in United States
North Haven, CT
10 November 2026

22097462R00122